Chin Music From
A Greyhound

THE CONFESSIONS OF A CIVIL WAR REENACTOR 1988-2000

Robert Talbott

authorHOUSE®

AuthorHouse™
1663 Liberty Drive
Bloomington, IN 47403
www.authorhouse.com
Phone: 1 (800) 839-8640

Published by AuthorHouse 05/06/2016

ISBN: 978-1-5246-0785-2 (sc)
ISBN: 978-1-5246-0784-5 (e)

Print information available on the last page.

Any people depicted in stock imagery provided by Thinkstock are models,
and such images are being used for illustrative purposes only.
Certain stock imagery © Thinkstock.

This book is printed on acid-free paper.

Because of the dynamic nature of the Internet, any web addresses or links contained in
this book may have changed since publication and may no longer be valid. The views
expressed in this work are solely those of the author and do not necessarily reflect the views
of the publisher, and the publisher hereby disclaims any responsibility for them.

TABLE OF CONTENTS

ACKNOWLEDGMENTS

Once again, I am grateful for the influence and input from so many people, otherwise this book would not have been possible.

First and foremost, I again thank Dr. Leslie Anders, who first created an interest in me with his lectures on Civil War History. To my wife Mona and daughter, Katie who has put up with the expenses and the wild weekends this hobby demands. To Gregg Higginbotham, John Maki, Dave Bennett, Gary Crane, Steve Hall, Mike Gosser, Jon Isaacson, Ralph Monaco, Pat McCarthy, Mark Olson, and John Peterson for their helpful input in composing this story. To Gail Higginbotham for using her teaching skills to edit this book. Finally, to all past and present members of Holmes Brigade, the LUAS, Crowley's Clay County Company, the Western Brigade and all the nameless and faceless individuals I've had the honor to associate with these two dozen years. I feel truly blessed to have known you all and I will always cherish the memories I have for this strange little hobby called Civil War Reenacting.

INTRODUCTION

"When Dickson Stauffer went away,
His wife came in the family way.

The only thing that she could say,

Was blame the Union Army!"
Too-ra-loo-ra-loo-ra-loo
They're looking for monkeys up in the zoo
and if I had a face like you
I'd join the Holmes Brigade."
The Holmes Brigade Song-Steve Allee and Doug Sloan

When I began composing the first volume of Chin Music, I stated that it would cover my early years up to 1987. I did not realize until I had completed the work, that I was also chronicling the regime of Dickson Stauffer. Dick resigned in 1987 and Don Strother took over as Captain of Holmes Brigade. Don's regime lasted until 1995. It is fitting that as I continue my memoirs, I should use this vessel as a means of commenting on the Don Strother years as well. Don was from a whole different cut of cloth when compared to Dick. Whereas Dick was more like one of the boys and could out drink most of us, Don Strother was more tightly laced and preferred his own company after hours. He was a very authoritative figure, dressed smartly, and was a very much "by the books officer". Don would have made someone a great clerk or staff officer in the regular army. Everyone in Holmes Brigade has an opinion of Don Strother-some positive, some not so. In my dealings with Don, he did not belittle me, look down on me, or patronize me either. In reading the following volume, you'll have to form your own opinion of Don Strother.

If you've read my first volume, I explained to you how I got into the hobby, my first event, and the dozens upon dozens of characters I've met along the way. By 1988, Holmes Brigade had grown to such an extent that we could field 60 or more men at any given time. We began to get invited to events, which were listed as "by invitation only," meaning only the most serious-minded and authentic reenactors were sought. A group needed a good reputation to attend many future events, in particular living history programs at National Park sites. We could still be found willing to knock off a "cold one" after hours, but during the day when the public came through, it was 100% total devotion to the impression.

With the passing of time, many fine details have escaped me. As with Volume One, I have referred to old newsletters, newspaper clippings, magazine articles, photographs, and personal accounts from my Holmes Brigade pards to help tell this story. For those gaps in my memory or the written record, I've bent the truth a small fraction and exaggerated slightly for the sake of continuity. If there are any glaring mistakes or if anyone has been offended, I apologize.

Once again, I am grateful for the development of some memorable friendships in this funny hobby. Holmes Brigade would be blessed with even more colorful characters over the next several years, one or two that I'd become very close to. Between the years 1988 to 2000, there would be many grand adventures for Holmes Brigade and me, mixed in with laughter, anger, tears, and death.

CHAPTER ONE

The Road to Gettysburg

The road to Gettysburg actually began in March of 1988, when Mona and I bought our mini-van. During the 1980's, mini-vans were all the rage. It seems, to my way of thinking, that most young couples with small children had one. By 1988, Mona and Katie had been in the hobby several years and had collected many articles of clothing. We had a couple of John Maki wooden bread boxes to hold these many outfits, but we sadly realized that a small pickup would not do for all the clothing, tents, rope beds, blankets, and the all important chamber pot. As plans for Gettysburg began to pick up momentum, it was our intention to combine a site-seeing trip with the reenactment. I would be taking two whole weeks off from work and once the reenactment was concluded, we would visit a number of historic sites in Virginia including Mt. Vernon, Yorktown, and Colonial Williamsburg. We also planned on spending a day in the Nation's Capitol.

But the first order of business was to shop for a new vehicle. Several friends, who owned mini vans, suggested we go to the Ford dealership in Buckner, MO. *Buckner is located 15 minutes east of Independence.* The overhead/cost for a new vehicle would not be as high (*so we reasoned*) as if shopping in the metropolitan area. We also wanted to trade in our 1983 AMC Renault. Mona was not as happy with it, as she hoped, when we first bought it. It had front wheel drive and child proof locks, but it had some serious mechanical problems that didn't become evident until after the warranty ran out. Periodically we would take it into the shop to get the front-end realigned; it wanted to wobble ever so slightly at times and the steering wheel would vibrate.

So one crisp weekend in March, we went out to MATT FORD and sealed the deal on a blue and silver colored FORD AEROSTAR mini van. The van could seat 7 people, including driver and co-pilot. The rear passenger seats could be folded down into one long bed or they could be taken out all together with that empty space used for cargo. It had power everything, including cruise control and it really spoiled us once we took our long road trips.

We put the Ford Aerostar through its first long distance test, when we all went down to the Wilson's Creek National Battlefield on April 16-17, 1988. Aaron Racine went with Mona, Katie, and I. Aaron was still partial to those nasty Chic-o-sticks and he brought several to snack on during the 3-hour trip. Fortunately, he DID NOT bring any Cinnamon Schnapps. After Perryville, he was cured from that.

The impression for the Holmes Brigade this time around was in the portrayal of soldiers from Company D, 1st Kansas Infantry. While most equipage, weapons, and accoutrements would remain the same as most generic impressions go, we were told not to bring any dog tents, relying instead on A frame or the Sibley tents. The 1st Kansas came to Wilson's Creek, in August 1861, attired in a hodge podge of military and civilian clothing, the government not having enough funds or material to completely outfit all. The majority of the men had the issue fatigue jacket or frock coat with civilian trousers and some sort of hat or cap.

By this time, most in Holmes Brigade had done a civilian impression as either a pro-slavery ruffian or as an abolitionist under John Brown for Territorial Days in Kansas. Others had done some living history at 1855 Missouri Town. The Brigade reported to Wilson's Creek that April wearing an array of trousers including colored wool, plaids, checks, jean material, and even some made of canvas. I wore a pair of white canvas drop front trousers. *I had just started doing an 1812 militia muster at Ft. Osage in which I wore a buckskin jacket, an Amish hat, and these pants. In 1988, I didn't own any other trousers, other than the Mexican War sky blue pants.*

The white canvas pants where a bit tight across the crotch and buttocks, but I made due that weekend. I did get a lot of weird looks from the boys and girls however and I was careful how I sat or bent over.

Joining us in this living history encampment at Wilson's Creek was the Missouri Confederates, the Ladies Union Aid Society, and the Confederate Ladies Organization. To be perfectly honest, we really didn't do a whole hellova lot at this event except drill and have a firing demonstration of muskets and artillery. I think both ladies groups orchestrated a fashion show up at the Ray House and we had a night firing demonstration, but beyond that, nada. I nearly forgot...our own Terry Forsyth popped the question to his girlfriend, Kay Turner, and the ladies had a fancy engagement party on their behalf-everyone got a piece of cake.

I think this was our first visit to Wilson's Creek since 1983. By now the park had its brand new visitor's center completed. Gone was the old trailer that housed a few meager objects. The new building had an auditorium, which could seat nearly 100 people. It had two walls of original paintings and other artwork, including a diorama; plus it had battle relics in display cases and an electric light show. The latter was a 3D topographical map of the Wilson's Creek battlefield, built in a round display case in the center of the back room. Once the lights dimmed, visitors gathered around it on all sides and were treated to the sight of colored lights moving across the 3 dimensional map, which represented troop movement during the battle. A taped narrative played in sync with the action that was going on. There are only a few Civil War battlefields that use an electronic map to help tell the story of the battle and Wilson's Creek has one of the finest-for my money.

By now, Dave Bennett was a member of Holmes Brigade. Just a year earlier, he had been commanding a battalion of Johnny Rebs at Shiloh as a full Colonel. Now he was just a plain ordinary Union private. How did this come about you ask? Let Dave explain it:

*"I worked my way up as commander of the "**Missouri Brigade**" which all of the Missouri Confederate units belonged to. As the prestige of the Brigade grew, so did the egos of a few of the Confederate company commanders. Politics invaded my*

world, but I survived, and so did the Missouri Brigade. I commanded a Confederate Infantry battalion at the Movie set of North/South II. I was also offered command of one of the three Confederate battalions at the 125th Battle of Manassas or Bull Run. The following year, I recruited an Infantry Brigade for the 125th Battle of Shiloh. At this event, I commanded over 950 men on the Battlefield, including the tactical command of the Cavalry and light Artillery.

"The politics with the Confederate units, and a reluctance to improve their impressions drove me to the point that I simply had enough. I wanted to leave the Missouri Confederate Brigade in good hands, however, and was working with Jay Jackson to bring him back as Commander. After Shiloh, I announced my resignation, and with glee, joined the Holmes Brigade as a private soldier. What a relief to drop the burden of responsibility and unending political bull crap.

"I will never forget my tenure with the Confederates, the Missouri Brigade, 125th Manassas, and 125th Shiloh. We had fostered a great cooperation with Dickson Stauffer and the Holmes Brigade and could always work together. The boys in the Missouri Brigade and my Battalions that honored me with command, I will never forget. That same year, I attended the battle of Pilot Knob for the first time as a Federal. Dickson honored me by appointing me as his adjutant. It was unbelievable to be in Fort Davidson for the first time to watch as the hordes of Johnny's were slaughtered before my very own eyes.

"Leaving the Missouri Brigade was difficult, yet my choice to join my pards in the Holmes made it an easy transition. Now it was the Life of Riley, spooning with my pards, drinking popskull, and generally causing trouble wherever we went. My first reenactment life was full of responsibility, and my second was one of total enjoyment.

"From Confederate Colonel to Federal Private, I've done it and have the T-shirt and video to prove it."

May 14-15, 1988 Ft. Scott, KS

I have written a whole chapter in the previous volume about events at the National Historic Site at Fort Scott, Kansas, but I would like to relate an incident that occurred on Saturday morning before moving on to the grand Gettysburg adventure.

As with most trips to any event site, the prime activity on Friday night is to get corned. After setting up tents and changing into wool, we would go over to the nearest saloon. By sunup, most of us were feeling pretty well hung over, including yours truly. However, Fort Scott NHS Superintendent Arnold Schofield, wanted Holmes Brigade to participate in a ceremony that Saturday morning at the National Cemetery.

*A brief description of Arnold Schofield is in order before proceeding. He has been running Fort Scott for as long as I can remember, well over 20 years. During the living history weekend, he will usually be dressed in the parade ground uniform of a sergeant major of dragoons from the time period 1847, complete with a large shako (*dress hat*) on his head. Arnold is a huge bull of a man, has a loud drill sergeant voice when he wants your attention and has worn the same large white beard as long as I've known him. He is not one to be trifled with, but he can be a softy once you get to know him. Recently we had a candlelight event at the fort, one scenario which dealt with a "farmer" who came to the fort to complain about the railroad wanting to move him and his family off their land. This play actor told me he was going to get in Arnold's face during the scenario and argue. I tried to tell him he better watch out, but he pooh-poohed my warnings. Sure enough, once the public arrived at our scenario, the fellow acted up like I'd feared. He got within two inches of Arnold's nose and began screaming about the railroad and his farm. He barely got two syllables out before Arnold closed one meaty paw around the collar of his coat and lifted him up on his toes. Keeping it within first person all the way, Arnold read the "farmer" the riot act right then and there. He said you will move yourself off the land, you will not harass the railroad people, and you will not cause the army any more problems. During this exchange, I stood back with my mouth open in shock. After the candlelight tour had concluded, I told the guy he had better not try that stuff again, even if it was only playacting. Arnold will definitely tear you a new one if you try to get into his face.*

Coming back to the proposed ceremony at the National Cemetery, we assembled at 8 AM for a five-mile bus ride to the other side of town. Once we got to within 'a quarter-mile' of the cemetery, we disembarked and formed ranks for the march in. A four-man honor guard was assigned to march about five paces ahead of everyone else. Two men on the flanks carried their musket's reversed-butts to the front, barrel facing down and to the rear. The two inside men carried flags. I was asked to carry one of the ceremonial flags. It may have been the Kansas state flag, but I don't recall, because I was woozy and feared I would vomit at any moment, because of last night's debauchery.

I recall we had a stiff wind that morning, our flags snapping in the breeze as we wound our way in solemn procession. About half way to the cemetery, the flagpole I was holding suddenly came apart in the center. The upper end-with the Kansas flag-dropped to the pavement, but I caught it in one bounce and without breaking stride, I reinserted the two ends back together and continued marching. Where the two pieces of the flagpole were joined together, the carpenter devised a male/female coupling but the male end was only an inch long. And just like in sex, if your male end is only an inch long, you're not going to stay in very long.

All the rest of the way to the cemetery and through the half-hour presentation with several speakers, I battled that flagpole. The wind was still brisk and many times I thought the flagpole would separate and get away from me. I had a grip on both ends of that quivering pole till my knucklebones nearly popped through my skin. I forgot all about my pounding headache and nausea from last night's drunk. Finally the ceremony was concluded we were dismissed, and the first person who came up to me was Arnold Schofield. He'd been as nervous as a cat, but was relieved and congratulated me on my battle with the flagpole. It took me a short while till I could get my fingers to work again.

The craziest thing happened to me about one week after Ft. Scott that demands it's telling. It almost complicated my trip to Gettysburg. I was at work, at Missouri Poster, involved in my normal screen making duties, when I suddenly felt ill and nauseous. I was overwhelmed with an urge to vomit and I did. At the same time, I felt very uncomfortable on my right side. It took me about a second to realize that I had an ailment similar to one I'd had ten years earlier. I had a kidney stone!

I couldn't very well stay at the shop and vomit. It seems the pressure of the kidney stone caused me nausea. I left work and went straight home. I may have had to pull the truck over to vomit during the half-hour trip. Anyway, once I told Mona of the goings on, we went straight over to the doctor's office. I couldn't go directly to the hospital without a visit to the doctor first! I had to wait nearly an hour before seeing the doctor and in the meantime, I made frequent visits to the restroom to spew. The restroom door was not soundproof. Everyone in the doctor's waiting room knew what I was doing, but I couldn't give a shit!

Finally I was let in. The doctor was a big boned gal in her thirties. I told her of the ailment and nausea and that I was positive that it was caused by a kidney stone. She had to give me an examination nevertheless, including an x-ray and a squeeze of my crank. Yes, she wanted to touch my penis to make sure there was no pain there, so I said, "Go ahead." Realizing that I suffered no stiffness anywhere else, she gave me a form to take to the emergency room. By this time, I was still heaving, but very little came up.

To make a long story short, I had to spend the night in the hospital and early next morning I was wheeled into the operating room where the Urologist ran a pipe cleaner up my crank to dislodge the stone. You see, x-rays showed that the stone was stuck on the tissue wall of the canal that goes from the kidney to the bladder. I was sedated (thank God!) and a skinny metal rod went up the pee hole. There is a medical name for this procedure, but I don't recall what that name is. (*Note: In 1978, I'd passed the kidney stone, this time I couldn't*)

I woke up groggy and disorientated about an hour later, spent another night in the hospital, and when it was decided I would no longer pee blood, I was discharged. My crank was sore for the longest time. The Urologist left a flexible tube in my urinary tract called a stint. After two weeks, I went back to his office where he pulled it out. A string hung out of my pee hole, the other end attached to the stint, which was about two feet long. He pulled it out and as it came out inch by inch, it felt like a pipe cleaner wrapped in sandpaper. I almost went into orbit. Anyway, this little medical adventure would have kept me from going to Gettysburg, if it had occurred a few weeks later. Praise the Lord the stone came when it did!

June 20-July 4, 1988 Gettysburg, PA

As I stated at the beginning of this chapter, the family and I were planning on incorporating the 125th anniversary battle reenactment of Gettysburg with a site-seeing adventure through historic Virginia, Maryland, and the Nation's Capitol. We'd taken the back seat out of the mini van and filled that empty space-nearly to the roof-with boxes, suitcases, tents, blankets, and etc. and began our adventure on Monday, June 20th. Once again we had Tony the house sitter watching the place in our absence.

That first day, leaving about 7 or 8 in the morning, we drove twelve straight hours till we stopped in Columbus, Ohio, for the night. Six-year-old Katie was supplied with tons of coloring books, dolls, and other time consuming knickknacks, so she didn't fuss too much. Mona and I took turns driving-using the new fangled cruise control quite a bit. The next morning, we drove up into Pennsylvania and stopped for the night at Chambersburg. We actually arrived in the afternoon and we could have driven a dozen or so more miles to Gettysburg, but figured we'd spend one more night in a motel, eat a hearty breakfast, then face the event in the light of a new day. *Reenactors were asked be to on site by Thursday morning, if possible, especially the infantry boys. The battle reenactment would begin on Friday morning, so Thursday was viewed as a day to form the battalions and learn the drill.* At Chambersburg that Tuesday night, we had supper, and then found a nearby movie theatre in town that was showing <u>WHO FRAMED ROGER RABBIT</u>.

Wednesday morning, we drove into Gettysburg, the Mecca of all things Civil War. People from around the world are drawn to Gettysburg as if it were the Holy City of Jerusalem. I guess one reason is because so many books have been written about it, Picket's famous charge, and especially Abe's little talk…"four score," etc., etc. The locals have turned Gettysburg into an obscene tourist trap. Vendors and shopkeepers of all kinds have souvenir stands, antique shops, wax museums, bed and breakfasts, and drive thru restaurants. There are even Off-Broadway productions, most notably one fellow who does an Abe Lincoln one man show for a dinner theatre crowd. The way the locals attempt to turn a buck on the site of America's greatest battlefield is almost as obscene a display as if driving thru Branson, Missouri. Nevertheless, if a major battle had been fought on the front yard of MY hometown, I suppose I'd try to turn a buck as well. Maybe open up a hot dog stand or sell dirt at a dollar a bucket.

In the National Park itself, we visited the museum, the Cyclorama, wandered the battlefield up to Little Round Top, and even went up the Gettysburg observation tower (*this eyesore, purist said, detracted from the historical look of the battlefield and sometime in the late 1990's it was demolished*).

By midday, we pulled into a burger place and bumped into Gail Higginbotham of all people. I think her, Gregg, and Hillari were staying at the Gettysburg Motel 6. They had reserved lodging a year in advance. She said there were a butt load of people at the reenactment site lined up to register and we should get over there soon. She said we might have to stand in line for an hour or better. So we hopped back into the Aerostar and drove the 5.5 miles south on the Emmitsburg Road till we found the turn off into the site.

Other than the Gettysburg reenactment, the National Park was hosting a rededication ceremony on the original battlefield, which would take place a week later on the anniversary date. Another ceremony was planned, at around the same time as the NPS event, on some property just northwest of Gettysburg. During the Franklin Delano Roosevelt administration in 1938, a monument to peace was erected. For the fiftieth anniversary, President Ronald Reagan and past President Jimmy Carter were expected to attend, along with 150,000 spectators. An additional draw to the Peace Light Memorial ceremony was an expected outdoor concert like a Woodstock. I think the entertainment would be along the lines of a Joan Baez or something non-threatening. Hotel/motel rooms had been booked for months.

Before proceeding with our arrival at the event, a word should be said that almost one year earlier, two Gettysburg's were proposed. One event was being organized by a group called the Gettysburg National Memorial Committee / Eastern Battalion / National Regiment, while the other Gettysburg was being proposed by a new group called Napoleonic Tactics Incorporated / American Civil War Commemorative Committee. Both sides claimed **they** would have the ultimate Gettysburg experience and reenactors should support them and not the other. In several letters to Camp Chase Gazette, members of the eastern faction claimed NTI was not interested in putting on a quality event. They claimed head organizer Pat Massengill an egotist, was only concerned with lining his own pockets, and was employing "back door wheeling and dealing" to get his event pushed through.

A couple of things in Pat Massengill's favor were he had organized the 125th Manassas back in '86 and it was a spectacular! Secondly he was from the Midwest and he'd quit his job in order to devote his entire energies to putting together mega-sized Civil War events. In September of '87, NTI had put together its first mega-event in the shape of Antietam. All hands were waiting to see how that event panned out before committing to one of the Gettysburg's. I definitely recall someone from either NTI or the National Regiment group coming to the Perryville reenactment of October '87 to soapbox campaign for their upcoming Gettysburg event. Aaron Racine had just been out east the past summer, where he'd met Pat McDermott and friends, and he was well acquainted with the National Regiment boys. Naturally, he was affected with eastern bias. For the rest of us, we stated we would wait to see what the feedback would be from last month's NTI Antietam event before making a decision.

For months people wondered if there'd be a Gettysburg event at all or perhaps two or three small ones instead. Then came the after action reports on Antietam:

"*...No proof of allegations against NTI*"

"*Antietam wins hands down!*"

"*Fantastic job at Antietam...most enjoyable reenactment!*"

"*Antietam...excellent event...most pleasurable event I've attended!*"

"*All the politics against Mr. Massengill, is, in our opinion, Bull!*"

"*Hats off!*"

"*Three hearty huzzahs to ACWCC / NTI for the Antietam event!*"

"*AWESOME! TREMENDOUS! MAGNIFICENT!*"

"*The ACWCC / NTI Gettysburg is the only one to attend in June!*"

Finally on Nov 21st, 1987, at an Eastern Battalion / National Regiment conference, the members voted unanimously to suspend plans for their Gettysburg event. There was just too much positive feedback about the NTI, Pat Massengill and the handling of the Antietam event. To continue on would be ludicrous. Instead, all vowed to support the Massengill event. We would at last have the large Gettysburg everyone dreamed of.

After a brief, but scenic drive south in our mini-van, we reached the turn off into the event site. The location was barely spittin' distance from the Maryland state line. Two "rent-a-cops" waved us through the narrow gate, over the rough dirt driveway and indicated to us where we could park and where registration was. It was like trying to enter the parking lot of a football stadium with folks in colored jerseys telling you where to go. The reenactment would be held on approximately 700 acres of property soon to be turned into an industrial complex. A rough map of the event site, which was included in the registration packet, indicates that spectator parking alone would consume about one hundred acres. Reenactor parking was 30 acres.

After we found a place to park, we walked a short distance to the huge registration tent where we stood in an endless line of humanity for no less than an hour. Finally, the three of us were able to "belly up" to a huge table where a dozen volunteers stood behind stacks and stacks of forms. Waiver's had to be signed (so you wouldn't sue Napoleonic Tactics if you got hurt during the course of the event), plus forms had to be filled out citing next of kin (where to send the body). You also had to list which unit you were with. Finally parking passes were issued, plus coupons and directional road maps so you knew where you were at and where you were going.

Back to the mini-van, we drove to the where the camps were located. The road to the campsite was narrow, barely allowing for two cars to pass each other. Halfway to the camp, we drove through a small city populated with hundreds of campers, RV's, and pop-up tents. Also in this area were the modern vendors, looking like so many 'carpetbaggers' or leeches. The goal of these vampires was to suck the dollars from thousands of visiting spectators with over priced bottled water, t-shirts, cotton candy, funnel cakes, and any two-bit piece of junk with a GETTYSBURG decal on it. Mobile kitchens were already filling the air with the aroma of overcooked food while re-recorded Civil War music warbled from cassette players. It looked straight out of the Missouri State Fair. The only thing not offered was the Ferris wheel, bumper cars, and the freak show. On second thought, the reenactors **were the freak show!**

At least ten thousand reenactors were expected for the G'burg shindig. This included 300 cavalry, 100 full scale guns, 2,000 civilians, and over 100 authentic sutlers. I personally counted ten rows of sutler tents with each row approximately 100 yards long. These peddlers offered "everything from biscuits to bullets". There were leather merchants, clothing merchants, hat makers, boot makers, saddle makers, gun smiths, tin smiths, dealers who sold ladies apparel, Pat McDermott with his paper products, and one or two photographers taking tin types and paper CDV's. And this is only to name a few!

When speaking of civilian impressions, not all came as refugees, Sanitary Commission workers, or politicians. I believe there was a lady in an old fashioned nun's habit, a parson or two, someone in the robes of a Catholic priest, and an "undertaker" who advertised embalming with a pine box set outside his tent. *If a soldier was fearful of his own mortality and wanted his remains properly cared for after death, the undertaker promised that, for a modest fee, proper care would be maintained using the most scientific methods of embalming.* Attending a reenactment does not always mean putting on a uniform and totting a musket. For some it is perfectly okay to interpret the nineteenth century as a civilian, as long as you can legitimize the impression and pay the registration.

Obviously someone who is doing a civilian impression will not participate in the battles that are planned. The battle reenactment occupied only a small fraction of the 4-day festival. There would be band music, fashion shows, a barn dance, an ice cream social, medical demonstrations, a ballet class, a Temperance Rally (*Holmes Brigade play:* ***YIELD NOT TO TEMPTATION***), children's activities, sing-a-longs, lectures, Civil War film festivals, and church services. Pat Massengill did not plan on anyone having a dull time while at his Gettysburg event. A few activities, including the film festivals, the barn dance, and the band concert, did not begin till after 9 PM. All this for only five dollars registration!

While on the subject of civilians, our own Ladies Union Aid Society had an area designated for their own use, but landscapers had not had time to clear the tall weeds. Borrowing a weed whacker from the event people, Higgy cleared the area himself. This might have been on Tuesday that he did this. By the time we arrived in the mini-van late Wednesday afternoon, the area had been leveled.

And so the wall tent was set up, the rope beds were assembled, and all the boxes and clothes for both Mona and Katie were unloaded from the mini-van and placed in the tent along with all of Gail and Hillari's stuff. After about an hour getting the girls comfortable, I drove "just a quarter-mile more" to the Federal encampment- located just to the south of the civilian area.

Once again, Holmes Brigade was part of the Western Brigade under the command of Chris Craft. *Approximately 600 infantrymen had registered with the Western Brigade, which was divided into two battalions. There would be six companies in each battalion, so it is safe to say each company was composed of at least 50 men.* Mark Upton commanded First battalion, which included Holmes Brigade, Logans Brigade (*Illinois sucker boys*), 14th Indiana, and the Mudsills. Dave Shackleford commanded the second battalion, which had some cats from Ohio, Indiana, Minnesota, and Arizona. I'll have more to say about the illustrious Shackleford at a later time.

Small wooden signs had been placed to indicate where each battalion/company was to set up. It was imperative that each unit stayed in their assigned area. The Western Brigade was one part of a two part Federal Division commanded by Mike Krause. Not sure who commanded the other Brigade, but it was probably some eastern puke.

The entire Federal Division occupied an area about twice as big as a football field. The Confederates, I'm sure, had an equal strength of numbers, maybe more. I quickly located the Western Brigade part of the field, and then had to find the sign where Holmes could camp, and then I put up my dog tent and settled in. I had two uniform coats, one or two blankets, and the usual accoutrements of an infantryman. I might have had one small wooden ammunition box or quite possibly the hardpack. I had about 300 pre-rolled cartridges for the event, plus a few minor necessities including pipe and tobacco, so I would have kept them in some sort of container-other than just crammed in my pockets. After unloading my "poop," I went ahead and changed into my wool duds, and then I took the van back to reenactor parking, locked it up, and walked back to the camp-a distance of about a mile and a half, as the crow flies. A few more Holmes Brigade boys had come in while I was gone and had set up their shelter tents in shebang fashion; looking more like Indian lean-tos or awnings to crawl under.

Dave Bennett, Don Whitson, and a few others had taken a commercial flight and had rented a car. One of their traveling companions, David Bailey, had had his baggage lost at the airport, so I tore off my sergeant's chevrons and loaned him my sack coat. A few hours later, Bailey's lost baggage was recovered, so I had to sew the chevrons back on! While the boys were setting up their shebangs, Higginbotham drove over from the ladies area and ran over six muskets as they lay on the ground. Fortunately, the muskets were lying flat and the tires gently rolled over them with no damage done. Higgy and all the rest of us breathed a sigh of relief. Catastrophe avoided!

Throughout Wednesday evening and well into the wee hours of Thursday morning, vehicles continued to come in and out. It was next to impossible to sleep that first night-the tent stakes that were being pounded into the ground sounded like the mating call of thousands of iron clad crickets. Add the artificial light from automobiles and/or hand held flashlights that swept the air all night and it's like a scene from CLOSE ENCOUNTERS OF THE THIRD KIND. Once these same people set up their canvas homes, they'd put on their 19th century duds and spend the rest of the evening around blazing campfires shouting, singing, laughing, and getting reacquainted with other recently arrived comrades with the sharing of alcohol. Most are too excited to sleep that first night. *Holmes Brigade has historically done the same thing the first night of any event, which is to drink popskull and gossip.* Because it was the 125th anniversary reenactment of GETTYSBURG, by damn, you could feel the electricity in the air that first night. It was like being on a high, half of it alcohol induced I'm sure.

The Thursday morning sun rose on an ocean of white canvas. As far as the eye could see, there were these little puffy clouds, the tents looking like mushrooms that'd materialized during the night. Bleary eyed men crawled out from under these tents, faces stretched into yawns, fists rubbing the sleep from red rimmed eyes. These early risers made a beeline to the portable toilets, while they were still somewhat fresh and didn't stink too bad. Others shrugged into shoes, trousers, and jackets, and began searching for the elusive coffeepot. Within fifteen minutes after reveille, the boys staggered to their feet to answer the first roll call of the day.

One hundred men had registered with Holmes Brigade. These were divided into Companies A and B with Don Strother commander of A Company and Bill Fannin, commander of B Company. I was First Sergeant of the former, while Frank Kirtley was the top soldier of the latter. Among the duties of First Sergeant was the taking of roll call, the assigning of fatigue details, and making morning reports to the battalion sergeant major. I also had to keep a record of how many black powder cartridges the men had, and how many were fired throughout the day. For example, if the company fired ten cartridges during drill, I had to add that number by 50, or 500 rounds expended by the company. This was then reported to the ordinance officer by the sergeant major.

It was determined that my company alone had a total of 6651 black powder cartridges between 50 men. Each man had an average of 150 to 250 cartridges apiece. By the time of Pickett's Charge on the final day of the reenactment, the men of Company A had already fired 3815 cartridges *(I still have some old notes, newsletters, and ledger as First Sergeant)*.

We still had not learned how to mess campaign style, relying instead on a company mess cook to fix chow for us. It would be yet another year before we learned how to eat out of our haversacks. What we did for Gettysburg was, each man anted up six bucks apiece to Darrell Wilson and he brought several grocery bags full of treats for us. Only those that paid got to eat. However, Darrell only had chow for Friday, Saturday, and Sunday. I don't know what we did on Thursday, but we were on our own as far as chow. Some of us may have wandered to the Ladies camp to beg for scraps of food or went shamefaced down to the carnival area for funnel cakes and cotton candy. I'll readily admit to sharing a funnel cake and lemonade one afternoon with Dave Bennett. There might have been sardines, hardtack, and jerked beef, but beyond that, I don't now what the heck we did for eatin' on Thursday.

On the first Brigade drill of the day, we marched through a field of waist high weeds. The pollen flew like a snowstorm as we kicked our way through. Holmes Brigade member Bob Potts suddenly halted and did a complete about face. It seems he'd gotten an immediate reaction from the ragweed pollen. His face got as swollen and red as a balloon. Bob left the event and did not return. What a tragedy! To come all the way from Missouri and turn around and leave after only a few moments in the summer weeds.

We had marched out of camp with fixed bayonets and at the right shoulder shift. After covering an area of several dozens yards and halting, Colonel Chris Craft told everyone to remove the bayonet. Sergeant Chuck Warnick still had his bayonet on and I brought it to his attention. He merely said, "Thank you," but left it on just the same. He might have been the sergeant major of the other battalion, but anyway, he looked at me like I was some kind of jackass. I mentally said, "Fuck you" and I have not forgotten this ever since.

It was during this early drill that the Brigade selected right and left guides. These soldiers would not have to fire their muskets during the entire event. Instead they would carry little US flags on a stick, which were stuck inside the barrel of their musket. The guides would march in a straight line, as directed by the colonel. Let me attempt to explain how the "guide" worked:

When marching in a column of fours, the men on the left of the line will march as if their left shoulder was rubbing along a wall-an imaginary wall if you will. The line of men in each column will stretch out to the right, but the anchor is the left. One guide will march on the left front of the Brigade and another will march at the left rear of the Brigade, with two more guides' left center where the two battalions break. For the most part, the men of the Brigade will turn on their left when wheeling or when forming a solid line of battle. It was paramount that the line was straight or unit cohesion would evaporate. Once at the halt, the colonel would admonish the men to step up or instruct each guide to move one way or another till the rank was as straight as the keen edge of a razor blade.

I hope I've explained the importance of guides during drill and in battle. The reason I mention guides at all is because Don Whitson became a guide. In fact he was placed in the front and marched alongside Battalion Commander Mark Upton or sometimes the Battalion Adjutant. Our battalion led the entire Brigade in drill and to the battlefield. Don Whitson, in effect, led us into and out of glory.

During one of the first battalion drills, Don was marching straight ahead. As First Sergeant, I was only about two paces behind Don, with Captain Strother on my left. Where Don Whitson led, I followed and the men of the battalion followed me. As Don tells it, an artillery crew, with a full-scale cannon and caisson, came rumbling past with Don immediately noticing, with shock and a loud exclamation, that one of the crew was female. Her bosom must have been such, that a well-buttoned tunic could not keep them confined, nor could it disguise her gender. With eyeballs and trousers bulging, Don did not notice the rock in his path until he stumbled over it. Down fell Don! Colonel Craft expressed some concern and as we all inquired if he was okay, Don said, "Did you see that woman?" Don dusted himself off, but seemed to suffer no injury. Instead, it was noticed, the pole of his little flag had broken. Embarrassed perhaps at his folly, Don mumbled an apology and quickly lashed what was left of his little flag to the barrel of his musket. When Frank Kirtley heard about this "accident," he gave Don a harmless ration of shit. Until he left Holmes Brigade about 1990, there wasn't a day that went by that Frank wasn't there to remind Don of the day he dropped the flag in the dirt. I think Frank ragged on Don just so he could see him get defensive and shrink up like a fetus. Whatever the case, dropping the flag at Gettysburg remains Don Whitson's greatest claim to infamy.

Thursday soon gave way to Friday, the first official day of the reenactment. The event strategists determined that the Friday battle would be a recreation of the first day of Gettysburg, July 1. On this day, we would be portraying elements of the famed Iron Brigade. To be specific, our battalion would be the 19th Indiana. We were asked to dress in frock coat and tall Hardee hat for this day. With the uniform of the day came the decree that "Corp badges" would be issued. These were pieces of red felt cut into a circle. We would sew/pin these to the front of our blouse.

At First Sergeants' call, the battalion sergeant major handed out these Corp badges with the provision that they were to be passed out to the men at the next formation. I returned with about 50 red circles of felt. These "Corp badges" were strung together by a single thread of string. As I entered our camp, I dangled the "Corp badges" in front of the boys like I'd just come back from the creek with the catch of the day. I should have known better. It was like dangling meat in front of hungry dogs. Higgy said, "Give us those Corp badges!" I said, "No, I'll hand them out at the next roll call." I was gang tackled by at least a dozen ruffians, thrown to the ground, and abused like I was a bitch in prison. Within moments I had been robbed of all the Corp badges except one which I was allowed to keep for myself. I staggered to my feet, dusted myself off, and admitted to the captain that I'd been defeated. He could only shake his head and remark that at least I hadn't been eaten.

Unfortunately, the battle would not commence till 5PM! Wow, what the hell were we to do all day? Fortunately, we had many more hours of drill time in front of us, plus a number of civilian/living history activities were to take place throughout the day. Many of us wandered over to **Las Vegas** (or sutler mall) where novelties were admired and purchased. I bought a new sack coat from Bruce Frazier-a C&D Jarnigan distributor, plus a lounge cap. Some of the fellows probably called it the "smoking cap." *When a soldier is wearing his "lounge or smoking cap," so the story goes, he is supposedly on his own time and exempt* *from any fatigue duties.* The cap resembles a "fez", worn by the Shriners or Egyptians from the old Mummy movies. It was made of carpet and was fitted with a hanging tassel. All the guys in Holmes Brigade got one, for about five bucks apiece. Later we posed for a group photo, each of us with our "smoking caps" and a "chin dangler"- *slang for smoking pipe.*

A battle reenactment consists of a lot of shooting, marching, running, and falling down. The only difference this time was the shooting, marching, running, and falling down would be on a much larger scale. What is best remembered are the little things that occur during this organized mayhem.

The Western Brigade was portraying elements of the Iron Brigade, as I'd already mentioned, which fought on July 1. After nearly an hour running around through sections of the field, "The Iron Brigade" entered a copse of woods-designated McPhersons Woods-and formed on the other side. Going through the foliage had an effect of fragmenting our column of companies. Once on the other side, we reformed the ranks and went into a line of battle facing left. I believe we were ordered to take a knee, so we reclined against the embankment and waited for the ball to open. Nearby was a group of fellows who were portraying Hiram Berdan's Sharpshooters. *With a uniform of dull green, possibly to blend into nature, these men had been recruited into this special unit, about 1862, because of their ability as marksmen.* There were about 50 of these soldiers and I believe they all had the Sharp's breechloading carbine. While we sat and waited, a few of the company wags started up with some harmless name-calling. The boys in green heard themselves called, "Green Beans," "Sprouts," "Sweet Peas," and "Pickles." They were good sports and took the ribbing with no ill effects. Once the ball opened up and the Confederates began their advance, the boys of Berdan's would make those carbines sing.

I believe our battalion had not yet fired. However, the sound of musketry was slowing advancing in our direction with the noise sounding like a giant popcorn popper. I distinctly remember making that comment to anyone within earshot. I don't recall seeing anything of the enemy, only the rolling thunder of thousands of popping muskets. The enemy might have been over the brow of the next hill. I don't know where the rest of the Federal army was positioned, off on another part of the field no likely. *The battlefield looked like a chessboard with each battalion, both Blue and Gray, a pawn on that chessboard and controlled by the hand of the commanding general. Some pieces moved one way, some another. It was not a pretty sight.* For my part, all I can remember is that suddenly a thousand Confederates came over the hill, about a hundred yards from us, slowly advancing with battle flags snapping in the breeze.

Once given the order, the men of our battalion commenced firing by volley and by individual. We did manage to check the advance of the Confederates for a brief time. For the next half-hour, black powder was blown back and forth between friend and foe. At a preordained point in the scenario, the Confederates renewed their slow walk towards us and we saw the need to vacate the area. We were on low ground and as we looked up, the long gray wall seemed to tower over us and nearly blot out the sun. Their line must have been a quarter mile long and it looked like every one of those Confederates had a musket aimed right at my heart. Dozens of casualties had been taken by this time, but most of us opted to try to get on the other side of McPherson's Woods. We nearly waited to the last minute before giving up the ghost. Once the word was given, we fell back through the woods. Unit cohesion had evaporated. It was tough getting through the tangled growth anyway, so it was "get through as best as you can and then reform on the other side".

Before proceeding I should mention the unofficial mascot of the Holmes Brigade, a little black rag doll, named John Henry. Actually, John Henry was the stepchild of our old pal Mark Gardner from Colorado. The rag doll was only about six inches tall and as black as the inside of a cow with dreadlocks that looked like the arms of an octopus. A red checked shirt and bib overalls completed his appearance. John Henry, the rag doll, first made his appearance at an early Pilot Knob event, I think. While Mark Gardner played on his banjo, Higgy would make the doll dance. John Henry came to Gettysburg, along with his master, but Higgy carried it around on his person. During a break in drill, Higgy would produce John Henry from a pocket or haversack and bounce him around on someone's head like he was doing a funky dance.

As you might have guessed, John Henry was with us on the first day of the Gettysburg reenactment. I believe Higgy had tied him to his canteen strap by the black dreadlocks. As we retreated through the confusion of limbs and brush that was "McPhersons Woods," John Henry came loose and fell on the forest floor. You should have seen the look of alarm that spread over Higgy's face as he realized his rag doll comrade was missing. Despite the fact that a thousand Confederates were nipping at our heels and worming through the woods from the opposite side, Higgy went back in to save the Holmes Brigade mascot.

The battalion was in shambles, but we managed to form a ragged line facing the woods we'd just come out of. About this time we were joined all around us by the rest of the Brigade, who'd fought near us but were separated by the grove of trees. Above the din of roaring muskets and cannon, coming from other parts of the "chessboard," came a great crashing from the woods as if King Kong were lumbering through, smashing everything in his path. Battalion Staff officers ran up and down the makeshift line with frantic orders telling us to quickly load and come to the ready. While in this feverish act of loading our weapons, there suddenly came an unholy scream, as if from the souls of the damned. It was the dreaded Rebel yell coming from a thousand throats. The effect of that chilling cry was like an ice water enema. A shout from Commander Mark Upton and we leveled our muskets at where we expected the enemy to appear. Suddenly, like a rabbit bolting from his hole, came Gregg Higginbotham with John Henry rescued. Less than ten paces behind him, the gray clad legions of the Confederate Army appeared. They seemed to ooze out of the woods like shit squeezed between a fat man's toes.

The enemy was less than fifty yards from us as they came out of the woods, so for safety sake, we were obligated to "elevate our fire." *This means we lift the musket slightly so the discharge of black powder does not fly into the face of the enemy. At a reenactment, safety is Job One. If you can see the white of your foe's eyes, you and he are too close to fire safely. That is when you lift the musket and fire over his head. Nothing is worse than getting a face full of black powder from an over zealous reenactor. It's happened to me once, in 1982, and I had blurred vision for nearly six hours afterwards.*

We fired our volley, into the tree tops, then we skeedaddled. **Every man for himself**! I had taken no more than ten steps when the Confederate demons unleashed their weapons upon our fleeing backsides. Like dozens of others, I collapsed and went into my death throes. The survivors of our Brigade continued to trade volleys with the foe-even as the "dead and dying" lay in no man's land. The muskets from both armies continued to explode and I could feel the wash of heat over my body at each discharge. Finally, I heard shouted commands and the Confederate line advanced till they passed by me. Someone rifled through my cartridge box, but other than the loss of a few rounds, I was not violated. The enemy pressed on past me. My face was in the dirt, but I could hear them continue on in the pursuit of my comrades.

I think I lay there for fifteen minutes while the battle continued to rage all around me. Slowly, the gunfire began to "peter out" and lose its intensity. It then became so quiet it was deafening. "Resurrection Day!" This shout meant GAME OVER and we all could rise from the dead. Thousands of spectators pounded their hands together as all the casualties of the battle rose to their feet. I slapped the Pennsylvania dust off my frock coat and located my musket. As I tilted my head back and drank in some warm canteen water, I noticed all around me the hundreds of boys who had played "dead" as I had. Bodies of both armies lay on that huge field as thick as fleas on a dog's back with barely two paces between each man. Higgy lay about ten yards from me, the doll John Henry tucked securely inside his coat and out of sight of prying Confederate eyes. That completed the adventures for day one.

I think the LUAS had cold lemonade and snack cookies waiting for all of us fagged out boy's right after the fight. I don't know exactly how the ladies occupied most of their time, but as I'd mentioned earlier, a number of civilian activities were available. The two little girls, my Katie and Hillari Higginbotham, found diversions of their own to occupy their time. A china tea set was one such diversion. At a little table, they served tea (or water), cookies, and hard crackers to themselves or to any friendly face who wandered into the camp. The rugged outdoors was just another adventure for the two seven year olds. They never seemed bothered with living in a tent, running around in camp dresses, or eating badly cooked campfire food. The girls loved horses and they could usually get a ride from a friendly cavalryman with just one smile.

Day two (Saturday) began with the sound of "reveille," blasted at the ungodly hour of 5AM. Roll call was taken, which included a tally of black powder cartridges from each man. Plus, fatigue details were assigned for men to gather wood, water, or help with the kitchen clean up. Once all these petty assignments had been taken care of, a visit was made by the captain to appraise us of the plan of the day. Those of us in the ranks, who stood like tired scarecrows, stank of sweat and campfire smoke. No one cut a more dapper figure, however, than Captain Don Strother, dressed in a uniform that looked as if it had been made in New York City. Don strolled over from Brigade headquarters with all the regal pomp and circumstance of a Turkish prince. Every button on his frock coat shined like polished glass. He wore his cap like a crown, but had it tilted at a rakish angle. Wound around his waspish waist was a scarlet sash. A belt rigging/harness was buckled over this sash, from which hung a Colt Navy revolver in a smooth holster and a saber in a scabbard the color of a black pearl. Don always walked ramrod straight, never slouched-it was if a two by four ran up his back. His features were fair, as was the color of his hair and beard. It wasn't even 6 AM, yet Captain Don already had a "dog turd" in his mouth! As he puffed away on that Corona, he announced we would be portraying elements from 3rd Corp, 1st Division, a unit originally under the command of General Dan Sickles. History states that this unit would find itself on the short end of the stick, by the close of the second day at Gettysburg.

"On this day, 3rd Corp commander Dan Sickles did not like the sector assigned to his men along Cemetery Ridge. It was too long and low to his liking and he unilaterally decided to advance to the Peach Orchard. If he had survived the battle unscathed he probably would have been court-martialed. But some claim that his advanced position absorbed the shock of Longstreet's assault before it could reach the ridge. This theory claims that if the assault had hit the ridge in full strength it would have broken the Union line. This is, however, highly debatable since his movement exposed his flanks to the enemy. "Always courageous on the field of battle, he was struck in the leg by a shell as his

command was beginning its withdrawal. The leg was amputated within half an hour. In 1867 he was breveted regular army major general for his role in the battle and three decades later was awarded the Congressional Medal of Honor. He donated his leg to an army medical museum and it is said in later years is said to have visited it."

Off came our frock coats and Hardee hats, and on came the sack coat, forage cap, and a different Corp badge. We were given the red trefoil. It looked like a club from a deck of playing cards. I didn't hand these Corp badges like I'd done the others. I learned my lesson. Someone else may have handed them out or the Captain passed them out that morning while we were in formation. The battle would not commence until 5PM, so once again the Brigade officers found diversions for us in the form of drill and more drill. In the early afternoon, the boys of Holmes Brigade and the LUAS put on the temperance rally, which included the aforementioned tableau vivant, YIELD NOT TO TEMPTATION.

The "battle" that we held at 5PM that day can best described as one in which we marched in one direction for a quarter mile, made a sharp left hand turn, marched another quarter mile, made another sharp turn, and so on. We probably covered four square miles in two hours. We began by marching in division formations (*120 men abreast*), then we wheeled left into line (*600 men abreast*), fired by the drum, and made a right wheel back into division formation. Then proceeded a bit further and when felt pressed by the enemy, we'd wheel left again into a line of battle (*600 men*) to send another perfectly fired volley into the gray masses. We really shined on firing by the drum this day. Every blue jacket that held a musket fired as one man. At the same time as us Western Brigade boys were going through our antics, the other boys in blue were moving about-some in opposite or parallel directions. Again, the movements of all participants had the look of a mad chessboard. Exploding muskets, artillery, and horsemen stampeding past with urgent dispatches, coupled with randomly placed ground charges and aerial bursts, created a wide screen Technicolor circus act of epic proportions. At one point our battalion came to a halt less than twenty yards from the spectators. I heard my name called and glancing over my right shoulder, I spied Mona and Katie sitting on a blanket with a picnic basket. Mona had the camera and had been snapping a few images of the battle. I was only a pace behind Don Whitson, the front guide of our battalion. As Mona squinted through the camera to frame her shot, I lifted the fabric of Don's little flag so Old Glory could be seen.

As God is my witness, this is all I can recall of Day Two of Gettysburg. We marched around the entire park, fired by the drum, and had our pictures taken. I'm not sure how the fight concluded, but assume us Federals were slowly whittled away (*just as in the original fight*). On the way back to camp, the volunteer fire department was working a hose over everyone that walked past. They had it adjusted to emit a fine mist and the relief was welcome because it was damn hot. Unfortunately the water was also getting our muskets wet, so a few of the boys voiced their displeasure and the hose was turned aside. Back at camp, we settled down for a steaming plate of stew (*or leper in a hot tub*) and cold lemonade. After a few minor activities, we then retired to our blankets for the night.

A word should be said here regarding a mysterious growth that invaded the Union camp. I don't know why these were not placed near the port-a-johns, but instead, two or three metal trash cans were placed smack dab in the middle of the grand Union army. I believe they were located in an area with several yards of open space on all sides, but they were right in the middle and an eyesore to any passersby. As time went along, the trash issue would become a bigger eyesore as well as a sore to the nostrils. It started with a plastic cup (probably brought up from the vendors), then a plastic bag, a few tin cans, and cardboard boxes. As I recall, no one came to pick up the trash. *Come to think of it, I don't even recall if the port-a-johns were emptied during our stay.* After four days the pile of trash was fifty feet long by four feet high. What I can't understand is what the make was up of all that trash? Did everybody bring their food in tin cans, plastic baggies, or cardboard boxes? Was alcohol consumed every night? Were those empty beer cans and whiskey bottles part of the trash heap? For a bunch of people striving for authenticity, we sure created a lot of modern looking trash.

The final day at Gettysburg, Sunday, June 26. The reenactment of Pickett's Grand Charge would commence at 2PM! A Grand Review was planned that morning for all the Union forces in the encampment, but at the last minute, it was canceled. It is rumored that a certain high ranking general could not find a horse "to sit on and look pretty"- *this quote comes from the Camp Gossip section of the newsletter Camp Chase Gazette.* I seem to recall we all were quite disappointed we could not show off for the spectators. I think the Confederates had a review, but our hopes for one came to an abrupt halt because of some miscommunication.

Earlier in the day, or possibly even the day before we all wondered where the "charge" would take place. That was when someone told me it would be in the field just north of sutler row. This was a field where we had done most of our drilling. It certainly was long enough, but did not seem very wide. However, at the opposite end stood a single tall, bushy tree. One hundred yards behind the single tree was spectator parking. When the fighting would commence here, us Yankee boys would be boxed in. Spectators were on our left, spectator parking was on our right and rear, and finally, Confederates was in our front. It was a narrow place to host the most memorable fight of the Gettysburg battle, but no other option was available *or attempted.* Our position was not unlike one that we held over a year earlier at Shiloh, when we were boxed in during the battle known as the Hornet's Nest.

Let me diagram the placement of the Union forces as I recall them. In the very front was a rail fence. Only about knee high and composed of cut tree limbs, this "wall" stretched from our right to our left nearly one hundred yards. In this small area, a 100-yard by 50-yard rectangle, all the Federals were packed in. Behind the fence would be a row of soldiers flat on their bellies. Behind these boys, were the artillery-about twenty guns strong. Behind the guns stood soldiers in column formation and in the rear stood another group of Federals in reserve.

For lunch we had ham and cheese sandwiches. The fire pit had been drowned and all the cook gear stowed away. We formed up about 12:30. We always had to get ready at least a good hour before the first shot of any battle reenactment.

We marched up from our camps, in column of fours, every single Union infantryman that could be mustered. We looked like a long dark blue snake as we went to our places, with bright smiling faces. I'll hazard a guess that there were more than 1,200 Yankee boys that day; maybe as many as two thousand. We took our assigned places, as preordained, at Brigade HQ-then we simply waited for the ball to open.

Over on the left, spectators were packed in an area an eighth of a mile long at least ten deep. There must have been tens of thousands of cooler carrying, lawn chair sitting; baby stroller pushing sweaty men, women, and kids who'd paid their few bucks to see this circus act. Witnessing the reenactments of the first two days of Gettysburg was one thing, but to be able to witness the grand climax, or Pickett's Charge, was icing on the cake with a cherry on top.

After what seemed an eternity, a single cannon roared. The crowd let out a collective gasp and squeal. The gun must have been a signal, because suddenly more than sixty Confederate guns belched. Their artillery was just on the edge of the tree line, some three hundred yards to our front. Our own twenty guns replied. *There was no one in front of our guns at the rail fence at this time. After the half-hour artillery duel finished, then the boys would move down.*

The Union artillery fired as a whole, in two's or three's at once, or sometimes one after the other from right to left. Randomly placed ground charges hurled potting soil and corkboard high into the air, while aerial bursts cracked with an ear splitting snap. The wind was blowing that rotten egg smell into the faces of all the men, women, and children behind the tape. Before long these spectators would be using their precious bottled water to wash the grit out of their eyes and teeth.

After dozens of loud artillery rounds had been vomited back and forth for about a half-hour, a calm settled over the scene. Ammunition limbers were wheeled away so they would not be in the line of fire once the infantry opened up. *You never want to get too close to an artillery ammunition box with a flashing musket. You're asking for a one way ticket to eternal damnation if a spark from your poorly aimed musket accidentally ignites the rounds in this ammo box.*

With the big guns silent, Union soldiers manned the split rail fence. Everyone else took positions as mentioned earlier, loaded their individual muskets, and anxiously awaited the appearance of Lee's Legions. I had been using John Maki's 1842 Springfield the entire weekend. I don't know why I didn't bring my own musket. I guess if John couldn't be at Gettysburg in person, then at least his musket would. I should also note that I'd brought 300 rounds with me to the event. However, as a rule, First Sergeants rarely fire their musket in combat. The First Sergeant normally looks after the needs of his men, whether it is in weapons repair, ammunition resupply, or getting the men in proper alignment during the heat of battle. I may have fired some cartridges during the previous two days or I may have loaned some out. Nevertheless, I had at least one hundred rounds available for day 3 and I planned on making my musket sizzle.

A sudden movement was detected from the tree line. Another gasp and squeal came from the crowd as the tree limbs parted, like the Red Sea, and out came the dreaded gray swarm; too many to count without taking your shoes off. They must have numbered nearly six thousand, for they were as many as the blades of grass. Quickly, but with precision, the Confederates formed lines of battle facing the Union lines. There were two or three lines in front of the formation with the rest following behind in reserve. Nearly a thousand men and at least six blood red battle flags were in each double rank of men. One hundred and twenty-five years earlier, the Union defenders on Cemetery Ridge had been awestruck on how grand the spectacle of the Confederate march looked. Here we were, in 1988, making the same comparisons. It was a thrilling site to behold, that massive gray wall inching slowly forward like an unstoppable tidal wave.

The Confederate legions were advancing and began presenting a wider front by some shifting of forces. It looked like an attempt to outflank us and try to draw our attention away from the heavier blunt force advancing up from the center. *I'm reminded of the tactics used by the ZULU warriors in the movie of the same name. The front rank of the attacking warriors was like the horns of an attacking bull, but the true strength lay in what was to follow-a type of battering ram up the center.* Whatever fears our commanding general had on the proceedings, he was quick to act by ordering an extra battalion to strengthen both flanks, while instructing the reserves to stand by.

The enemy continued their parade ground pace until they got to within one hundred yards of our lines, then they halted, and a hot debate with blazing muskets was commenced by both sides. It was load and fire as fast as you can. There was no firing by the drum or any other fancy trick shooting this day. Load and fire at will. Officers and file closers, in the rear of each company of men, ripped open fresh packs of cartridges as the men needed them or unclogged fouled muskets as they got dirty. Our battalion occupied part of the left wing of the Grand Union army. We were about mid-center. Thirty yards in front of us, our comrades in blue hugged the rail fence while we threw blazing volumes of smoke over their horizontal bodies. These boys dare not stand up!

All up and down the entire blue line it was the same story. Muskets roared from those that stood, knelt, or lay prone behind that long rail fence. *Ramrods are never used during a reenactment. For safety reasons someone might forget to pull it out, then just imagine the looks of embarrassment if the ramrod comes flying out when the musket is fired. During the battle reenactment, the powder is poured down the barrel then the empty paper cartridge is tossed aside. Most boys get overly excited during the heat of combat and will bite too much of the cartridge, getting a mouth full of black powder. After the battle reenactment is concluded it's not uncommon to see dozens of lads looking like they'd applied black lipstick.*

After about ten rounds through the musket, the barrel tends to get about as hot as a stove. It doesn't help that the summertime temperature is nearing the triple digits. You could wrap several strips of bacon around that musket barrel and fry 'em extra crispy. If you try to grab that barrel with your bare hand, "brother watch out!" Some boys will splash a little canteen water on the barrel, while others might wrap a rag or handkerchief around the offending steel. Whatever the case, when the musket gets red hot, beware of an accidental cook off! That's when the black powder blows up about half way down the hot barrel. If your face is hovering near the end of the musket barrel, you're in for a world of pain. For safety sake, the men have always been instructed to hold the musket away from the face when reloading. If it would cook off, only the fingers would get scorched.

Enough with the safety tips!

Back and forth the two sides blazed away at each other. At the feet of the combatants, lay empty paper cartridges piled so high they looked like drifts of snow. Both Union and Confederate infantry, nearly ten thousand men combined, were sending volumes of gun smoke in the air in such a degree, that a meteorologist would think a thunderstorm had settled down to earth. Most of the smoke wafted over to the exciting crowd of spectators who continued to "ooh" and "ahh." The men of Lee's Army had already begun taking fearful casualties during this stand up fight.

Finally, a shout from the gray ranks and the entire front wall surged forward at a trot. Unit cohesion had evaporated. Men were falling in heavy numbers. They fell one at a time, or in pairs; then they began to fall by the tens and dozens. The goal was to reach the center of the Union line. Onward they came. Fifty yards more! The men had more the appearance of a mob than anything resembling an army, but the dreaded howl of the Rebel yell spurred these scarecrows on and made us Union boys pause in wonder. Faster and faster they ran, but with each step, even more fell. With a last burst of sheer will power, the enemy was amongst us.

A small gray wedge of barely two hundred men had broken through the Union line. Too close to fire muskets safely, a violent hand to hand struggle broke out. At the same time, the commanding general of the Union army sent in his reserves. They advanced at a trot and collided with the invaders head on. Fists flew, muskets were used as clubs, and bodies fell. Those of us on the left lowered our muskets and became spectators ourselves, witnessing the last gasp of Pickett's Charge. After some frantic moments a hush began to descend on the panorama. Many Confederates limped away from the battle line, struggling back to Bobbie Lee with their tails between their legs. Others were welcomed in as prisoners of war, kindly accepting the offered canteen of water from a former enemy. Many others, numbering in the thousands, lay on the hard Pennsylvania dirt that afternoon, the dead and the dying.

Screams, moans, and of course the sobs of the broken hearted who had thought themselves invincible.

A great shout-'HUZZAH!'-came the cry from the blackened lips of us Union boys as the Commanding General and his staff rode out to the front of us waving a huge flag. 'HUZZAH!' we shouted. Three 'HUZZAHS' for the Union. A roar of approval and applause from the tens of thousands, who sat as our audience, washed over us like a tonic. Smiles, handshakes, and hugs were awarded to both friend and foe. We'd pulled it off! The grand Gettysburg extravaganza had become a reality!

While we were congratulating each other and ourselves, a shout was heard which caused all to pause. Somewhere bugle notes began playing. Hats came off and heads were bowed in reverence. It was at that moment that each of us truly understood what the real motivating factor was in recreating this horrible battle. It was to honor the sacrifices of those who had fought, bled, and died 125 years earlier. Not a noise could be heard, except for the gentle strains of TAPS and the whisper of battle flags caught in the summer breeze. The flags seemed to be whispering, "Remember us. Honor us."

We marched back to camp where Western Brigade Commander, Chris Craft, and Battalion Commander, Mark Upton, gave emotional farewell speeches. Among other words of praise, they said they were proud to have served, these last several days, with such gallant men as us. Three loud HUZZAHS we gave them. "BREAK RANKS, MARCH!" A madness of handshakes and hugs overwhelmed all, plus a few hats were tossed in the air, as the boys were ordered dismissed for the final time.

The worst part of any reenactment is when it's over. A feeling of sadness comes over everybody, coupled with numbing fatigue, because now you have to drag your tired feet back to the parking lot to get your vehicle. With at least ten thousand reenactors and fifty thousand spectators thinking the same thing, which is get to the car and get out, the best thing you can do is just wait it out. After about an hour of rest, some of the Holmes Brigade boys decided to go on up after their cars, so after a sip of warm canteen water, I joined them. I had taken my tent, blankets, and other non-essential stuff up to the van that morning. All I had on my back now was what I wore in the fight. After a brief word to my wife, I shouldered my musket and jumped into the human stream of traffic-all headed a mile and a half to the parking lot.

Chapter Two

The Road from Gettysburg

Several hours later, I put the Ford Aerostar into DRIVE and with Mona and Katie, we left the 125th anniversary reenactment of Gettysburg. I don't know what we did that very first afternoon, but it was still daylight-maybe 6 or 7 PM. I do know I drove back up to the National Park to visit the 19th Indiana monument (*we'd portrayed them on Day One*). After that we may have driven to a motel to cleanup, eat, and sleep.

This will be a short chapter of the events following the Gettysburg reenactment. Remember, Mona and I still had another week of vacation and we planned on seeing the sites in this area. I will try not to bore you too much, but since this is my book, you must bear with me. Unlike the previous week's agenda, I don't remember exactly which day we visited each individual site, but I guess it just doesn't matter. I'll just list them and for those that have a special meaning, I'll say an extra sentence or two about them.

One of the first places I recall we drove to was Fredericksburg, VA. It might have been on the very next day, after a night in a cheap motel. As I pulled into the Visitors Center parking lot of the National Battlefield site I beheld two familiar sites, the automobiles of the Higginbotham's and the Whitson's. Little Katie squealed with excitement, because she also recognized the Higginbotham car. She would get to see her playmate Hillari one more time. Even as we parked and got out, Mona warned Katie to "be on good behavior and don't act up while in the museum." Inside, we quickly spotted our friends who all shouted a joyful hello. Katie and Hillari found each other and started a playful dialogue. Meanwhile, Don Whitson had been back in the gift shop and was walking towards the check out register with an armload of Civil War books. I turned to face Don as he approached, gave an enthusiastic greeting, and yanked his baggy shorts down to his ankles. Time seemed to stand still. Everyone was in shock, the Higginbothams, Susan Whitson, Mona, the two little girls, and even the clerk behind the cash register. For a period which seemed to last a full minute, but was actually only a few seconds, Don just stood there. What else could he do? He had his arms wrapped around twenty pounds of books. At least he had on his briefs, so the vice squad didn't have to be called in. He finally shuffled the few remaining feet to the counter top of the desk, laid the books down next to the register, hitched up his drawers, and paid for his books. To this day, I don't know what possessed me to yank down his shorts. I might have been suffering under post-event syndrome. Then again, Don is extremely sensitive and a guy who's feathers are easily ruffled. He is the perfect target for practical jokes. After this comic episode, we climbed back in our Aerostar and resumed our journey towards the Chancellorsville, Wilderness, and Spotsylvannia corridor. *The Higginbotham's and the Whitson's had other plans so we bade them "adieu".*

I had heard that after Stonewall Jackson was wounded at Chancellorsville, he was moved southeast, but his amputated arm was buried at a nearby farm. I had done my research on this fact, and so after a moment or two viewing the remains of the old Chancellor House, I drove us south, into the Wilderness forest (which was on both sides of the two lane road). After a few miles, I took a left-hand turn onto a country road for another short mile or two, and then stopped at a wooden gate. On the other side of this gate, about a half-mile ahead was an old house and it was here, in a small plot, that Stonewall's arm had been buried. After I'd assured Mona that it'd be all right, the three of us climbed over the gate and proceeded up the lane on foot. She was worried that Leatherface would come out of the old house, but there seemed to be no one about. The stone marker, which was located about fifty yards on the other side of the house, was inscribed "Here lies Stonewall Jackson's arm." There were other scratch markings on it-dates, etc. I took a picture and we skeedaddled. To this day, Mona claims that was the weirdest experience she'd ever had.

We drove through Spotsylvania (you've seen one battlefield, you've seen them all), then drove further southeast to Guinea Station, where Stonewall Jackson died about a week after his wounding. The building where he died is all that remains of the old Chandler plantation. The National Park owns this property and has converted it into a shrine. On this day it was closed. Might have been after hours when we stopped.

On the following days, until we headed off into the sunset homeward bound, we visited such places as Monticello, Mount Vernon, spent a day in the Nation's Capitol (Smithsonian), drove up to Antietam National Battlefield (Katie and I lay in the sunken road while Mona took our picture). We also went through the Shenandoah Valley, stopped at New Market Battlefield, visited Yorktown, and spent a whole day at Colonial Williamsburg. We even took a ferry across the James River. At Williamsburg, we spent a night at a bed and breakfast, but I felt uncomfortable as it was in someone's house and we stayed in an upstairs bedroom. There were antique's all over. Mona and I shared a large bed, while Katie lay on a cot in that room. I'll admit that I'd much rather stayed in a motel room, which you can trash without feeling guilty.

CHAPTER THREE

"I'm Not Doing That Damn _____ Movie!"

After the Gettysburg 125th anniversary reenactment and the extra week visiting a number of historic places in Virginia, Maryland, and the Nation's Capitol, we returned back to Missouri and resumed our normal humdrum lives. The concluding months of 1988 saw us return to Lexington, Osawatomie, and Prairie Grove.

About the first of the year, the videotape documentary of Gettysburg, produced by Classic Images, came to my door. This was a similar production as the 1st Bull Run and Shiloh tapes; however it was about two hours long and featured even more speaking/acting parts. Reenactors assumed the roles of all the leading participants of the original battle, including General's Lee, Meade, JEB Stuart, Longstreet, and Colonel Joshua Chamberlain of the 20th Maine. The latter role was given to our ol' Colorado pal, Mark Gardner. Selection for all these roles was based on appearance, not acting ability.

Before proceeding with the next item of my adventures, I should take this opportunity to comment on the death of my father. Raymond Wilson Talbott died on April 4th, 1989 after a bout with cancer that first affected his brain, and then went into his lung. The radiation treatments helped him at first, but he gradually got weaker. Dad spent his last days in a nursing home in Sedalia, Missouri, where he lay in bed barely able to speak intelligently. He had always been a heavy smoker, was 20 years divorced from my mother, and had been somewhat of a heavy drinker after the fact. He died just about a month shy of his 59th birthday.

Shaking off the funk of my own personal tragedy, my wife assured me, would best be solved by going on down with the boys to yet another Civil War event. The next big thing was a major motion picture based on the exploits of the 54th Massachusetts, the first all black Union infantry regiment. Filming for the movie, GLORY, had already commenced in South Carolina at a beach side resort called Jekyll Island. This spit of ocean front sand was being turned into Fort Wagner, the place where the 54th Massachusetts achieved their greatest glory.

Meanwhile, the movie people were asking for at least 600 reenactors to come to Jonesboro, GA, to film one day -Saturday, April 22nd. They wished to recreate an episode from the battle of Antietam-an episode, which would be shown early in the movie. This scene would serve as a means to introduce the main character and future commander of the 54th, Robert Gould Shaw. This role was given to Matthew Broderick, best known from *Ferris Bueller's Day Off.*

Holmes Brigade was able to muster 40 men for the movie, including four galvanized Confederates from Crowley's Clay County Company. John Moloski, Richard Taylor, Tim Moore, and Clayton Murphy were willing to put on the blue in order to be in this movie. They later "complained" that the blue wool itched them, so they assumed it was lice infested. Hollywood was giving each participant 50 bucks apiece, so the Crowley's boys figured a few chiggers could be tolerated.

And so it was, on Thursday afternoon, four boys left Kansas City, and drove like the Devil, on down to Georgia. There was Pat McCarthy, who drove, Don Whitson, Dave Bennett, and finally, yours truly. We made good time; I think we got to Chattanooga in twelve hours. As a police officer from Leawood, Kansas, Pat probably knew all the perks and evasive tactics to elude the radar gun. I think he had a fuzz buster on the dashboard. Like I said, we made decent time-got to Chattanooga in time to visit a cocktail lounge before bedtime.

The next morning, after a brief splash of water to our nether regions and a hearty breakfast, we drove over to the National Battlefield Park at Chickamagua, visited Missionary Ridge, and even drove **up** to the top of Lookout Mountain. At the summit, we changed into our civil war duds and posed for a famous "standing on the very edge of the mountain" photo.

After this "photo op", we drove **down** Lookout Mountain and headed south towards Atlanta. In was mid-day and we didn't have to be on set till next morning, so on my suggestion, we entered the little burg of Kennesaw. I told the guys that in this town there was a Civil War Surplus store run by a strange character named Dent "**Wildman**" Myers. Way back in 1980, I had tried to buy an (original?) artillery shell jacket from this fellow, but was saddened to learn it had already been sold. Instead I received his current catalog-ten stapled together sheets. This catalog was illustrated with many pen and ink drawings of a few of his products as well as humorous anecdotes about himself or the Civil War. He also included a black and white image of himself in the role of a Turkish prince. A caption read-"Would you buy a used harem from this man?" Myers called his store **WILDMAN'S CIVIL WAR EMPORIUM** and he even boasted that it was "the best little war house in Georgia."

The place looked like it hadn't been dusted in 125 years. Wildman Dent Myers greeted us at the door as we came in. We still had on our "Yankee" clothes and he correctly assumed we on our way to the movie. When one of us asked if he was going to participate in the Hollywood production, he curtly responded, "**Hell no! I'm not doing that damn movie!**" Wildman was a short squat fellow, I recall. He hid behind a wild looking beard-kinda reminded me of John Maki. He also had a six-shooter strapped to his waist. I believe Kennesaw, Georgia, is one of the few places in the United States where it is ok to walk around packing heat.

To be polite, we walked around Wildman's little rummage store for the better part of an hour. Don may have found something to buy, but I contented myself with trying to keep the dust bunnies off my uniform jacket while I browsed. After this little adventure, we walked across the street to a museum that housed the old locomotive engine, THE GENERAL. In 1862, I believe, a group of Union spies captured the train and attempted to run off with it, but after a chase, it was recaptured and the Union men were tried and hung. Buster Keaton made a silent movie about THE GENERAL as did Fess Parker for Walt Disney studios. Anyway, the locomotive engine was in this building, along with several artifacts, wall paintings and posters. There may have also been a slideshow in an auditorium. We spent the better part of another hour here, and then decided to find a sit down restaurant before heading on down to Jonesboro and the movie.

Jonesboro is on the other side of Atlanta, so we were forced to make our way through the metropolis before turning off the interstate. On a two lane road we drove another dozen miles until we found a big sign and a camp ground packed with many canvas tents. On the horizon, about a mile away, we could see tractor trailers by the score, plus several big circus type tents. There were also several vehicles up there as well as folks milling about on foot and on horseback. That was where the movie people were set up. It was just about sunset by the time we arrived, so we couldn't see a whole lot else. After checking in, I set up my dog tent and the four of us crawled inside for a late night smoke.

Early the next morning, 6 AM, we were up and in formation with all the other Union reenactors who had shown up the night before. I believe some boys were already up at the site, but there was well over one hundred in our bunch. We would not be back at this spot till after dark, so we had to make sure we had everything before marching off. By this time, the galvanized boys from Crowley's had arrived, plus many of the guys from Holmes Brigade, including Bill Fannin, who was dressed out in his lieutenant's uniform. We even recognized about 18 boys from Logan's Brigade, including Randy 'By God' Jackson and Joe Covais-the head seamstress of New Columbia Mercantile (*endearing words had already been spoken regarding these two men whom I had served with during the Mexican War period of my hobby*).

Once everyone was through getting reacquainted and "grab-assing" was finished, we marched off in column of fours up the street to movie production central. As I mentioned, here were vans, semis, utility vehicles, generators, lighting and sound equipment, mobile homes for the cast and crew, and a mobile cafeteria. As mentioned in Volume

One, while I was on the NORTH AND SOUTH set, Hollywood goes all out when it comes to feeding its people. Buffet tables were loaded down with all the trappings of a large breakfast, including fruits of all varieties, cold cereal, donuts, juice and milk in box containers, and plenty of bottled water. Food handlers in white smocks and paper hats serviced a steam table in which sat stainless steel tubs of scrambled eggs, bacon, grits, biscuits and gravy, sausage (link and round), pancakes, French toast, hash browns, etc., and etc. Once we arrived at this central location, the reenactors were told to "pitch in" and then be on the set within an hour. Reenactors may be many things, but we're not bashful. We quickly stacked arms and stood in line with plastic trays in our mitts piled high with the cooked and the raw.

After breakfast everyone started to mosey up to the "set." This was an area a half mile away that we were told was to resemble a small portion of the Antietam battlefield. Off to one side of the field, Hollywood craftsmen had built a replica of the Dunker church. Don, Pat, Dave, and I posed for a picture by it. *As I recall, the Dunker building never made it in the final cut of the movie.* The field was fairly wide open, about three football fields in width and breadth. The field was not perfectly flat. It seemed to have one or two rolling folds, plus it rose to a slight elevation. During the filming of our scenes the Federals would be advancing uphill in three long lines, while the Confederate infantry would enjoy the comfort a barricade along with artillery support. Before filming here, an assistant director sent about fifty of us into the woods for some footage of us running, shooting, and falling, but those scenes ended up on the cutting room floor.

Directing GLORY would be Ed Zwick, who's previous claim to fame had been as director/producer of the TV series THIRTYSOMETHING. I think this was his first motion picture. Anyway, he came down and welcomed us all to his movie and gave us all instructions on what to expect and what to do. He told us if something went wrong or he needed to stop shooting, someone would yell, "CUT," or some type of flare would be launched if the battle noise got too loud for us to hear the order. He told us there would be ground charges in various places on this field-he pointed them out and told us to be aware of the wires and flash pots. Ed Zwick was very grateful for our involvement and wanted us to have a good time. He also told us that there'd be a lot of hurry up and wait between takes, but not to get bored or frustrated as that is how Hollywood does things.

We had a guy who was sort of the "middle-man" between Hollywood and the reenactors. This was a guy who was "one of us" but also worked, in a temporary capacity, for Hollywood. This man was Dale Fetzer. He had been around for many years, had some expertise in reenacting, so he was appointed coordinator of all the Federal infantry. He was made up as a brigadier general with wide muttonchops. Fetzer also carried a walkie-talkie in his haversack so he could communicate with the director.

After the little shoot in the woods, director Zwick had all the Federals form up in the large field for the big scene. Three battalions were formed, with roughly 150 men in each battalion. All the Holmes Brigade boys were in the first battalion in the far right company. The other two battalions were lined up behind us in equal numbers. As I'd mentioned earlier, the scenario called for all of us to march uphill into the teeth of enemy artillery and musket fire. After a pre-determined number of flash pots had detonated under our feet, we were supposed to panic and run around like scared little girls. It was NORTH AND SOUTH all over again.

We were all in our places, "with bright shining faces," when Mr. Cary Elwes came down the brow of the hill toward us. At the early point in his Hollywood career, he was mostly known for his role in The Princess Bride. There were whispers in the ranks that Mr. Elwes was a prima donna. Somebody suggested he was a prick, but I don't remember how that rumor began, although I think Don Whitson was the author of that observation. He obviously over heard someone say something negative about the actor, which Don took as gospel.

As Cary Elwes came closer, we could see he had on an officer's uniform, plus he was decked out with leather rigging and carrying a wicked blade. Although his face wouldn't be seen in this segment of GLORY, director Zwick wanted him in the ranks with us reenactors. He had a sheepish grin like he was half embarrassed to be here, but that smile quickly vanished when I playfully remarked," Is that uniform hot?"

Such comments as, "Is that beard real?" or "Is your coat dirty or do you own a parrot?" and others, including, "Is that coat hot?" are all little playful and harmless jabs us reenactors usually to say to one another. It's like saying, "How you doing?" or "How are the wife and kids?" It was an innocent way of poking fun at each other. Mr. Cary Elwes did not understand the humor in my comment. His eyes narrowed and his lips puckered like he'd bit into a lemon. He aimed a few derogatory remarks in my direction and then walked over a few paces to my right to a group of five men who were decked out in the uniform of Hiram Berdan's Sharpshooters. The "sweet peas" were sucking on filter tip cigarettes and they kindly offered the actor one.

Before Mr. Elwes got half of it smoked, word came via the walkie-talkie of Dale Fetzer that filming was about to start, and everyone was to stand by for "ACTION!" Cary Elwes walked to the front of our company, with his back to the camera, and held both arms straight out from his side-the saber in one hand. My guess was Matthew Broderick was on the left end of the battalion and would lead the men on his wing, the same way. When ACTION was shouted, Cary Elwes began walking backwards, arms still outstretched. *The object by most battalion officers, who do this, is to keep the battle line straight, by using sheer will power and out stretched arms.* It's not wise <u>not to</u> look where you're going, as Mr. Elwes would discover, the hard way. Acting company commander, Lt. Bill Fannin, tried to tell the actor he was going about it all wrong and he could possibly hurt himself if he continued to walk backwards, but Cary Elwes curtly responded with a "I know what I'm doing" remark.

Here is a comment from Pat McCarthy on what happened next: *"As you recall, we were instructed that we should take a hit if a ground charge went off close to us during filming. Prior to one of the takes, one of our guys (*Fannin*) noticed that Elwes was carrying his sword with his off hand on the blade. He had the audacity to mention to Elwes that this was dangerous and that he could hurt himself. Elwes responded by saying "I know what I'm doing"! Well, during the filming I had a ground charge go off almost between my legs, so I dutifully died on the spot. Shorting after, the charge faltered and the rout began. Through slitted eyes*

I watched as Elwes, "face to the enemy" and backing up, was headed right for me. Of course, his left hand was on the blade of his sword. Without moving my lips, I tried to shout, "Look out" several times, but he obviously couldn't hear me. Sure enough, he tripped over me and his elbow dug into the inside of my left thigh (it left a huge, deep purple bruise that lasted for weeks). *Anyway, Elwes rolled off me, looked at me with a funny look on his face, got up and started limping to the rear. My first thought was* "great, I've just maimed the co-star of the film!"

"After the take we got up and were brushing ourselves off when someone came running up to me saying that Elwes was looking for me. Well, I was PISSED OFF. I'd watched this prima donna strutting around all day and yelling at people, and I thought if he was going to shout at me that I'd take his head off. After all, I was hurting and it was his fault. Soon enough he came striding up to me, and I was ready to give him both barrels. But he <u>was</u> very apologetic and asked several times if I was all right. As it turned out, he thought his elbow had come down on my head. I told him I was ok and asked if he was, since I saw him limping afterward. He told me that he had affected the limp for the camera.

"About that time I noticed that his left hand was dripping blood, and asked him if that was affected for the cameras, too. He looked at his hand and got all pale. Sure enough, he cut his hand on his sword when he fell over me! Filming was held up for an hour while he had the hand treated! So much for my brush with fame!"

During the break, while the special effects people rebuilt all the ground charges and Cary Elwes was being treated for his cut, we soldiers milled around a bit like cattle, sat down and munched on snacks or played with some of the props lying about. Littering the "battlefield," was a number of dead horses and dead men. These were all fakes and stuffed with straw, although the horses looked like they had once been real and had come from a taxidermist. Don Whitson, Tim Moore, Joe Covais, and I became playful with one dead horse, while a few of the other boys, including Dave Bennett, turned a straw soldier into a pin cushion with their bayonets. I have the photographic proof! During the breaks, we also found time to get four or five of us in a picture with Cary Elwes and Matthew Broderick. Don shoved his camera into the hands of one of the Hollywood people while we crowded around Matt. The guy that Don rudely forced his camera on turned out that he was the producer. Don didn't know. He just saw some guy standing next to Matt with his hands in his pocket and said, "Here, take our picture!"

When Cary Elwes came back, a bit later, he had a cloth bandage wrapped around his hand plus his face was red with embarrassment. He walked back to us with his head sunk low and refused to meet our eyes. Instead he walked back over to the "sweet peas" for another filter tipped fag. There was one "sweet pea" who, after we'd come back from the last take, remarked to no one in particular, "I was in Vietnam." I remember that as he said this, I looked over at him and he had a glazed look in his eyes-that "thousand yard stare." Maybe the Hollywood ground charges going off under his feet caused him to have a flashback to his psychedelic days in Saigon with mama san!

Director Zwick had us do another charge up the slope. All three Federal battalions got about half way up, and then once again the earth opened up under our feet. At the same time, a long line of Confederate infantry, behind a rail fence, was pouring volumes of musket fire into our ranks. The Federals were instructed by Director Zwick not to return fire! Instead we were supposed to panic, play dead or "run off like scared little girls." However, as the third battalion came up over the slope and marched into the pandemonium, they began firing back! Boy was Zwick pissed! CUT! Red flares went off in all directions. With a forced smile, Zwick reminded us that, "**we were not supposed to return fire**!" All the ground charges had to be made up again. Another hour sitting on our hands. At some point we went to lunch. It may have been before the Federal firearm's fiasco. Once again, the amount of food laid out would have made King Henry the VIII envious.

A word should be said about the production crew who seemed to be about the laziest bunch of people on earth. They were all union workers, of course, who seemed to take their sweet time doing anything. As most people know, time is money. When working on a Hollywood movie, lost time can mean the film will go over budget. While getting ready to film a scene, the director can be waiting on the sun to be just right or for that airplane or other background noise to fade. He waits for the props and people to get in place and all the while, he's checking his clock. This was Saturday. Union people WILL NOT work on Sunday and the reenactors have to go back home to regular jobs, so he had to get his shots this day!

About twelve ground charges had been rebuilt. Marking sticks were placed in the ground, about ten paces apart, to indicate where each charge was. Before he could roll camera, someone had to pull all the stakes from the ground (otherwise they'd be in the shot). One of the union workers walked out to pry each one. I mean he casually strolled to each one, like it was a day in the park and not in any hurry. It seemed to me that he could have moved his ass, but director Zwick may have been too timid to yell at a union man, so he just bit his lower lip, glanced at his watch, and then glanced at the darkening skies. Finally, the old boy had completed his demanding task and filming could resume.

After a few more takes, word came that there would be one more shot. It would be a long shot of the Federal army marching off into the sunset. While we waited, Dale Fetzer sat on a "dead horse" and bored us with some lame humor. As I said earlier, Hollywood does not work on Sunday. However, they wanted the reenactors to stick around and work on Monday! Fetzer begged and pleaded with us, but we explained that we had to be back at work, at our real jobs, and could not stay one more hour. It was almost hilarious as Fetzer almost got down on his hands and knees, groveling like a beaten dog. He whined with tears nearly in his eyes, "You'll get an extra fifty dollars if you come back Monday!" We nearly laughed in his face.

We filmed the last scene, marching along a ridge at sunset, and then as twilight settled down, we marched down the road to the paymaster to get our copy of US Grant for our one day with Hollywood and Glory! On the way out of Jonesboro, it was unanimously decided that we'd find lodging for the night, shower, and have a hot meal. We all had worked up a sweat while on the Hollywood set, but for some reason, the boys claim I stunk the worst! Dave Bennett told me that I stunk worse than the ass of a dead skunk. For the next twenty miles, while I sat in the back of the van comfortable in my own funk, Pat, Don, and Dave did their best "dog with its head out the window" impression.

CHAPTER FOUR

Fresh Fish

By 1989, Holmes Brigade was at the top of its game. In just a few short years, we had conquered Missouri, Kansas, and Arkansas. We had taken large numbers to Mississippi and back. We had even been asked to attend the 125th anniversary spectaculars of 1st Bull Run, Shiloh, and Gettysburg. We were looking forward to continuing the 125th anniversary with a focus on the Price invasion of 1864. Several reenactments were planned for the summer and fall of 1989, including Pilot Knob, Glasgow, Westport (or Kansas City), and Mine Creek, Kansas. We were hoping we could lure some eastern folks over to the Missouri side of the river in 1989, so several volunteers came together to brainstorm that very dilemma. I was asked to serve on a board, hosted by Sonny Wells, to determine the site for the Westport reenactment. It was originally hoped we could have the reenactment at Loose Park, but there are too many nice houses nearby and loud cannon noise would shatter the fine windows. So it was decided to have it at Swope Park where the only thing we'd have to worry about would be upsetting the lions and bears at the nearby zoo. As I mentioned in Volume One, where once the old battle of Westport was fought, now sits tons of pavement, housing, and the Country Club Plaza. It's like fighting the battle of Gettysburg in a parking lot near high rise apartment buildings. But the story of Westport and the rest of the

Price Invasion Remembered must wait a chapter or two. Meanwhile, the Hollywood experience on the set of GLORY had ended and it was time to look ahead to the next Fort Scott.

By 1989, we had lost a few members but gained a few more. I believe most of the bagladies had graduated from high school and were looking ahead to higher learning. We still had most of the old guard, but we also gained some even more colorful characters.

As the wife and I came into Fort Scott that Friday evening (it was after dark), a figure came out of the darkness and asked us if he could help carry some of our gear. Mona had one or two boxes, baskets, hoop, and several dresses for herself and Katie. The ladies were situated upstairs in the infantry barracks and it was a chore to mount those two dozen steps. This fellow approached us and wanted to help and I said sure. He was a new recruit brought in by I don't who. The first thing I noticed was that his forage cap looked a little misshapen-like a pig's snout hanging off to the side. He had a wide-open smile and a hearty laugh, looking like a young Andy Griffith from the movie NO TIME FOR SERGEANTS. He introduced himself as Jon Isaacson and from that moment on he and I became close friends.

Jon was originally from Macon, Missouri, but lived in Kansas City. He worked for a quick printing company called KINKO. (*A few years later he would be printing the Holmes Brigade Dispatch, as its new editor. Using KINKO'S computer system he created a whole new look for the newsletter, making it more like a brochure than merely several typewritten sheets stapled together*).

Jon also had an unusual taste in music. One minute he would be listening to the country swing of Bob Wills and his Texas Playboys, then the next he would pop in a cassette of German WWII military music. Some of these cassette tapes contained speeches from Berlin Betty, Axis Sally, or Lord Haw Haw. Once I rode with Jon through the streets of Jackson, Mississippi with the Nazi music coming from his tape deck and the windows rolled down. We got many strange looks that day from the local rednecks. Our reason for cruising through Jackson, Mississippi was to look for comic books. While I was obsessed with OUR ARMY AT WAR featuring SGT. ROCK, Jon had his eye the comic series WEIRD WAR, tales of horror and the supernatural set during World War II.

Back on the subject of music, Jon also had an interest in spirited and lively tunes of life on the plantation during the mid-nineteenth century. He particularly loved the ballads that the Negroes made up or those that were written with the Negro in mind. Jon's favorite was songwriter Dan Emmett who wrote many tunes that would be considered politically incorrect by today's audience. Dan Emmett, and other artists of his ilk, would perform these songs while wearing blackface. *This was nearly one hundred years before Al Jolson.* The band might consist of one or two banjos, a tambourine, and possibly a set of "bones." The bones were in fact two rib bones taken from a cow with all the meat boiled off and dried. The musician placed the "bones" between a couple fingers of his right hand and shook his wrist, making the bones clack against each other in rhythm with the other musicians. One who was highly skilled with the bones might have an additional set going on his left hand.

Jon became so enamored with plantation music, that he built himself a crude banjo and within a short time he was serenading us boys around the campfire. Jon had the ability to sing from the gut. He would sing real low, with a deep bass voice. Other boys became infected with Jon's choice of music including Hig who would sing the "Cabbage Head" song, or "The Banks of the Ohio." On the matter of banjo making, Jon found a like-minded individual in George "Butch" Wunderlich. Butch lived all the way over on the other side of the state in St. Louis, but he and Jon became banjo-making fiends. I have no musical talent of my own, but Jon got me involved in a little shindig he arranged at Fort Scott one year which featured me and Dave Bennett on the "bones" and he and Butch on banjo. As time went along, Jon began coming to Civil War reenactments dressed not as a soldier, but in the civilian dress of a traveling entertainer with his banjo slung across his back.

Jon's obsession with plantation music took a turn when he decided to put on blackface himself. At Missouri Town one summer afternoon an impromptu concert was held on the porch of the tavern featuring the EBONY MELODIANS. With Jon Isaacson (on banjo), Joe

Anderson (on fiddle), and Don Whitson (on tambourine), came Fort Osage superintendent Grady Manus (playing the cow bones). The quartet played and sang plantation songs in blackface, and told jokes in voices that reminded me of a television episode of Amos and Andy. Before the performance, the audience (*invited by invitation only*) was given a warning what to expect-that this form of entertainment was part of early Americana. However some people were shocked or else hid that grin behind an upraised hand. This was the last and only performance by the EBONY MELODIANS.

The highlight of Jon's masquerade came one evening while we were at a reenactment at nearby Weston, Missouri or Bee Creek. Jon intended to crash the forthcoming dance, scheduled that night, by arriving in blackface and with a fright wig that stuck up in the air like a shark's fin. I escorted Jon to the dance and turned him loose like an animal unleashed. The look coming from the reenactors was priceless; especially the Confederate's who scowled when Jon started pawing on their women folk. Ol' Zip Coon or Cuffy, as Jon called himself, began to shuck and jive like he was infested with a fever. He kicked up his heels to more than one dance, then figured enough was enough and slunk off into the darkness to terrorize someone else. This may have been the last time he wore the make-up, to my knowledge. The other entertainment of the Bee Creek event came one afternoon, courtesy of six or seven ladies who pranced around in flimsy low-cut garments, proclaiming themselves the SOILED DOVES. The "doves" performed a risqué, but harmless burlesque show on stage for dozens of leering men.

From the moment Jon became involved in the Civil War reenactment family, he made it his goal to be right in the center of discussion. If a rumor was being spread about someone, he wanted to hear about it. If there was a discussion about the bylaws, an upcoming reenactment, the newsletter, officer and NCO elections, authenticity, or if he had an opinion on any individual, he'd let you know about it. Despite the fact he'd only been in the hobby a short time, Jon made it his goal to be heard, whether you liked it or not. Like Gregg Higginbotham, Jon was only trying to get members of Holmes Brigade to become more authentic-to get out of our frozen generic impression and reliance on company mess, for example. Jon was one of the first to try individual mess at an event, but Captain Don Strother chastised him in strong language, "We all voted to mess together as a company, so I'd appreciate it if you'd put out that fire!"

A wild bearded biker looking fellow from north of the Missouri River came aboard at about the same time as Jon. His name was Ray Woods, but he didn't stick around longer than a year or two. He had some issues, including the drinking of Wild Turkey before breakfast. Ray was the father of a mentally handicapped teenage boy. I think Jesse was not too severely handicapped, but maybe slow in the head and prone to getting himself into trouble with the law and the neighbors because of wild behavior. Ray told us there were times when he had to personally walk his boy to and from school. He was so concerned with the safety of his son, that most times Ray would be carrying a firearm under his jacket. Whenever we had an event and Ray Woods did not show up for it, Jon remarked with a grin, that "Ray had to take Jesse for a walk."

Around this same time, Mona and I decided that little Katie should take dancing lessons. We wanted her to have a well-rounded education and have all the opportunities we never had. In other words, we spoiled her. Two dance studios were within a short two miles of our house, including one that was in Raytown called Layton's Dance Academy. What caught my eye the first time we walked into the small studio was the blond instructor. Cindy Layton had big blond hair, a big smile with perfect teeth, and she was easy on the eyes! Her resume included several years dancing on stage at Worlds of Fun. This Kansas City amusement park had roller coasters and kiddie rides, but also featured indoor amusement (*for those wishing to get out of the heat and into air conditioning*). Pretty young people sang and danced to show tunes or hits from the 1950's. This was entertainment rated G and mostly aimed at the over 60 crowd. Senior citizens are usually the ones who are the first to tire of the summer heat.

So MY choice in where Katie would attend dance was based on how attractive the dance teacher was. We sat in on a dance class that

Cindy was teaching at that moment, watching little 6-year old girls toe tap. Katie seemed to like the place as well as I. Later, we met Connie Layton, the other sister and co-owner of the studio. Connie was just as attractive as her sister, but had not taken the trouble to bleach her hair. After some years dancing at the amusement park, both Layton girls opened this studio and based on their sex appeal, they soon had many students.

We enrolled Katie in tap, jazz, and ballet classes. Neither Cindy nor Connie taught the ballet portion of the dance. That went to another equally attractive Italian woman named Cindy Monaco. She had an even more impressive resume than her boss' did. I believe she had spent some years in New York City or somewhere on the East Coast, and had performed in some notable ballet productions. She was about thirty at this time and made Raytown her home. The Layton girls and Cindy Monaco must have grown up together or had shared a dance floor. Whatever the case, the three girls became partners in the studio.

As I got to know the ballet teacher even more I discovered that her brother, Ralph, sometimes hung out at Missouri Town. Ralph was a lawyer in real life, but sometimes liked to escape from reality (and possibly his wife) by going to Missouri Town for an afternoon to smoke cigars and dish out legal advice as an 1855 circuit lawyer. Within a short time, I was introduced to Ralph and an extremely handsome man who was Cindy's husband. His name was also Monaco, but pronounced differently (*MoNACO rather than MONaco*). When Cindy married Michael she didn't have to do much paper work-as far as worrying about name change. Michael is a doctor of internal medicine; an extremely handsome man who looks like he just stepped off the pages of GQ as a male model. I felt out of place surrounded by these two professional men, considering I'm only a sweat shop peon with unpleasant features. However, I was soon put as ease, because both love to drink popskull and are not afraid to look silly. Within a brief time, I convinced the duo to attend a Civil War reenactment where they met Higginbotham, Isaacson, John Maki, and all the rest of the maniacs. *Michael soon became involved with the Kansas City Chiefs football club as a sideline doctor and could no longer attend reenactments.*

At this time, Ralph was also a member of the Raytown School Board and a District Representative to the state capitol in Jefferson City. Always a warm and friendly soul, Ralph knew everyone in Jackson County and everyone in Jackson County knew Ralph. He would take your hand and introduce himself. You couldn't help but like the man.

Ralph attended his first event as a Civil War infantry soldier during the first weekend of August 1992 at Glasgow, MO. As most Italians go, Ralph and his family are very close. So close are they, that they drove all the way from Kansas City (maybe a two-hour drive), just to see their boy in action. After the event concluded Sunday afternoon, we arranged to meet for an early supper at a roadside café. Ralph's wife, his father, mother, and even his sister Cindy (and maybe Mike) all wanted to sit down over a hot barbecue sandwich and chips. I asked Jon Isaacson to come along only because I felt a tad uncomfortable with all those Italians and didn't want to be the only white boy under the microscope. I had seduced Ralph into becoming a Civil War reenactor, so I assume his family wanted to see exactly who the culprit was that had corrupted their boy. On the way from the event site to the restaurant, Ralph worked a cordless Norelco razor over the stubble on his chin. After two day's under the summer sun, he was worried his family would scold him about his unkempt look, so he took the extra effort to shave and comb his hair. With Jon acting all goofy and me talking about Katie, dance, and my Civil War ancestry, we all got along famously. It helped that we were in a casual restaurant with plastic forks rather than a fancy place. After all we still had on our smelly wool clothes on.

The following year we returned to Athens, MO. On the drive home Sunday afternoon, Ralph, Jon Isaacson, Pat McCarthy, and myself, decided on a supper in nearby Hannibal (*the boyhood home of Mark Twain*). I think three of us had already changed out of our CW clothes, but Ralph waited till we got to the parking lot of the restaurant. An elderly lady was walking past as Ralph peeled off his clothes. But he wasn't bashful, nor did he care if anyone saw his manhood. The three of us learned that day that Ralph is not Jewish. Isaacson said that Ralph's ding-dong looked like "a water squirting flower."

Once inside the diner, we ordered sandwiches and onion rings. After two days in the August sun, with little sleep, we'd become slaphappy. Only Pat McCarthy kept his composure while the rest of us tittered like schoolgirls. The other diners in the eatery must have thought us drunk or insane. When the waitress brought the chow, we noticed the onion rings were stacked on an upright wooden dowel rod. As we gazed at the display, I launched into that infamous joke: "Who is the most popular man in a nudist colony? The man who can carry a dozen onion rings and two cups of coffee." We all tittered till the tears streamed down our faces, forcing us to bury our faces in the tablecloth. At a nearby table, a young father tossed several greenbacks next to his unfinished dinner and hustled his wife and children out the front door. Meanwhile, Pat was explaining to the unsmiling waitress that we were all on a field trip from the rest home and he was the male nurse in charge of us. Between fits of uncontrollable laughter-brought on because of lack of sleep and heat exhaustion-we managed to wolf down the chow, onion rings and all, then we beat a hasty retreat before the cops could be called in.

Over the years, Ralph has been the center of several amusing episodes. Like the time at Pea Ridge when he lost his harmonica only to find another one. We went across the state line back into Missouri to find a tavern. Where we were at was a dry county-"no likker sold to solgers." Only ten miles north we crossed back into Missouri and found a tavern and a local barfly who, hard to believe, had in possession, a harmonica for only $20. Ralph bought it on the spot and before the weekend was over, he was tweeting and squeaking off-key notes once again.

Another time at Pilot Knob, Ralph decided to sleep outdoors next to the fire pit because he was chilled. Despite the quart of "anti-fogmatic" he'd poured down his throat, he insisted on snoozing near the embers. During the night, his gray wool blanket got too close to the fire and caught it on fire. I think Ralph would have slept through his own incineration except for the fact that Isaacson happened to get up to pee and had to stomp on the blanket and part of Ralph's leg just to get the flames out.

A number of characters came through Holmes Brigade during the turn of the decade, but one of the most unusual was a young pup I first met at a living history encampment at Pea Ridge, Arkansas about 1992. That year, Holmes was camped just off the tour road midway between the visitor's center and Elkhorn Tavern. As we had done years before, we'd interact with the public-as they came by, answering questions and such. A ceremony would occur during the day with words spoken, etc. Anyhow, we'd set up tents and started a campfire to warm our bones that'd become chilled in the March air. One of the fellows had a brand-new A frame tent, but the poles he'd brought were too long so a hand saw was borrowed from the park. (*This was when we first met the park ranger dwarf. He was barely three feet tall-definitely a little person. I don't recall his name, but he was dressed out in the full regalia of a park ranger-little shirt, little pants, and a little Smokey bear hat. As most dwarfs go, he could not walk too well; one leg might have been shorter than the other. To get around the park property, he used a walking stick. Dave Bennett named the little man, "tick with a stick." Despite this handicap, the little man was very intelligent on Civil War history, was very gracious and helpful to us, and we came to respect him a lot*).

So we were all settled for our first night under the Arkansas stars. Around the blazing fire we gathered to tell stories and drink beer. There were several new faces that had made Pea Ridge their first event, including this young pup that seemed all tickled and laughed like a little girl. Of course Higginbotham was in his element dancing on a John Maki breadbox while Jon Isaacson strummed on his banjo. The box had just when purchased by another recruit, but Higgy declared it needed scuffed up a bit so he jumped on it and did a tap dance.

So we were all having a jolly good time, courtesy of cold brew and retelling old war stories from the early days of Holmes Brigade. Whenever the stories got too wild or arrived at a racy episode, young pup would titter like a schoolgirl.

Finally I asked, "Who is this guy?"

"Oh, that's Roger Forsyth," someone replied.

One story that is told is of the night Roger "fell in love" with a gal from the ugly bar at Fort Scott and brought her back to camp. The story goes on to say that Roger, allegedly, woke his tent mate, forced him out into the cold night air, and brought the gal into the tent to play "hide the sausage." I was not a witness to this episode, but I'm sure by daybreak Roger was looking for some of that alcohol-based soap from the lavatory.

Among his other peculiarities, Roger was a novice poet. He became editor of the Dispatch a few years later and for a brief time; he included some of his prose in our newsletter. He was also hard at work on "the great American novel" as he phrased it. He was so wrapped up in his novel that I feel the newsletter suffered. After a while, the newsletter resembled pages of handwriting. He did not make the effort to type the articles, he merely wrote them out in long hand.

We have had many people come and go over the years. Some have completely fallen off the face of the earth like Roger Forsyth and Ray Woods. Some have suffered serious medical problems-heart attacks and open heart surgery. A few have died along the way. Jon Isaacson got married and moved to Harper's Ferry sometime after 1996. He's still very deep into living history and occasionally he'll show up in Missouri just to say hello. Ralph is still very much involved with living history, but prefers events where he can dress as a gentleman of the 1850's. Places like the 1859 jail, the Elmwood Cemetery in Kansas City, Missouri Town, and the old Jackson County Courthouse are some of the places Ralph likes to hang out. Of the many living history venues he attends or sponsors, he particularly loves to get involved in political discussion as it pertains to 1855 and Missouri. Whenever I'm introduced to one of Ralph's friends, he always says to them," This is Bob Talbott, the guy who first got me into the hobby."

These men are only a sample of the great personalities that became part of the hobby and the Holmes Brigade family during the period 1989-1995. Other men of equal personality came through to be sure, but none that had more of an impact on me than Jon and Ralph. During the next few chapters, and on up to 1995, you will find Jon Isaacson, Roger Forsyth, Ralph Monaco, and other 'fresh fish' mentioned, but in less detail than I've given here. I will end this chapter on the new recruits of Holmes Brigade and return to 1989 with a discussion of the 125th anniversary battles of Sterling Price's 1864 Invasion of Missouri.

CHAPTER FIVE

Price Invasion Revisited

Ask someone on the street to name a Civil War campaign, other than one Lee took up North during the summer of 1863 that resulted in the fiasco at Gettysburg, and you might get a few responses. Billy Sherman's March to the Sea, the Vicksburg Campaign, or Stonewall Jackson's Shenandoah Valley Campaign perhaps?

How about the Price Campaign of 1864 to retake Missouri? To the casual observer, the Civil War was fought in the eastern part of the United States or, in rare exceptions, near the Mississippi River. It wasn't until 1978 that I found out that Missouri had its share of fighting by both the Blue and the Gray. If you've read Volume One of Chin Music, I've already told you how I found out about Missouri's involvement in the war.

In the autumn of 1864, Uncle Billy Sherman was about to begin his famous "March to the Sea." Meanwhile, US Grant had Bobbie Lee bottled up in Petersburg, Virginia. The Confederacy was breathing its last gasp, but for one last desperate attempt by an old familiar Missourian. General Sterling Price had been away from his beloved home state for close to three years. After the defeat at Pea Ridge, Arkansas, in March 1862, "Old Pap" and his boys were needed east of the Mississippi. Missouri was firmly in the hands of the Union, with the exception of some minor harassment by Quantrill's guerrillas. Price and his "orphans" felt

Missouri had been abandoned to its fate and longed for the day when they could return to her.

As events were unfolding in Georgia and Virginia, Price saw this opportunity to try to retake Missouri while Federal forces were occupied in these two hotly contested states. If he could raise enough of an alarm by threatening St. Louis and Jefferson City, perhaps the Union would send men after him, thereby easing the pressure on his southern comrades on the eastern front. After some cussing and discussing, Jeff Davis gave "Old Pap" the greenlight to launch his invasion. With an army of about ten thousand, only two-thirds being armed, Price slipped across the state line in late September 1864, to claim his long lost prize.

The following has been a bastardized history of the prelude to the Price Invasion. Better histories can be read elsewhere. My goal was merely to get you to think and go, "hmmm!"

History states that Confederate General Sterling Price first attacked Fort Davidson in Pilot Knob. After his defeat there, he headed into the central part of the state and eventually west into Kansas. These turns of events occurred within a span of approximately thirty days. We planned on reenacting four battles of the Price Invasion, but for an odd reason, the host and the MCWRA placed Glasgow in August. *This battle had been fought on the 15th of October 1864.* This was the same Glasgow, MO event I'd attended nine years previously, when I'd "seen the elephant." Pilot Knob would be the end of September, on the anniversary date (this was a state of Missouri sponsored event, so the date was firm). In late October, we'd have the battle of Westport (in Kansas City), followed in November by Mine Creek near Pleasanton, Kansas.

August 12-13, 1989, Glasgow, MO.

We did not camp behind St. Mary's Catholic Church as we'd done in 1980. There were too many reenactors this year, so the camps were located on the extreme eastern end of town where there was a wide-open field for us to camp and have the battle. At 10 AM Saturday morning there was a memorial service at the local cemetery. We may have all been bused down for that, because it was at least a good two miles to the southern end of town, by the railroad tracks. Following this, we all marched in a parade down Main Street. We passed the same bank with time and temperature sign as I recall from 1980. Don't know if it registered into the triple digits this year or only in the upper nineties. It was hot nevertheless, plus it hadn't rained in the area for some weeks.

Despite the summer heat, the whole town came out. The local historical society made it possible for visitors to see several of the Victorian homes in the area. Historical pamphlets and arts and crafts knickknacks littered dozens of folding tables all along the bus route from the town to the Civil War camps. There were also concessions and souvenir stands to tempt the unsuspecting visitor. I'm sure Sonny Wells, the peddler, had a prime piece of real estate-his table loaded down with cardboard kepis, flags on a stick, toy soldiers, and T-shirts with the MCWRA logo. I believe John Zaharias was one of the few authentic sutlers here.

The battle was slated to run from 1:30 to 2:30 PM. After the half-mile parade through downtown, we barely had time to hop back on the bus, get back to camp, eat a quick lunch, and then head out a quarter-mile to the makeshift battlefield. Following the battle would be a Medical Demonstration, a ladies fashion show, and then later that night, a dance. By the time the infantry soldiers finished tramping around in the hot, humid air, who felt like dancing? Most of us would welcome a cold popskull and a piece of shade. Mona was not at Glasgow, so I didn't have to worry about keeping her company. I had my dog tent, which I shared with Isaacson, and that evening, after some adult refreshment, I had no trouble slipping off into dreamland.

Sunday continued with historical tours and a visit to the "battlefield" and camps by tour buses. Again it was shaping up to be another hot day. Our activity was limited, as we didn't want to tire ourselves out two days in a row. After lunch we again marched up the park lane, one-quarter mile, to the large field designated for the "battle."

Let me remind you that high temperatures and no rain had made the ground very dry. Any campfires set by us or any other campers had to be strictly watched. Come to think of it, I don't recall if we had anyone watching our camp during the battle. Usually the company cook only fixed cold cut sandwiches for our noon meal; the campfire already doused. As our "dog robber" was Darrell Wilson, he had the habit of joining us on the field for the Sunday battle. So my guess is, there was no one in the camp to keep an eye on things, but I may be mistaken. There may have been one or two souls who were napping in the shade because of heat exhaustion. Nevertheless, lack of proper security in a reenactor's camp can sometimes be a prescription for disaster, as we would soon find out to our extreme horror.

No sooner had we completed the generic fight, and then we marched back to our camp to see a sight that turned our blood cold. A fire had started in the straw and had spread to at least two tents. One of the tents belonged to Captain Don Strother. The second thing I noticed was one of our pards-one of the skulkers who'd stayed in camp-walking towards us holding a six-foot wooden staff with burnt material at one end. I blinked once, then twice, and then realized that this burnt wooden pole was all that was left of our beloved National colors. The flag had been left inside Don's tent. That magnificent silk flag with the hand painted gold stars that Dickson Stauffer and Bill Fannin had collaborated on and had presented to us at the Higginsville event in 1982 was gone! Gone by the wayward spark of an errant flame.

The fire had started behind Don's tent. The wall tent had been set up so the back was up against a wire mesh cattle fence. Someone suggested that they'd seen a couple of teenagers playing with matches. No proof could ever be found that the fire had been set deliberately, but whatever the cause, we all felt like we'd been kicked in the belly. Other than the loss of the colors, Captain Don had lost most of his personal effects-clothing, etc. Bad news travels fast, people say. Within a few minutes, we had dozens of folk "rubber neckin'" about like they'd come to see a train wreck. Words of condolence were mumbled, and then a fist full of dollars was pressed into Don's hand. In the Confederate and ladies camps, a hat had been passed so Don could buy some new clothes. One month later, at Pilot Knob, the LUAS raised over $300 in a picnic basket auction for the purchase of not one, but two flags: a National and a Regimental. The Regimental flag was envisioned as a solid medium blue field with an eagle clutching a scroll painted on it. Anyway, that was the plan but it would not be carried out for at least a year or two.

September 23-24, 1989 Pilot Knob, MO

A couple of things make this Pilot Knob memorable. We had nearly 230 infantry, 60 cavalry, and 8 full-scale guns. Don Strother became the overall battalion commander; but I suspect he might have asked for advice, on drill and such, from Dick Stauffer-who made his first appearance since Perryville, one year ago. Bill Fannin and John Maki each commanded a company in the battalion and I believe I was first sergeant under John. I remember we had a drill including the popular- "by right of companies, to the rear into column" and it was a sight to see all those companies turning and maneuvering here on a Missouri field for a change, rather than out east.

The other significant change took place within Holmes Brigade during the annual election. For the last two years, Frank Kirtley had been our First Sergeant. He was a member of the United States Marine Corps. His duty to Uncle Sam sometimes kept him away from many reenactments and I found myself assuming those top soldier duties in his absence. Now he was being ordered to Georgia to a new duty station. He had already announced his resignation with Holmes and on the evening of September 23rd, I was nominated and elected as the new First Sergeant.

October 20-22, 1989 Kansas City, MO (Westport)

In the previous chapter I mentioned the "board" I was asked to serve on to locate and plan the "Battle of Westport." Sonny Wells was the main driving force behind this planned spectacular and he envisioned it as the grandest thing on earth! Westport would be talked about for generations, he declared. I told you that the only sizable space logistically available to hold all the reenactors and stage the battle was at the huge Swope Park, near the old Byram's Ford crossing. Constructed in 1896 through a generous donation of land by millionaire Thomas H. Swope, the park encompasses an area of 1,769 acres. Aside from the zoo, Swope Park is also home to <u>Starlight Theater</u>, an outdoor amphitheater for plays and concerts. There are also two golf courses and several outdoor playing fields set aside for softball and soccer. For the casual visitor there are picnic areas, trails for hiking and horseback riding, and finally, a lake for fishing. These activities, naturally, occupied a large balance of Swope Park. The reenactors who came to Swope Park for the battle of Westport would find themselves confined to the Northwest corner, in an area measuring less than one-fourth of the entire park.

For this late war event, I decided to come dressed in the ugliest set of rags I could lay my hands on. I took a knife to my old Jarnigan frock coat and cut off the lower skirt and wore it as a shell jacket. To complete my uniform, I wore a patched up pair of britches, tall boots, a battered Hardee hat, and a shiny green vest with glass buttons. The patch job I'd made on my britches, most notably on the crotch area, caused Dave Bennett to remark that it looked like I had vagina hair.

I only lived a short distance from Swope Park, so it was no big deal from me to drive to and from the event. Later, I found myself returning home because I'd forgotten tent poles or something. Every military reenactor that registered that Friday night and early Saturday morning received a pair of wooden "dog tags." These were similar to ones modern GI's get today but made out of wood. I wonder who came up with that idea. Beside the "dog tags," each person who registered received an envelope full of coupons. A free mucket of Pepsi (with the purchase of a Pizza Hut pizza), one free bag of ice, or a half bale of straw, were just a few of the things you could use a coupon for. There were also coupons for a discount on Westport 125th anniversary commemorative merchandise such as T-shirts, bumper stickers, belt buckles, or medals. Or, as Jon Isaacson would later testify, you could use the coupons to wipe your ass.

Other than the wild zoo animals roaring in the night, there is little worth noting about the 125th Westport. Just before Sunday's battle, we received several new faces. I had never seen these fellows before, although John Maki seemed to think they were from Nebraska. One odd joker, who wasn't affiliated with anyone, joined our company about an hour before we marched out. He had a decent looking uniform on him, but he seemed a little odd. He kept talking about how excited he was about being able to shoot his gun at the "good ole boys." I hoped this trigger-happy fool wouldn't be a problem.

No sooner had we arrived on the battlefield and began a wheeling movement into the Confederates, than there came a rifle shot from our ranks. Sure enough, it was the yokel. He fired his musket from the hip, while we were still wheeling our line! Once we came to a halt, I ran down the length of the line and tore up his ass! I used these words:

"You don't fire until you're ordered to! We don't play cowboy stuff here!"

I asked the file closer, a sergeant from Nebraska, "Is this one of your men?"

He said no, but I told him to keep an eye on the soldier anyway. Boy was I hot about that. After the event was over and we all went our separate ways to our cars, I admitted to Bill Fannin that I felt sorta bad that I'd jumped that guy's ass. Bill said the guy deserved it and that's part about being a First Sergeant. By the way, the guy whose ass I jumped never came to another MCWRA or Holmes Brigade event again.

November 11-12, 1989 Mine Creek, KS.

Just about two miles south of Pleasanton, Kansas, just off state highway 69, is a short road that leads to an area wild with prairie grass and thick woods. A shallow creek, measuring about fifty yards wide in some places, cuts through these woods. The creek does not flow in a straight line, rather it has more bends and twists to it than a snake's back. While the banks of the creek bed are not too high, there are only a few places where it can be easily forded. This was the dilemma facing Sterling Price's army as he retreated from Missouri.

If it hadn't been for the wagon train, carrying mostly ill-gotten gains taken from loyal Missourians, his army might have escaped the pursuing Federal cavalry. The wagons would not be abandoned, he stubbornly declared. After so many failures: the bloodbath at Pilot Knob, the failure to take St. Louis or Jefferson City, and the defeat at Westport; the possession of the wagons, loaded with stolen contraband was the only prize of the campaign! With the enemy nipping at his heels, Price found the unforgiving banks of swollen Mine Creek another enemy. Crossing his wagons would become a nightmare. It would be the final act to this tragic drama.

Though the reenactment at Mine Creek was sponsored by the state of Kansas and the Linn County Historical Society, the one person who did the most pre-planning for this event was John Maki. For nearly a full year, John drove back and forth from Kansas City to Linn County nearly every spare chance he could get, coordinating with local, county, and state officials to get this 125th anniversary event going. I believe the National Historic Site at Fort Scott also put in a good word on behalf of the reenactors participating in the Mine Creek event. As a result of all this good will and trust, the reenactors were allowed to use one half of the original battlefield to camp and wage war *(the other half of the original battlefield was on the other side of Hwy 69)*. Unlike Pilot Knob, Glasgow, or Westport; which had the events right in or on the edge of town; Mine Creek was virtually out in the middle of nowhere. The highway was about a half-mile to the east and the town of Pleasanton was two miles north. However, you could see neither from our location, deep within prairie grass and woods.

Coming into the site on that Friday night, the reenactors were treated to a bowl of deer chili. One of the locals from the area boiled up 30 gallons of the stuff that night. It sure was tasty and a source of much honking during the night! The Confederate area was located near the tree line, near the bank of Mine Creek. The Federals had their camp about one hundred yards north of that position, in an open area near a pond. The civilian/refugee camp and sutler row was off to one side of this arena. The weather for early November was very pleasant although each man broke out his greatcoat after dark.

No battle was planned on Saturday although we may have had a rehearsal of some hand-to-hand play that would occur Sunday. Rather Saturday was a day for speechifying, rededication, and honoring of the dead. Several descendants of soldiers who had fought at Mine Creek were on hand to receive words, accept flowers, and shed a tear. One such descendant was a fellow whose great grandfather had captured Confederate General Marmaduke at Mine Creek. Since the original fight had been mostly a cavalry action, *(on the Federal part)* most of us would act like we'd just "dismounted" from our nags and were advancing against the foe on foot. Another fifty or so Federals *(probably Shelby's 5th Missourians wearing the blue or Karl Luthins 7th Illinois boys)* would remain mounted and gallop down into the gray clad masses.

Over two thousand people came through on Saturday-to hear, see, and smell the Civil War. Besides the generous amount of "chin music" shed about that glorious day, ancestors, etc., the Civil War Roundtable of Kansas City graciously led visitors on a walking tour of the Mine Creek battlefield. Some time after breakfast, Captain Don marched us out of camp and into the woods where a footbridge took us over the creek. We followed a winding path for about a quarter mile through the wildest woods ever seen. There were many old trees here; it's possible some might have been around during the battle. It's safe to assume that the woods we walked through probably still had many hidden treasures left to be found-artillery rounds and bullets. John Maki had been all over the area during his months putting the event together and was quick to point out some landmarks such as the area where many of Price's wagons tried to ford. We spent a good hour looking around the wilderness, and then we followed the path back across the footbridge and back to camp.

Saturday night we had our annual end of the season toast in which we gathered around the campfire and threw back shots of peach brandy, wine, whiskey, or whatever else we could splash in our tin cup. During these toasts we took the time to honor some past deeds, person, or things that had happened that year-even it was only to celebrate an erection. From out of the darkness, one of the boys joined our group at the fire with pieces of fabric. Remember I told you of the tragedy at Glasgow that resulted in the loss of our flag? Several small pieces, about half the size of paper napkins, had been salvaged from that inferno. Like some sort of Viking funeral, these pieces were gently laid on the fire one by one. Each of us stared at the crackling fire, as if in a trance and lost in our own thoughts, as the flames caught those pieces of Old Glory and sent the embers heavenward. A much larger piece of fabric, one that still had a hand sewn gold painted star attached, had been mounted in an 8x10 glassed frame and it was presented to Bill Fannin. We were all a bit choked up by these proceedings, though Bill was even more humbled and overwhelmed by the presentation. He probably mumbled a few words, then his emotions got the better of him and he retired to his tent. The rest of us finished our drinks and then we all retired for the night.

Sunday, the day of the battle! After church services, a bus took us into Mound City, five miles to the west, to the National Cemetery. I think there are some boys buried in this cemetery who were at the 1864 battle of Mine Creek. Don't recall what all went on during this ceremony, but I'm sure words were said by a district politician, followed by a musket volley. Afterwards, we were bused back to camp where we had our pre-battle lunch of baloney and cheese sandwiches.

What I recall of the battle was the mounted US cavalry appeared on top of the hill-in one long single line of about fifty boys. At a command, they came down the hill at a trot, pistols popping in each man's fist. Those of us who were "dismounted" were also spread out in a single line of battle, but we were firing the infantry long rifle. Our foe, the Confederates, were massed near the back of the woods and huddled around several wagons and artillery pieces. After a lengthy duel in which many volumes of gun smoke was spewed, we forced the Confederates to surrender. As we approached these survivors of Price's ill-fated army, it was noticed many of these boys were wearing Union overcoats. A hasty trial forced us to come to the conclusion that the clothing the Confederates were wearing had been stripped from our dead comrades, so the judgment was to execute these men on the spot. At least a dozen men were cut down like dogs, before calmer heads came forward to interrupt the slaughter. In one or two of the wagons we looked into, we found sides of ham, bags of grain, sugar, barrels of molasses, clothing, dinnerware, brass candlesticks, a metal wash tub, and a piano. These were just a few of the items taken by Sterling Price's army during his path of destruction through Missouri.

I briefly mentioned the fellow whose ancestor had captured Confederate General Marmaduke. Between Maki and I and a few other Holmes Brigader's, we got this fellow outfitted in a blue uniform, gave him a musket and let him reenact his great grandfather's shining moment. By the way, both ancestor and descendant had the same name: James Dunlevy. Afterwards, the reenactor James Dunlevy became emotional and thanked us for allowing him a chance to "walk in his ancestor's shoes."

And so the battle reenactment of Mine Creek came to a close. It also closed the chapter on our observation of the Sterling Price Invasion of Missouri of 1864. For all the boasting and bragging that had preceded all of the events this year, the one true success story clearly was the event at Mine Creek. While Pilot Knob can always be counted on as being good, the event at Glasgow was soured by our loss of the flag, and Westport was plagued by its location. There is just no place in metropolitan Kansas City to put on a nineteenth century outdoor drama when you're surrounded by urban sprawl. In my opinion, Mine Creek succeeded not merely because of its location in the middle of prairie Kansas, nor because it was the first major reenactment ever held in Kansas (*not counting Baxter Springs, which was a guerrilla action*). It succeeded because of the efforts of the Linn County Historical Society, the Kansas State Historical Society, the battle of Mine Creek descendants, and John Maki.

CHAPTER SIX

The End of the Eighties

December 1-3, 1989 Franklin, TN

The final act of the decade of the eighties would close on an episode, from 125 years earlier, that resulted in the death of an army. While Billy Sherman was marching to the sea, Grant had Lee bottled up in Petersburg, and Price was running for his life from Missouri; Confederate General John Bell Hood decided on a campaign to retake Tennessee. After the fall of Atlanta, he could have sent his army after Sherman, but instead he turned away and led his men northward. Hood had been severely wounded at Gettysburg and again at Chickamauga. These wounds may have caused him great pain and it's possible they affected his judgment. Many fine books on the Hood campaign into Tennessee can be found and I will not attempt to give you another history lesson. Suffice to say the Union was able to assemble an army from the Nashville area in sufficient numbers to slow Hood down and eventually cause many Confederate lads needless suffering along the works at Franklin.

Much to my wife's displeasure, I decided I would go to Franklin. Little Katie was in her first dance recital, although she only a small part in one dance number, Mona was slightly annoyed that I would not be around to see it. I was torn between my obligation as a father and my desire to go to Tennessee, so the wife said go! Since a video of the recital would be available for purchase at a later date, I said I'd see the dance number then. In later years, I would attend all the dance recitals, as Katie would be more and more involved with each passing year.

I took Friday, Dec 1ˢᵗ and Monday, Dec 4ᵗʰ off from work. That Thursday night, the 30ᵗʰ of November, I met Jon Isaacson and Steve Hall in Steve's van for the trip east. Just on the other side of Columbia, Mo., along Interstate 70 and near the town of Millersburg, we picked up Andy Papen. *Both Papen and Steve Hall had joined a few years earlier. I went to New Madrid '87 with Steve.* Our taste in cassette entertainment went from bad to worse during this trip. Not content to listen to Nazi, Ragtime, or country swing music, Isaacson assaulted our ears with the adult humor of Sam Kennison. If you're not familiar with his brand of low comedy, Sam Kennison tells jokes about sex, drugs, religion, and other taboo subjects, all punctuated with coarse language and a lot of screaming. Before the weekend was over, we were using words like "Leper Whore" and "Whisker Biscuit" as part of our normal conversation.

After an all night drive (we may have sacked out for a few hours at a truck stop or roadside rest stop), we entered the little burg of Franklin and sought out the Carter House. It was this old family home that saw some of the hottest action of the battle. On a couple of the buildings, visitors can count nearly two hundred bullet holes. Nearby was a museum that housed old bullets, cannonballs, swords, rifles, paintings, and photographs from this bloody day. At the time we arrived, Classic Images Video was doing some filming around the house. The filming here included some armed soldiers running around the yard in various stages of panic. Another scene had members of the Carter family huddled in the root cellar. These scenes would be added to yet another videotape that would be made available to a paying public.

We "dicked" around till just past noon, had a bite to eat, then drove northeast about five miles to the event site which was located on 800 acres (*three years after the event, this property was turned into an 18-hole golf course*). The event was boxed in on four sides with roadways, but was hidden from the traffic by well-placed trees. By the way, this event was not sponsored by Napoleonic Tactics or American Civil War

Commemorative Committee. They had suffered a serious financial setback back in September 1988 when their effort at Chickamauga was literally drenched by Hurricane Hugo. Due to the circumstances, as dictated by the wayward hand of Mother Nature, NTI lost more than $75,000. Other issues, including the mismanagement of funds and poor bookkeeping since April 1987, caused NTI founder Pat Massengill to consider bankruptcy. At the start of 1989 the event organizers only had a working balance of $21. With several lawsuits and unpaid bills hanging over their head, ACWCC and NTI parted company. The two separate entities attempted new venues, but the event at Wilderness lost money due to lack of planning and overspending on advertisement, while Atlanta just barely paid for itself. After several resignations, lawsuits, and other headaches, Pat Massengill allowed Napleonic Tactics to die a peaceful, but quick death. As of March 1990, ACWCC was still fighting a war with creditors.

A group simply known as the Battle of Franklin Reenactment Association Incorporated, Nashville, TN, was handling this event. This was a much smaller event as compared to Gettysburg. There would be only one civilian camp, for example. All camps would be within easy walking distance from one another, with a much abbreviated sutler row in the middle somewhere. Gone were the giant US and CS camps. One after action report suggests there were 3000 Confederates and only 600 Federals (*infantry, artillery, and cavalry combined*).

This would be the first event (*for me*) in which we would have to take care of our own eating. I did not attend the early September Atlanta event, but those that went had to make due with what was in the haversack. I did not own a skillet and was only used to eating cold stuff such as sardines, jerky, and hardtack. With the exception of one evening meal, I don't know what I did for grub from Friday to Sunday afternoon. It's possible I had Steve Hall pick me up some things from FRITZ, an old fashioned butcher shop on State Line Rd. in Kansas City. In the past Steve was used to buying beef jerky and pre-cooked salami snacks. The latter came as a linked meat product, which looked like a small intestine. I probably had those items, plus the aforementioned sardines and hardtack to complete my diet. I'm fairly sure I didn't have anything hot to eat, with the one exception I'll mention later. Anything else I may have thrown down my neck may have been along the line of a hot dog or funnel cake from sutler row.

Jon Isaacson and Andy Papen went into town that Friday evening and picked up a few groceries for themselves and a few other boys. "*I distinctly remember Papen and I stood in different aisles tossing vegetables back and forth over the stock.*" Jon also states for the record, "*I took my last heated crap for the weekend at that grocery store, with my shoes in a puddle of water from the overflowing toilet in the next stall.*"

It seemed like reenactor parking was fairly close to where we camped-no more than two hundred yards away at best and on the other side of a wide expanse of trees. Upon arrival, some Federals were already forming up for the 2 PM skirmish, or "the action at Columbia." Someone asked us if we wanted to get dressed and come along to play, but we declined.

As this was a late war event, reenactors were asked to bring only shelter tents. Officers would be allowed the larger tents. Most of us set our shelters up in "shebang" fashion, much as we had done at Gettysburg over a year earlier. Event organizers expected the weather to be mild during the day, with temperatures near 50. However, we were quick to discover that with the fall of night, the temperature would plunge like a fallen rock into the teens. Thankfully common sense had prevailed, and we had all come prepared for uncomfortable nights under the December skies.

I think I had two wool blankets, two quilts, and a lamb's wool comforter, plus two rubberized gum blankets. I shared my shebang with Isaacson and I'm pretty sure he had a like number of covers. We would spend those two nights not only under all those blankets and huddled together like conjoined twins, but with every stitch of clothing we had including the wearing of greatcoats, mittens, and fur hats. I may have used one cover as a windbreak to cover a draft where the canvas gapped open. During those nights, I believe some reenactors managed a few hours of sleep, but for the majority, the shivering and teeth rattling got to be too much. In the end the unfortunate wretches would shuck off the 50 pounds of covers and join a growing mob of humanity around the feeble embers of a fire. Some would stamp or flap their arms about for circulation. Others would fire up a cigar or pipe, perhaps thinking that the tobacco ash would warm them up. Most of us who huddled around the fire pit were too numb to move. At times like this we looked more like wild animals (swaddled in our greatcoats, scarves, and mittens) than anything remotely human.

Since most of us got very little sleep during the chill of night, we used as much of the daylight hours as we could to nap. Once again we were commanded by Chris Craft, who orchestrated battalion and Brigade drills, plus a Grand Review on Sunday morning. As first sergeant, I was responsible for making company reports and just as I had done at Gettysburg, I had to list ammunition amounts from each man. *Our company had a combined total of nearly 3,000 rounds or 100 rounds per man.* I also had to make a report on company strength. This was done when the battalion was formed up on the "color line." The first sergeant from each company stepped to the center of the battalion and reported to the Colonel or Adjutant if his company was "all present and accounted for." After this formality, the captain of each company was called forward to make his report and listen for the plan of the day. *The Federal infantry probably numbered 400 men.* At the first formation on Saturday morning, Colonel Craft first welcomed us all, appraised us on what was planned for the day including drill and what to expect during the afternoon battle. Then he surprised us all when he announced he would not seek command of the Western Brigade next year. After five years as Colonel he said it was time to step aside.

A successor was named in February 1990 and that man turned out to be Dave Shackleford from Ohio. I first met this Shackleford at First Bull Run then again at Gettysburg. He seemed cut from the same cloth as our own Don Strother which meant he was very bookish, was more show and less substance, and kept to himself most of the time, but was known to rant and lose his temper over the littlest detail. Over the next couple of years, we would bear witness to his actions as our commander and within time a low opinion of the man would develop. As many of my comrades in Holmes Brigade would later testify, Dave Shackleford was probably not the best man to fill Chris Craft's shoes.

In the meantime, we had completed brief instructions and maneuvers on company, battalion, and Brigade drills. We completed these drills before the hour of 10:00 AM! We were supposed to leave camp following drill for the Spring Hill fight, so each man had to make sure that besides a full cartridge box, each had lunch rations to nibble. We would not return till after 2:00 PM!

Before preceding one more step, I should acknowledge just a few of the men who came to Franklin and served with Holmes Brigade. We had a company strength of 30. Beside McCarthy, Whitson, Bill Fannin, Don Strother, Steve Hall, Papen, Isaacson, and I, we were blessed with the presence of Gary Crane, Randy Rogers, Ed MacDonald, Mike and Ray Gosser, John Zaharias' personal piss boy Mike Watson, and representing the "bagladies" Charlie Pautler. Some of the Illinois sucker boys also came to Franklin including Randy "By God" Jackson. My old grade school buddy Ted Mueller did not make the trip, unfortunately.

Of those mentioned, I think I should describe Randy Rogers. Think of a fat Frankenstein monster and that about sums up Randy. Perhaps it's unfair to call Randy fat, in the general sense of the word. Rather it would be correct for me to say he is as wide as he is tall. He is so big the fabric for his uniform could be used to reupholster furniture. Calling Iowa his home, I believe Randy worked in some type of law enforcement or security field (*I'm told he's also worked as a hospital or nursing home orderly*). Over the years he has tangled with his share of trouble and has the scars to prove it. Jon Isaacson once saw Randy naked and said the man probably has had more staples in him than Office Depot. As of late, Randy had begun to sport a shaggy black beard, where, it is said, he hides bits of old greasy food. Despite his appearance, Randy Rogers has always been a pleasant sort of fellow; reminding one of "Mongo," the Alex Karas character from BLAZING SADDLES. He does not feel sorry for himself due to his looks. In that mind of his, this is under that matted mess of greasy hair is a fountain of Civil War knowledge. And just like "Mongo," Randy Rogers can be a teddy bear once you look beyond that rough exterior.

The Spring Hill fight is memorable for only one reason. First of all we arrived on site in plenty of time to stand at ease for nearly an hour.

Arms were stacked and we were allowed to sit on our duffs. Most of us took this opportunity to dig jerky, apples, and hardtack out of our haversacks. I distinctly remember I worked on repairing a haversack strap during the interim. As I didn't own a knapsack, I brought two haversacks. One had rations, while the other carried black powder cartridges and some personal effects including a sewing kit. It took me a good thirty minutes to tenderly repair that leather strap, and then I may have used the needle on a rip in some trouser fabric or to sew on a button. The four hundred of us Yankees lolly-gagged on that ground for what seemed like forever, but the guys seemed content and some took naps right there on that hard ground with barely a whimper.

All too soon came the call to arms. Our muskets were taken from the stacks and we began turning our lines in various evolutions to meet the enemy. I believe there was an artillery duel and quite possibly the horse soldiers clashed sabers. At some point Colonel Craft ordered the Brigade forward, four battalions at a time in one long line. The other two battalions I believe were held in reserve. The Confederates were less than one hundred yards from us and the noise was terrific. Shouted words could not be heard, so we fired by the drum. At some point, we were called upon to fall back, then to lie face down on the ground while our artillery roared behind us. After a few hot rounds had passed over us, Colonel Craft ordered the cannoneers to cease-fire and once again he had us on our feet. "The enemy is stunned after that bombardment," so our Colonel reasoned as we resumed the offensive.

As the musketry returned to rip the air between the two armies, a sudden grass fire erupted right before our eyes. The grass was obviously very dry, despite the December climate. Evidence suggests that the fire was a result of guys putting the cartridge paper down the barrel with the gunpowder, but it's anybody's guess whether it came from the US or CS line. *During the actual Civil War, the infantry soldier sometimes included the paper wrapper when he rammed the powder and ball down the barrel. When the musket is fired, the paper flies out, and when it does it usually comes out hot. The use of paper wadding in reenactments is not recommended for those very reasons. Usually the paper refuse is tossed aside.* In the case of the Spring Hill fight, it was as if the grass had been soaked in gasoline. In a matter of seconds, a fifty-foot wall of flames had sprung up. Both Federals and Confederates ceased firing, dropped their muskets and proceeded to lend a hand in extinguishing the blaze.

During this moment of high drama, Randy Rogers created a quite the spectacle of himself when he bolted from our line and ran back towards the reserves and Colonel Craft. He may have been going after someone with a walkie-talkie to get emergency assistance. Picture if you will a large man, running as fast as his stubby legs will carry him, with all his leather accoutrements flapping against his body as he runs. You would have to be there, but most everyone agreed it was a vision of some merriment. However, the high winds whipping over the dry grass conspired to turn this humorous little incident into a serious problem. Within a few minutes, the Franklin Fire Department was on the scene and brought things under control.

However, play was not resumed with as much enthusiasm as before due to the near tragedy. A number of less than spirited volleys rang out, then by mutual agreement and under a flag of truce, both commanders decided to end the contest for the day. Despite the fact we had to cut the drama a few minutes short, the spectators who witnessed the "battle" seemed to enjoy the show-especially the "live fire." Applause and loud cheering came from the sidelines; most of it for the Confederates, as they marched past the crowd with blood red banners snapping in the breeze. We were in Tennessee where the bias is typical for the area.

We made it back to camp; thanks in due part to the spirited fife and drum corps. The lively and patriotic tunes were such a tonic to us foot sore lads that it seemed to provide us with an extra spring in our step. Drum music has always had that affect, at least on me. You can't help but fall into step-that is if the music is performed with mechanical precision.

It was near 2 PM when we were dismissed. We would have a dress parade in two hours, but that was merely a formality in which roll call would be taken and a report on ammunition used by each company would be reported to the battalion sergeant major. In the meantime, we could fag out or think about dinner.

As I lay there under my tent puffing on my cherry wood pipe, I heard a female voice asking someone if Bob Talbott was here. Crawling out from under the canvas, a smile broke across my face as I beheld the sweet face of Cousin Patty. A few months earlier, I had phoned my dear cousin and told her of my planned visit for the Franklin reenactment. As we had not seen each other in years, she was giddy with excitement and said we would have to have dinner.

My dad and her mother were brother and sister. Patty's father had been a career military man, like my dad, but Uncle Vernon Whittle had been in the army. I can still recall several times Dad driving us to Fort Leonard Wood to visit them back in the sixties. The Whittle's had two girls, Clarinda Jo, born in 1949 and Patty, born the same year as me, 1953. I remember both girls had quite a collection of Barbie and Ken dolls and sometimes, for the lack of anything better to do, my brother Bill and I played with those dolls. The girls also had a fondness for the surf music of Jan and Dean. I can still hear "Little ol' lady from Pasadena," as if it was only yesterday.

Patty told me over the phone that she had put on a few pounds, and I might be disappointed when I saw her, but when I crawled out of my tent to face her she looked as sweet as a peach. I told Patty we had one more formation at 4 PM, but after that I would be on free time. After a warm hug and some affectionate words, she promised to come back with the car and take me to dinner.

When she came back later, it was just turning dark and colder. I told the boys not to wait up for me, and with a tip of my hat I plopped my ass in the family car. Patty was married to a guy named Gary Fitzhugh. I had met the lad some years back, so it wasn't like I was meeting a total stranger. Also in the car were Patty's two teenage daughters. Both of these girls were very easy on the eyes! The oldest, Tara, was blond and about 17, while the youngest, Erin, was probably about 13, had dark hair and was as cute as a pixie.

For dinner they recommended a Mexican restaurant in Franklin. As we went into the place, I felt all eyes on me. I was dressed in my Yankee uniform, sky blue overcoat, and slouch hat. I suppose a bug-eyed

Martian would have received the same amount of stares as I did. It was here that I had my very first Margarita "on the rocks."

Over plates of steaming refried beans, chimichangas, and taco salads, we traded stories of life, home, and the Civil War. Afterwards, I was taken on a driving tour of Franklin, which included a stop at Carnton Mansion. Patty told me that this house was supposedly haunted, because after the battle of Franklin, it was used as a hospital. Plus, the dead bodies of five Confederate generals, slain on the field, were laid out on the porch. The two girls, Erin and Tara, on a dare, wanted to run up on the porch and jump around. Perhaps they hoped to provoke the ghosts. As the girls went up to the porch, Gary backed the car away, acting as if he would leave them there. The girls squealed and came running.

From here, I was taken to the family home. I think Gary went to bed because he had to work the next morning and I think the two girls had a date or something else going on that night. Patty and I sat at the kitchen table for about an hour and again talked about life, home, and our families. She mentioned my dad's death. We talked about when our parents would get together to play canasta, or the board game with marbles- a homemade version of SORRY! When the dice was dropped on the floor, my dad always shouted, "No crapping on the floor!"

About ten o'clock, Patty drove me back to camp. Knowing how cold it would be, she had offered me a blanket to take back, but I said I would manage. With one last hug, she promised she would come by after the battle Sunday afternoon. We said our goodnights and I walked the brief one hundred yards to the glow of the campfire.

During the night, the wind came down from the north. Despite the fact I'd downed almost a quart of alcohol, it was not enough anti-freeze to sustain me throughout the chill of the night. Plus, I found the thin canvas material of our shelter tent a poor insulation from the whispering winds. Pat McCarthy confessed to me that, he and Don Whitson…*"snuck out of camp at about 2 AM and found a motel room. We slept in a warm bed, showered and ate a hot breakfast, and were back in camp before anyone knew we'd left."*

Meanwhile, some enterprising clods in a neighboring camp built a windbreak by stacking several large bales of straw until there was a wall five feet high by thirty feet in length. In the wee hours of the morning I was jolted out of dreamland by the cry of "FIRE!" Staggering to my stocking feet I beheld an inferno roaring only 20 feet from my face. Men were dancing around the hot red glow in various stages of panic, much like the damned in Hades. In a second, I realized what had happened. Our neighbors in the adjoining camp had stoked their fire before retiring for the night and left the blaze unattended. A sudden shift in the wind lifted sparks from that fire onto those stacked bales. I think the whole Union Army was awake and trying to beat the flames out. A "staff officer" came out of his headquarters tent with a fire extinguisher, unfortunately and with some horror, it was discovered that the contents of the fire extinguisher had frozen. After some frantic moments, scorched blankets, and the workings of shovels and a bucket brigade, the fire was put out. Despite the chill of the night, we had all been sweating in panic. It was lucky that only a couple bales went up. The straw was moved far away from the fire and the rest of us tried to rediscover dreamland or clean underwear. An after action report states that at least a dozen tents in various camps were accidentally burned over the weekend.

Upon awakening that frosty Sunday morning, we were shocked to learn that during the night someone had died! A bunch of us were huddled around the fire pit and watched as the meat wagon came through. Only fifty yards away, in a camp occupied by a group of Federals from Ohio, lay Mr. Stanley J. Kahrl flat on his back. The story that came back to me was sometime during the night, Mr. Kahrl stepped outside his tent to pee and had a heart attack right on the spot. His tent mate was fast asleep and didn't discover the body till first light. By then Mr. Kahrl was as blue as a pair of army trousers. The county coroner had to come out to pronounce the body dead, and then it was loaded in the ambulance and taken away. We were all lost in our thoughts-no words seemed appropriate. Finally, Isaacson broke the ice by saying; perhaps we should go molest the dead body. Several of us giggled at the suggestion. Jon was only trying to lighten the mood, but one old boy-a half-breed Indian buddy of Randy Rogers- said we should have respect for the dead and then he walked away in disgust.

The temperature remained as cold as the mood. Word came that today's high would only be in the teens. The sky was cloudless and was the color of dull steel. The winds that came through during the night remained in the area and gave everyone an excuse to stay bundled up. During the Grand Review later that morning, most every soul was wrapped tighter than a tick with greatcoat, muffler, and mittens. Gripping the bare metal of the musket could be pure agony if you didn't have something over your hands. In the absence of mittens, some fellows rolled the cuffs of their greatcoat sleeves down over their knuckles.

The Grand Review seemed to last an eternity. The Confederates had as many flags as they did people on the field. In the mean time, the icy winds buffeted us, whipped our greatcoats around our ankles, and caused our teeth to chatter, our fingers to grow numb, and the snot to freeze to our face. We were supposed to be at attention or parade rest, but I'll wager a few of us had the lower limb trembles holding back a weak bladder.

After the "review" was finally over, we were allowed the luxury of returning to camp for a hasty lunch, and then we reformed about 11:30 AM for the march to Franklin. The fight wouldn't commence till 1PM, but we always had to be on site at least a good hour before kickoff.

At the conclusion of the original 1864 Spring Hill fight, the Union Army waited for the cover of darkness and was able to slip past the sleeping Confederates and made their way northward to heavily fortified Franklin. Upon learning that his enemy had disappeared out from under his very nose, General Hood threw a shit fit and accused his subordinates of dereliction of duty, and then he ordered all his troops forward. Ignoring the advice from his generals, whom he already distrusted after the lost opportunity at Spring Hill, Hood sent 19,000 men against an entrenched Union Army, most who were in line near the Carter House.

The Battle of Franklin Reenactment Association built a scale model of both the family home and the nearby cotton gin. Between both buildings, a log and lumber breastwork was built extending at least one hundred yards in length. When the reenactors arrived on scene, we were detailed to help finish a section of the wall. Imagine four hundred guys running around like blue coated beavers, each taking lumber from one pile and putting it in another.

During the battle, our battalion (about four companies or approximately ninety men) sat in reserve behind the "Carter House." We were told we would be portraying members of Colonel Emerson Opdyke's Brigade who, during the 1864 battle, rushed into the fray like cavalry to the rescue, to plug a gap where Confederates had broken through. We were told that "Opdyke's Tigers" pretty much saved the day for the Union. However, for the first forty-five minutes of the battle reenactment our battalion sat on its collective asses. Meanwhile, a special company of about 20 to 30 Union soldiers came equipped with the Henry Rifle.

This brass framed 13 shot repeating rifle had been developed in 1860, but only a select number of men were armed with this formidable weapon. Why weren't more infantrymen armed with repeaters? Because the government thought it would be a waste of ammunition if issued to all soldiers. Plus repeaters were more expensive to make. Single shot muzzleloaders made between 1842 and 1861, the military brass concluded, was good enough for the common foot soldier.

Anyway, those of us with "Opdyke's Tigers" sat behind the Carter House while the war was going on in front of us. We were actually looking at the backs of our comrades as they blazed away at an unseen enemy. Unseen by us that is! By the way, this is the only reenactment I've ever attended in my 25-year history in which the reenactors fought the battle in greatcoats. It was still damn cold.

After about forty-five minutes into the battle reenactment of Franklin, "Opdyke's Tigers" were summoned. We leaped to our feet with a hearty HUZZAH, took arms and bolted forward. The colonel wanted us on the far right of the Union line. We tore around the front corner of the "house," and formed a double line facing the enemy. Spread out before our eyes, like Sunday dinner on a tablecloth, was the panorama of battle. Dead and wounded Confederates lay all about the field 300 yards square. There was still a good number of the living, but they were slowly being cut down under the withering fire of the boys in blue. Our artillery was silent, as the enemy was too damn close for safe fire. Off to the far left, I could see the spectators, but they were placed on the horizon and I doubt if they could see too well.

We were perched up on the parapet on the far right. I distinctly remember taking two packs of cartridges, or twenty rounds, and placing them on the top of the fence where I could get them easy. We began firing at will and I think I fired three rounds, when play was halted. What! The battle was over? All up and down the line, men shouted to cease fire, then taps was played to remember the original fallen of the November 30, 1864 battle. Needless to say, those of us who'd been waiting in reserve for the last forty-five minutes felt cheated. However, after suffering two sleepless nights, shivering in the cold, battling a runaway brush fire, and seeing a dead man, I had plenty of excitement for my eight-dollar registration fee.

After Colonel Craft dismissed us for the last time, came the difficult task of loading up to go home. It is the same story after every event. After the emotional high of a two or three day battle reenactment, facing the reality of going back to the 20th Century can be a real struggle emotionally, as well as, physically. That's when the fatigue really sets in.

On the way out of the event, Cousin Patty and her daughter Erin came by to give me a hug and wish me a safe journey back to Missouri. I promised to write and especially to call her Mom and Dad went I got back home. Fortunately, I didn't have to drive.

It was well after 5PM by the time we got out of the event. We drove quite a distance through Tennessee and were probably well into Illinois when we pulled into a Pizza Hut to eat. The restaurant was selling funny looking sunglasses as part of a promotion for the Back to the Future Part II movie. Do you remember when Marty McFly went to the future and ran into those futuristic tough kids with the hoverboards? Well, those tough kids were wearing those sunglasses. Isaacson and I both bought a pair. I still have mine as of this writing.

So after the Pizza Hut meal we were on our way back to Missouri, when just on the other side of St. Louis, we ran into a severe rainstorm.

Now I may have been asleep at the time or the episode was so traumatic that I've shut it from my mind. Jon Isaacson has a fantastic version in which "*...Steve was driving and decided to stop in the middle of Interstate 70 because he couldn't see.*" Jon further claims that a semi was behind us and "*We all started screaming like banshees for Steve to pull off the road.*" The way Steve Hall remembers the incident differs slightly from the frenzy Isaacson seemed to recall. Steve told me, "*It started hailing heavily with medium-sized hail stones. I slowed to pull under an interstate overpass, but there was already a car on the shoulder. A look in the rear view mirror showed that no one was behind me in my lane. A semi-truck was barreling along in the other lane, but not mine. I knew exactly what I was doing when I stopped in the right lane under the bridge – constantly checking the rear view mirror. After about 3-4 minutes it was all over and we continued on a solid roadway of hailstones.*"

When standing around a blazing fire pit, like the one at Franklin, one tends to get lost in his own thoughts. Usually the dancing flames have a hypnotic effect and will lull a person into a dreamlike trance. Your mind becomes relaxed and at ease, just by staring at the simplistic beauty of fire. Sounds like poetry from a pyromaniac, huh? I'm no arsonist, but I enjoy the calming effect a campfire has on a soul. Add one or two beers and a cigar and you have a recipe for relaxation. It was while I was thus relaxed that I realized that Franklin was the last event of the eighties. The end of the eighties! It was with great fondness and some melancholy that as I gazed into the fire and watched those tiny sparks fly heavenward, I came to remember the last ten years. The decade of Higginbotham, Maki, the Bagladies, the North and South miniseries, the Mexican War, the 125th anniversary reenactments, and all the great people and places I've seen during the eighties. I expressed my sadness to Charlie Pautler, one of the few who knew what was in my heart, because he also began the hobby at the start of 1980 as a little drummer boy. Now he was a high school graduate on the way to higher learning.

I was unsure what to expect in the next decade, because I thought I'd already experienced the best the hobby has to offer. In some respects, I would be right. After Franklin, Bill Fannin would resign as editor of the Holmes Brigade Dispatch and then a few months after that, both he and Gary Crane would go under the knife for heart by-pass surgery. Franklin would be the last time most of us would see Bill, as he would not take the field again until the following August. Gary Crane, however, would bounce back much quicker, returning to us by Fort Scott in May. Aaron Racine would become the newsletter editor for about two years; even finding time to work on it while at Stanford University.

And so this chapter brings an end to the decade of the 1980's. Next year we would start remembering the 130th anniversary of the Civil War. 130th! Doesn't have quite the same ring as 100th, 125th, or even 150th. In the early 1990's we would return to Wilson's Creek, Perryville, Champion's Hill, Kentucky, and Louisiana, among others. In the early 1990's, I would lose two jobs, become tempted into accepting another, and find myself in possession of not only a new car, but a new home as well.

CHAPTER SEVEN

"Shall we dance?"

One evening out of every winter, several hundred reenactors from all over the Midwest would gather in one place, not to wage war, but to dance. This was the one time out of the entire year in which the ladies could shine. Many weekends, these tireless ladies would follow along with their soldier husbands to swampy, humid, dusty, or muddy environments for Civil War reenactments. With nary a complaint, these ladies would set up their tent communities, with other "reenactor widows," and would watch from afar as the boys went off to play noisy games. To occupy themselves while the men "did their thing," the ladies would have tea parties and fashion shows, as well as other amusements.

Barely one year after the birth of the group and acceptance into the MCWRA, the Ladies Union Aid Society, under the leadership of Constance Soper, Kathleen Fannin, and other fine ladies, decided to stage a fancy dress military ball. *Mention has already been made, in the first volume of Chin Music, on a dress ball we had in the Fayette Missouri High School, in late 1982. It was probably the genesis of future dress balls we've had since*. Wherever the inspiration came from is immaterial. Suffice to say that within two months, the very first Twelfth Night Ball was being planned.

The word Twelfth Night refers to the 12th night after Christmas, or King's Day, when the three wise men of the Bible are said to have visited the Christ Child. Twelfth Night has been celebrated by English speaking people for centuries for it is viewed as a time for gayety, drinking, dining, and dancing. In fact, the festivities usually continue on until the advent of Mardi gras, a few weeks later. The most symbolic part of Twelfth Night is when a dessert known as the King's Cake is served. Legend states that one bean is placed in the batter and if a man finds that bean in his piece of cake, he is proclaimed Twelfth Night king! On the other hand, if a lady finds the bean in her piece, she must bake next year's cake! I suppose these footloose and carefree festivities might seem somewhat pagan considering it claims as its roots the three wise men and the gift of the Magi. Then again, aren't most traditions and rituals, in today's society, based in some degree on a pagan ceremony from a bygone age?

On the subject of the Twelfth Night, as it relates to the LUAS, these ladies wanted to follow tradition and decided that this ball or any dress ball in the future should be in the early part of the year, before the reenactment season began. It not only gave everyone a chance to see one another after several months away from the hobby, but it was also viewed as the one event that was solely being put on for the reenactors, rather than for the amusement of public.

So the first Twelfth Night Ball was held at the Odd Fellow's Hall in Liberty, Missouri, on Saturday evening, January 8, 1983. I believe a small fee of eight dollars was charged to each couple. With this minor donation, the guests were treated to a six-piece chamber orchestra, playing period music, plus each lady who entered received a printed dance card. The card was tied to the wrist of the lady by a ribbon. The card not only had a list of all the dances planned for the evening, but there were spaces on the card where the lady could write in the name of any suitor who wished to dance with her. About one hour before the ball there was dance instruction. I believe there were about six different dances that we would be doing, including the waltz, polkas, Virginia reel, and the Grand March.

The Virginia reel is the only dance not done as a one-on-one couple dance; it reminds one of square dancing. Two long lines face one another, the men in one line facing a line of women. The two lines step forward, "dosey-doe," swing around one way, then another, make another leg move or two, then one couple trots down the line and back, then forms an arch for the other dancers to crawl under. Then it starts over again. It is very exhaustive work if you have over one hundred people. The real challenge is twirling around in those wide hoop skirts.

There was a number of finger snacks and liquid refreshment including the famous "fish house punch." This was a concoction in a cut glass crystal bowl, the ingredients that remain a mystery to this day. Connie Soper might have been the author of this witches' brew. Nevertheless, all the soldier boys were drawn to the punch bowl like bees to a honey pot.

After an evening of dance, and for those who'd come a great distance, lodging was sought in the area. Arrangements were usually made many days in advance of the gala occasion and some hotels/motels offered discounts for the reenactors. Lodging was extremely important as it provided a place, especially for the ladies, to dress into and out of the volumes of clothing. Before retiring for the night, however, most of us would seek an "open all night" restaurant. When twenty or thirty people walk into an IHOP or DENNY'S restaurant all at the same time, wearing fancy dress uniforms and the ladies in wide hoop skirts, just imagine the looks we got!

The following year the Confederate Ladies Organization put together the winter ball. It was held in February and announced as a **St. Valentine's Day Ball!** The CLO was able to obtain the use of the Capitol Rotunda of the Missouri State Capitol building in Jefferson City. The use of the rotunda is a rare privilege granted to only a few groups. At the time, our own Bill Fannin was curator of the State Capitol Museum, so it's possible he pulled a few strings.

Once again, couples were asked for a measly eight dollars to help cover the cost of a band, decorations, dance instruction, and other minor arrangements such as the printing of dance cards. At this time, since I was the only person affiliated with print business, I was asked to print up the cards. Under the watchful eye of Constance Soper, I designed the look and contents of the four-page dance card, and then I asked a friend at Sign Craft to run off several hundred on his printing press. A special insert called the "Etiquette of the Ballroom" was included. It was a list of proper etiquette and gentlemanly behavior as suggested for the dance floor. For example, everyone wore kid gloves. A gentleman on the dance floor never touched a lady with his bare hand. Over the next several years, I would be asked time and again to print up the dance cards.

When attending the Capitol Rotunda ball, in the mid to late eighties, lodging was sought at the Hotel Governor, an old ten story hotel built I believe in the 1920's. Most reenactors preferred to stay at the Hotel Governor, as it was a short two blocks from the Capitol. In the early part of February, the weather was quite pleasant with the stroll in the evening air very invigorating. *In 1984 the cost of a room was only about thirty dollars.*

Even though the Hotel Governor seemed big, ten stories tall, I seem to recall the rooms were not so big. The elevator, I know for a fact, was small. It could hold four people or six if they were naked. If two of those women happened to be dressed in wide hoop skirts, you better take a deep breath because it was like being in a mineshaft. I made the mistake once of breaking wind in the elevator. Boy, did I get an earful!

I think it was that particular Saturday night, February the 11th; we celebrated Gregg Higginbotham's birthday. Actually, his birthday is on February the 12th, the same day as Abraham Lincoln. Nevertheless, with a bunch of his closest friends on hand, time was set aside for a piece of cake. Don't know who made it, nor do I recall if we ate the cake before or after the dance. I do know Gregg cut the cake with his officer's saber.

One half hour before the ball was to commence, we all left the hotel, arm in arm with our ladies, and walked the brief two blocks to a doorway under the massive stone steps which front the Capitol. Once we handed the doorman our dance tickets, we walked toward the central rotunda area. The area set aside for the dance was a wide polished floor about fifty yard's square (*I may be exaggerating slightly*). A rounded marble staircase, beginning on either side of the hall, went up to the second floor. Patriotic banners, and flags from all the US and CS units in the MCWRA littered the walls of this political palace.

After an hour of instruction by Peter Lippincott of St. Louis, we all formed up for the Grand March! This begins with the men entering the hall from one end and the ladies entering from the opposite end. The two lines weave in and out like snakes, go up the stairs, down another passageway, double back, and enter the hallway from another way. It's all very confusing and a great way to slip and fall in the haste to get from one area to another. In fact, most male reenactors put duct tape on the bottom of their brogans because of the heel plates. The floor is so polished with wax, and then buffed up that many of us have stumbled during the course of the night. During one dance at the Capitol Rotunda, my feet went out from under me and I landed hard on my back. The only ailment I suffered was that it knocked the wind out of me and I had to sit down to rest for fifteen minutes or so.

The very first ball we had at the Capitol Rotunda was a resounding success, with numbers estimated about at 250! Since that night in 1984, based own our conduct inside the Rotunda building (*we didn't tear anything up*), we were allowed to return several more times.

The last time I recall attending a ball in Jefferson City was right after the Franklin event, which was February 3, 1990. The Hotel Governor was closed down for remodeling, so we had to seek lodging elsewhere in town. Jon Isaacson brought this raven-haired beauty to the dance. I mean she was a real eye-opener! She may have been a co-worker, or friend of the family, but she was not his steady girlfriend. When they checked into the motel, it was discovered Jon had only requested one room! She was very pissed and I don't blame her. She wasn't about to shack up with Jon who she hardly knew! I told her she could room with my wife and I'd bunk with Jon. However, after the dance ended about midnight she made Jon drive her all the way back to Kansas City. Adding insult to Jon's bruised ego, the weather had turned for the worse and it was snowing like a bastard! There wasn't much stuck to the ground yet, but the flakes were coming fast and furious in a horizontal flight path. The last I saw of Jon and his "date" they were driving away until the red taillights of his car were swallowed up by the white fury. I never saw her again.

The post-Franklin ball was also where a special presentation was made to John Maki. While wandering up sutler row during the Franklin weekend, Isaacson and I spotted an officer's saber complete with scabbard. It was only about 2-foot long and priced at fifty dollars. A bunch of us from the company chipped in and bought the thing on the spot and gave it to Maki at the ball. We had always teased John Maki about his height because he is less than five feet tall-a hobbit really. He accepted the tiny saber all in good humor and a wide grin.

In 1985, we had the ball on the campus of the University of Missouri in Columbia.

In 1986, we returned to the Capitol Rotunda in Jefferson City, Missouri.

On January 10, 1987, we had the ball in Excelsior Springs, Missouri.

Having the ball in the Kansas City area certainly did not set well with the St. Louis crowd. In the Loyal Ladies Annunciator, several letters to the editor complained of an assumed bias towards the eastern part of the state. I'm sure Connie was hard pressed to find a suitable place to host the dance and was little concerned in what part of the state it was held. Most of our membership resides in the southwestern, western, or central portion of the state, but provisions were made to consider St. Louis as a future site of the Twelfth Night Ball.

"Located only 35 minutes from the famous Country Club Plaza, the Inn on Crescent Lake, in Excelsior Springs, beckons to visitors looking to experience a bit of the unusual. This stately 1915 three-story Georgian Colonial sits on 22 acres of wooded land that is perfect for romantic, leisurely strolls any season of the year. The Inn on Crescent Lake appears unexpectedly like a vision out of The Great Gatsby, *and overlooks an estate-sized lawn where Canadian geese strut self-assuredly on their way to one of two crescent-shaped ponds."*-From a newspaper article from the Kansas City Star.

It was another beautiful night, the house looked like something from Gone with the Wind, plus it was far back away from the regular flow of traffic where one could almost get a sense of having traveled back in time. About a week before the event, several of us walked the grounds and toured the house. I remember Connie saying that it would be grand if we could have a horse drawn buggy to bring people up the drive to the door of the manor. At this time, the only people living in the house were a young caretaker and his wife. They would be out of town or on some other business. The actual owner of the home gave Connie the permission for us to use the lower rooms of the house to host our ball.

If my feeble memory serves me, just inside and to the left was a room with a long hall. It was determined the dance would be here. A wide wooden staircase went up to the upper floors in which the caretaker and his wife lived. In the rear of the house was a narrow set of stairs that went from the upper floors down into the kitchen. The servants most likely used this as they moved about the house, from kitchen duties to housekeeping.

On the night of the ball, a horse drawn sleigh was indeed employed, bringing guests *"across a snowy expanse of lawn to the candle-lit mansion filled with warm laughter and music."* Inside, the tables over-flowed with period refreshments, punch, cut flowers, and a special Twelfth Night cake. Instead of a bean, a small coin was placed in the batter to be found by the one and only Gregg Higginbotham. Amidst peals of laughter and much merriment, Higgy was led to a "throne" then crowned as Twelfth Night King with a laurel wreath upon his head. Everyone seemed to be having a grand time and the ball was on its way to being another success. Then the caretaker and his wife made an unannounced visit to check on us.

The first thing the caretaker was pissed about was somebody had taken his and his wife's anniversary champagne out of the refrigerator. The bottle had been sucked dry. Upstairs in a third floor room was a pool table. Some of the Holmes Brigade boys discovered it and were hunched over the green felt like a bunch of pool hall junkies. The caretaker was not amused by this display. I was walking down the stairwell as he and his wife were peering into the room. I did not want to hear the dialogue that I knew was sure to come. The final complaint came after the conclusion of the dance. It seems there was a carpet in the hallway where we had the dance. All the heel plates on our shoes literally cut that fabric to ribbons. I also believe the kitchen was in a sad state and it took the ladies and some volunteers some time to straighten things up.

Later we all went to Perkins for a midnight snack. I think Connie felt bad about the way things turned out, due to the fact that the reenactors wandered about the house and got into stuff that we shouldn't have. I'm sure the caretaker did not have too many kind words to say about the way we treated the house, especially the carpet. All I remember was, as we sat at the restaurant, we all felt sorry for Connie. She sort of had her head hung low over the dinner table as we all commented on the conclusion of the ball and how the caretaker and his wife had hard words to say. I suppose word would eventually reach the owner of the home and its possible Connie was afraid of any lawsuits that might result. She had already stated months earlier that this would be the last time she would head the ball committee. It was probably just as well. The job involves trying to please everyone and keeping an eye on everything at the same time. If something happens and it did, whether she was directly involved or not, Connie was ultimately held responsible. I wouldn't want the job!

The next ball was planned by the Confederate Ladies Organization, but the Capitol Rotunda would not be available on the dates in early 1988 that we wanted. If memory serves me, a new Governor was having his inaugural ball around the same time, so the reenactors were given the boot. Instead the CLO planned the ball in historic Lawrence, Kansas, the home of abolitionism and John Brown during the days of Bleeding Kansas 1855 to 1859. I don't know why the Confederate ladies decided on Lawrence to host the ball, but I'm willing to bet their Rebel ancestors were rolling in their graves.

The ball was held at the historic Eldridge Hotel on December 31, 1988, and was billed, strangely enough, as the New Year's Eve Ball. As stated, the CLO had the duties of putting on the shindig. Tickets for the dance had jumped from $8 a couple to $18 a couple, but the price included a midnight supper. This was certainly more appealing than going to a DENNY'S or IHOP. The meal would be right in the hotel dinning room.

Because I can't help myself, here is a brief history of the Eldridge Hotel.

"The original building on this site was the Free State Hotel, built in 1855 by settlers from the New England Emigrant Aid Society. The Free State Hotel was intended as temporary quarters for those settlers who came here from Boston and other areas while their homes were being built. It was named the Free State Hotel to make clear the intent of those early settlers: that Kansas should come into the Union as a free state.

"In 1856, the Free State Hotel was attacked and burned to the ground by the infamous Sheriff Sam Jones, heading a group of pro-slavery forces. Colonel Shalor Eldridge rebuilt the hotel and added another floor, vowing to do the same every time it was destroyed. The hotel stood until 1863 when it was attacked and destroyed once again, this time by Quantrill and his Raiders. Quantrill and his men rode into the community of Lawrence and killed over 150 men, women, and children. They tragically burned and destroyed the city that stood as a proud symbol and home for the Free State of Kansas and the freedom and rights of individuals everywhere.

"Colonel Eldridge promptly rebuilt the hotel and gave it his name, The Hotel Eldridge. The city of Lawrence took the phoenix rising from the ashes and the motto "from ashes to immortality," as their symbol and motto to exhibit our determination to stand and fight for the rights and dignity of people everywhere.

"The Eldridge Hotel stood until 1925 as one of the finest hotels this side of the Mississippi and continued to play an important role in the early development of Lawrence and the State of Kansas. By 1925, the hotel had begun to deteriorate. A group of Lawrence business leaders was organized by Billy Hutson to tear down and rebuild the Eldridge Hotel because of its importance to the city of Lawrence, and restore it to its former place of dignity and elegance. Billy Hutson fully committed himself and his life savings to the project. The community stepped forward and made the investment necessary to insure the success of this important undertaking.

"By the late 1960's, trends had changed, motels were springing up all over the country and downtown hotels were becoming less prevalent. The Eldridge Hotel was not immune to these forces and it finally closed its doors as a hotel on July 1, 1970 (in fact a key had to be made to lock the front door because it had been lost many years earlier). *The hotel was converted to apartments and so it remained until 1985. Then Lawrence developer Robert W. Phillips organized a group of investors to rebuild the hotel. The City of Lawrence supported this project*

by committing two million dollars in Industrial Revenue Bonds to match the one million dollars in private money raised by Phillips and the investors. The top four floors of the hotel were completely rebuilt and converted into 48 two-room luxury suites. The lobby restored. To pay tribute to the people who played such important roles in our history and heritage, the Eldridge Hotel named each of its 48 suites in their memory."----From eldridgehotel.com/History.htm

The Eldridge Hotel probably had only been reopened less than a year or two when the reenactors showed up for the New Year's Eve dance. I believe most every one who attended the dance also spent the night here. The hotel people were very courteous and bent over backwards to make sure our stay was pleasant.

Of the dance, I can recall very little. Oh, Mona and I danced to be sure, but at some point I was seduced into going to the downstairs bar where Kevin Wells (the son of souvenir hustler Sonny Wells) had everyone drink shots of Tequila. I think the shots were only a dollar apiece. We had the lime and a lick of salt to go with it. I think all of Holmes Brigade wandered down to the bar at some point. I'm sure the bagladies were there.

I probably had ten shots of Tequila, but didn't feel all that bad until morning. By first light I was puking up my socks! I felt like death warmed over. Mona just sort of laughed as I stumbled about in my misery. At some point that morning I wandered over to the room in which the Higginbotham's were staying. Gregg was eating breakfast and watching a Marx Brothers' movie on TV. After a spell, I felt my stomach had settled enough to try a few eggs and bacon. That is my fondest memory of New Year's Eve at the Eldridge Hotel-getting corned!

In 1989, we traveled down south to Eureka Springs, Arkansas, and arranged to have the Twelfth Night Ball at the 1905 Basin Park Hotel (*thumbing our noses at St. Louis once again*). The new dance committee chairperson was Connie Winfrey of Joplin, Missouri. Connie's claim to fame was she and her husband Will owned the historic Rothanbarger House, the site of tarot card readings, seances by candlelight, floating hatchets, and thrown chicken drumsticks.

Once again we were blessed with the mildest of weather on this 7th day of January. It was practically shirtsleeve weather! In Volume One I've already talked about the history of Eureka Springs, the healing waters, shops, etc. During the spring and summer season, when the senior citizens come through, it becomes a real tourist trap, but at the time we arrived, there wasn't more than two or three people in town.

We arrived very early in the day; it was just past noon I guess. We all had time to wander up and down the boulevard, peer into the shops, and even had a meal at The Other Place. That was the name of cafe-THE OTHER PLACE. While walking up and down the streets, John Maki fell in love with a boarded up building that had once been a machine shop or carpenter shop. It wasn't that well sealed off and we were able to walk around inside and look at some of the equipment and junk lying about. I think there was the upper torso of a mannequin somewhere and I picked it up and dropped it down the staircase into the cellar. John proclaimed that he intended to move to Eureka Springs, buy this old building, and turn it into a shop where he could make boxes and stuff. However, his dream did not bear fruit. He never came back, nor did he buy the building.

Mona and I shared a room with Dan Hadley (my co-worker from Missouri Poster) and his wife Rhonda. I think Gail Higginbotham was here, but Gregg would be coming in later that day. He had been hired to work on a documentary of Jesse James or Wild Bill Hickok, for one of the cable channels-TNT, A&E, DISCOVERY, or the HISTORY CHANNEL.

Of the actual dance, there is little worth mentioning. Later that afternoon, Gregg did indeed show up, dressed not in military attire, but as a country gentleman wearing clothes that he might have wore at 1855 Missouri Town. By this time Gregg had fallen back in the ranks of the Holmes Brigade as a private. It wouldn't do for him to wear a common private's uniform to a fancy dress ball. If he could no longer dress as an officer, a nineteenth century gentleman of leisure would be better suited to his taste. Of course to complete his attire, Gregg wore his world famous rattlesnake necktie.

About 11 PM, the dance was suspended so we could eat a supper in the fancy downstairs dining hall. We crowded into the hall and quickly found seats at one of a dozen wide tables. Each table could probably seat 30 or more. For the next hour we feasted on the bill of fare. Elbows flapped about like bat wings while cutlery skittered noisily across china plates in an attempt to rearrange meat, potatoes, vegetables, and bread, into bite size morsels. Gallons of coffee, water, or tea were on hand to wash anything aside that got stuck in the windpipe. Between bites, a running dialogue of humor, jokes, and commentary passed among the diners.

Before long some of us started to get so silly that the wives had to step and take control. It was well after two in the morning when the wives hustled us to our rooms and to sleep. This is really all I have to say about the dance at Eureka Springs, Arkansas.

In 1990, we returned to the Capitol Rotunda in Jefferson City, Missouri.

In 1991, we had the ball at the Elms Hotel in Excelsior Springs, Missouri.

Of this ball, I can recall very little. I think we had the dinner first, then the Grand March into the dance hall. The Elms Hotel has a heated indoor pool and after all the festivities were over, several of the boys took a late night dip. By now, Jon Isaacson was sweet on a young lady by the name of Becky Rowles. She was fairly attractive, but seemed a little light-headed. Just the kind of girl Jon likes, one he can manipulate. He doesn't go for women that are smarter than him, because they'll quickly kick him to the curb like an old dog.

This was the last time Mona and I attended a military ball. I don't know why, but several factors might have contributed to our indifference. Don Whitson and his wife split up. John Maki and his live-in girlfriend, Linda Fetterling, finally called it "quits" after ten years. John's bachelorhood would be brief because he would soon find himself falling in love with an attractive divorcee from Ft. Scott. In a ceremony about a year later the two would marry. Meanwhile, Gregg was so firmly enmeshed in the goings on at Missouri Town and making documentaries for the HISTORY CHANNEL that he found he couldn't get away to do Civil War stuff much less attend a dance. My daughter Katie was more and more active in dance, school, and other activities, so Mona felt it best to attend to **her** needs. So after 1991, both girls left the hobby. Gail Higginbotham also felt the pressure of child rearing, because in 1988, she had given birth to a daughter, Shelby. With two girls to care for, plus teaching full time, Gail also dropped out from the hobby. Without John Maki, the Whitson's and the Higginbotham's, the dance lost its appeal. Another factor was Holmes Brigade's decreased involvement with the MCWRA.

The association did not seem as authentic or as authentically run as had been prevalent during the eighties. Most of it had to do with the way its membership conducted itself on the field at events. However, this is not a time to air dirty laundry. Instead, I like to say that I truly enjoyed the times I had on the dance floor, even when I fell on my ass. The military balls were the one chance in which everyone could dress up and look pretty, even the men. All in all the experience was great exercise with great people. Sorry it ended so quickly.

CHAPTER EIGHT

1990

Happy New Year! Happy New Decade!

The birth of the new decade was heralded with one of the last parties at Constance Soper's house. Of course we lamented the passing of the eighties, that great decade when we all discovered the hobby. We were all ten years older. Would we be able to carry over that enthusiasm for Civil War reenacting into this new decade?

Holmes Brigade was also ten years old. Through a series of invitations at quality events, including National and State Historic sites, Holmes had built and established a solid reputation. It was almost a self-sustaining entity meaning a member could go to any site, say he is a member of Holmes Brigade, and the host would have nothing to fear. With our foundation in place, what events could Holmes Brigade look forward to in the 90's?

Gregg Higginbotham recently told me, "*I don't remember anything about the nineties!*" That's because he was either at Missouri Town or making movies during most of this decade. At first glance, the nineties are not that special to me either, but after racking my brain and with the help of the old newsletters, I think I'm capable of putting together an argument in which the decade of the nineties is very interesting indeed. Otherwise this will be a very short book!

After the February ball at the Capitol Rotunda in Jefferson City, nothing was done until the May muster at Fort Scott, Kansas. True to form, Gary Crane returned to us, looking no worse for wear. He did show us the long scar running down the middle of his chest where the surgeon had cracked him open. Exactly one week later, Holmes Brigade and Gary Crane, was heading down south for an MCWRA maximum effort event in fire ant country.

May 18-20, 1990 Champion's Hill, MS.

The legend of Champion's Hill of years past had made its way around all the new recruits and "fresh fish" in Holmes Brigade. All wanted to see what the shouting was all about. However, we only mustered 25 boys in our company.

This was another one of those weekends where we wanted to leave Thursday night, drive twelve hours straight, pull into Vicksburg National Military Park on Friday, then go to the event site later that evening. This was a carbon copy itinerary of the old bus trip of '82 and '83, but without "Johnny Reb" or beer cans rolling in the aisle. This go around we'd drive ourselves.

The plan that John Maki and I intended on was to drive through Springfield, down through Arkansas and eastern Louisiana-just as we had done with the bus and when we had participated in the miniseries NORTH AND SOUTH near Natchez, Mississippi. However, Isaacson wanted to pick up Andy Papen at his home in Millersburg, which meant we would have to drive via Interstate 70 and then swing south at St. Louis. The interstate may be faster than taking the back roads into Arkansas, but it also made the trip longer.

The goal when we left Kansas City was that we'd follow each other, try to stay within sight of one another in case one of us decided to pull off the road for gas or food. Maki rode with me in my Mitsubishi, while Isaacson drove his own car with Randy Rogers and Mike Gosser as his traveling companions.

No sooner had I told Isaacson, *"Go ahead and I'll follow you,"* than he took off like a bat out of hell driving as fast as 90 MPH down the highway. My Mitsubishi only has a 4-cylinder engine in it and could not keep up. In less than a minute, Isaacson's car was a mere speck on the distant horizon. Maki and I never saw his car again until we got to Mississippi.

I could have turned the truck around and gone the way south as Maki and I had previously planned, but there was hope we'd run into Isaacson after he picked up Papen. So we pressed on. I only had an AM radio in the Mitsubishi, which was poor entertainment for the next 12 hours. I borrowed my daughter Katie's tape player, a handful of C batteries, and about six cassette tapes, including THE SHADOW, INNER SANCTUM, and some other old dramas from the golden age of radio. Between cold soda pop, sugary snacks, and the cold voices of Orson Welles, Vincent Price, and Basil Rathbone coming from a two-inch speaker, Maki and I managed to stay awake during the long night.

Early the next morning, Maki and I found ourselves once again inside the Vicksburg National Military Park; this being our fourth visit in eight years. Waiting for us was Jon Isaacson and company who I suspect had been parked many hours. Of course between the four of them, they'd probably taken turns driving during the night because they looked as fresh as daisies. Maki and I could only spell each other during the long drive, so we had these large bags under our eyes, plus it was difficult to talk without yawning.

I think we had a bite of breakfast at the Waffle House then we took the tour. While I'm sure Randy Rogers had been through this area before, I don't believe Isaacson, Papen, or Mike Gosser had. Maki and I were bushed, but we couldn't very well say to hell with the rest of you, so we found ourselves led along with the rest. As my mind was probably clouded with fatigue, I recall few details of this Vicksburg adventure.

But Isaacson remembers that,"...*we toured the U.S.S. Cairo, the museum, the Old Courthouse downtown, and then Papen took us on a blow-by-blow tour of the battlefield. As the day, and patience drug on, Papen was just getting started. You and Maki in the peanut gallery started getting restless and soon the razzing began. I think you all attempted to run him over at one stop so we could get out to the event site.*"

At some point that day, we drove the extra hour to the event site. It was the same as I'd remembered it. After finding a place to park, we had to walk up the old narrow dirt path past the pond filled with green scum. Most of us had shelter halves and these were set up shebang fashion. We did not have to pitch our camp on the opposite side of Baker's Creek as we had done in 1982 and 83. This year, the Union boys were allowed in the Garden of Eden or rather that spot which had some semblance of vegetation and a few trees. I think the all-you-can-eat fish fry was in full swing, but it was located closer to camp, just down the road, rather than at the Cactus Plantation. That first night, Friday, after we'd gotten our fill of the beer battered fish; it was very easy indeed to slip off into dreamland.

John Zaharias was at Champion's Hill along with his right hand man, or personal piss boy, Mike Watson. I think about this time, Mike started bringing his little roly-poly son to events. He was a dirty little cuss about six years old who always wanted to mess with us or just generally get in the way. I seem to think Watson was divorced and had custody of the kid that weekend. Since he already had plans to attend the Champion's Hill event, Mike thought he could baby sit the kid, make a few bucks selling pre-rolled paper cartridges, shoot his gun, and possibly drink a beer all at the same time. Mike didn't think the kid would get into too much trouble as long as he stayed within line of sight of in the Federal camp. The little Watson kid (don't remember what his name was), didn't bother us too bad, although when he spotted any member of Holmes Brigade, he would shout at us, "hey soldier!" The kid reminded me of little Clint Howard from the Andy Griffith TV show who was always trying to give Andy or Barney a bite of his jelly sandwich.

Also on hand was Tommy Rye and his traveling medicine wagon of potions, balms, ointments, pills, and medicated powders. I think T. Rye lived in this part of Mississippi. Of course he remembered John Maki and me from years earlier when we used some of his medicated crotch powder. This year he had another instrument of entertainment in the form of a dancing stick doll. It was a wood carved Abraham Lincoln doll with bendable arms and legs that flipped and flopped when Tommy Rye made the doll dance. Poked in a hole in the doll's back was a long thin wooden dowel rod, which he held in one hand, then he bounced the feet of the doll on a flat piece of wood like a cedar shingle. The dancing doll toy was quite amusing and as it danced and shuffled to the time of Jon Isaacson's strumming banjo, I got the inspiration to make a doll of my own. In less than two months, I would have my own dancing doll.

Upon our arrival at Champion's Hill, we were pleased to see Frank Kirtley with his brand new artillery piece, a full scale 6 pound James gun. Not exactly sure what a James gun is, but Frank purchased it while in Georgia. Originally it may have been an iron tube but Frank, in his infinite wisdom, decided to apply a finish to it to make the tube look bronze. The end result was the tube had a weird orange-gold-green look to it. Despite the appearance of the gun, Frank was very proud and protective of it. Without thinking, some joker was leaning up against the gun carriage and propped his muddy brogan on the axle. I was not around to hear the heated exchange but I understand Frank went ballistic. "I don't step on your musket, so you don't step on my gun!" His Marine Corp blood rose past the boiling point. Needless to say, the offending culprit was quick to find a rag to wipe off the Mississippi mud from Frank's prize. Although Frank might have exercised a loving hand in the care of his gun, the same cannot be said in the choice he'd made for his hand picked crew. The team Frank assembled for Champion's Hill looked like they'd just been bailed out of jail or were used to spending most of their hours in a biker bar. These were no Marine Corp poster boys, nor did they look like they'd seen the inside of a barbershop in many years. More than likely his gun crew was assembled from guys already used to working cannon in another unit, possibly as Confederates. Frank spent most of the afternoon making rounds for his cannon. He mixed a quarter pound of black powder into aluminum foil balls. While I'm sure Frank's gun "spoke" during the battle, he also fired his gun during a nighttime demonstration. That's all I recall about Frank Kirtley and his gun.

Of the actual battles that were staged over this weekend, nothing stands out that is worthy of mention. What else is new? I'm sure the required number of musket volleys and artillery rounds were fired. There was no rain to drown us nor did we have to hike a mile or more away from the comfort of our immediate area. However, there are several comic and unusual episodes while we were on the Champion's Hill event site that **is** worthy of mention.

It was while we were in company formation, during drill or prior to our deployment into battle, that a large copperhead snake went slithering past our feet. I think Robbie Piatt actually stepped on it. Already disturbed from its nest by all the humans tramping about and probably just as scared to see us as we him, the creature was suffering the further indignity of being stepped on. Rather than apologize to the serpent and back away, our own Captain Don drew his blade and proceeded to hack at the beast till it was in six or eight pieces. Of course, we were all stunned, but some clod in another company tried to come to the snake's defense by saying it was part of wildlife and we should not have destroyed it. Screw that! We're all lucky no one got bit plus I'll bet Robbie had to empty his drawers after that exciting episode. This was also the event in which Pat McCarthy crawled into his tent in time to see *"a five foot snake crawling out the other end."*

The Mississippi State bug, the fire ant, also made us feel at home by his presence. The event sponsors tried once again to exterminate several colonies, but those fire ants are as stubborn to control as a fat man at an all-you-can-eat buffet. One of the company wags thought it was funny when he poked at an anthill with his bayonet, but when a dozen of those flaming red bastards flew up his arm it was a different story. Snakes, ants, chiggers, and spiders all conspired to make our visit an unwelcome one. I don't know if anyone was bothered by the Brown Recluse spider, as Higgy had been in '83, but Pat McCarthy *"woke up one night and looked down the length of my body and thought the moonlight was playing tricks on me - everything was moving. I struck a match and found I was covered in wolf spiders."*

In a previous chapter I told you about Jon Isaacson and me leaving the Champion's Hill event and driving to Jackson, Mississippi to buy comic books. We left that morning after drill. We had to be back just before the one o'clock battle. John Maki was the elected lieutenant and he said he would write us up if we were late. Isaacson drove his car, going about 80 MPH. Jackson was only about 45 minutes away. After we returned to the event, some hours later, I think we only had seconds to spare before roll call. Jon and I quickly bailed out of the parking lot, running like the demons of hell were after us, and we hitched a ride on an ATV that the event people were riding on. One of those guys was Bob Bond, a guy I'd met in 1980 on the way to my first event in Makanda, Illinois, with the 13th Missouri Infantry. By the way, Isaacson and I arrived just in the nick of time for roll call.

The temperature in central Mississippi in mid-May is very hot and sticky. After an hour or two on the drill field or in battle, we are bathed in sweat. Once we are excused from the ranks, most of us drop like lazy hound dogs. With twenty or thirty guys flat on their backs snoozing in the shade, one is reminded of the TV show "Hee Haw" except there were no pretty girls with plunging necklines and short shorts in the background. No sooner had the jacket come off and a hat is placed low over the eyes to sleep, someone announces he is going to make a trip to the beer wagon. Like zombies crawling from out of the grave, the guys would rise to unsteady feet, find their battered tin cups and join a procession for the sweet nectar of barley and hops that only Budweiser can provide.

The beer wagon was actually a U Haul sized trailer with 3 spigots on the side. It was provided and brought to the event by the local Bud distributor. It sat down the hill from camp over by the green pond of scum water. I think the price of beer was only a dollar. John Maki visited the beer wagon Friday evening just as they had finished setting up. From what John remembers and told me, he walked over to one of the spigots and helped himself. The vendor may have been in a nearby lawn chair under an umbrella or awning, but he watched Maki with some curious amusement and calmly asked John if he intended to pay for that beer.

"Why no," John declared matter-of-factly, *"I'm the duly appointed taste tester for the Federal army assigned to see whether this beer is acceptable for consumption by the men and stuff."*

When asked if he found the beer to his liking, John stated that it had too much foam in it. After a third refill, he smacked his lips and gave the beer man a nod as his stamp of approval.

"Aren't you afraid that the beer might be poisoned?"

"*Well, if it is,*" John calmly said, "*then only I will suffer rather than the men.*" Perhaps a smile came to the face of the Budweiser man. Perhaps he was thinking, "This little Yankee man has a large set of gonads! First of all what gall to just walk up and help himself to my beer and then he just stands there filling my head with a ridiculous story! I suppose if he'd been smiling the whole time, I might have been tempted to call the police. He hasn't smiled once, so he must be dead serious or touched by the heat, so I'll not press the issue." The episode may have been the most interesting of the day for the beer man, because he invited Maki to come back later that evening for a free supper of pan fried chicken.

Now going back to the subject of women, the only women folk within a stone's throw were a hard looking bunch in the civilian camp. It was our misfortune to be only fifty yards from them, with porta-johns between here and there. Isaacson's current girlfriend, Becky Rowles, was here. I was rudely disturbed from a nice little sit down in one of the porta-john's by at least two or more people shaking it till the blue water tickled my bare backside. I thought they would tip it over and then I'd be in a sorry looking state. A few unkind words directed at my tormentors and I was left in peace. I never was quite sure where to place the blame, but I suspect Jon Isaacson and his girlfriend Becky were the masterminds behind the "foul" deed.

Since 1986, Pat McCarthy and Don Whitson had become inseparable pards. They lived in the same general area of Johnson County, Kansas, so they became quite close. They always traveled together and shared the same tent at all the events. Don was beginning to have marital problems and the strain was beginning to show in his conduct on the field. At Champion's Hill, Pat found his own patience tested by an episode involving Don and a hay bale. Pat states that Don, "*...was trying to get into a bale of straw that was bound with wire. He asked if he could use my bayonet, and I told him he could* (not knowing what he wanted it for). *He was smart enough not to risk his own bayonet, so he tried to pry the wire off the bale with mine. I was talking to another pard and turned around in time to see Don trying to straighten my bayonet out - it was bent in two different directions and looked like a pretzel. I grabbed it away from him and told him I'd use it on him if I* *thought it would kill anything anymore. I had to use that bayonet for months before I found a replacement".*

Despite these amusing distractions- bugs, snakes, and beer -most everyone agreed that the 1990 Champion's Hill event was flat. No matter how much Maki, Don Strother, and I tried to play up the past accomplishments of Holmes Brigade on this field, Isaacson and some of the other "fresh fish," who were attending for the first time, simply shrugged their shoulders and said, "Ehh, big deal!" No one walked away from Champion's Hill with a hard-on. We did not leave empty handed, though.

After the final battle on Sunday afternoon, we had to march past sutler row on the way back to camp. As we passed John Zaharias' tent business, Mike Watson hollered and threw a handful of stale Marsh Wheeling cigars our way. Mike would have to help Z pack up his wares, so he probably thought the cigars would be one less item to pack up. Plus they'd been exposed to the humid Mississippi air all weekend so who'd wanna buy 'em?

A couple of weeks later, on June 2nd, Connie and Will Winfrey hosted a one day only living history in Joplin, Missouri, at the historic Rothanbarger House. I rode down with Isaacson, but the only thing worth mentioning at all about this event was when Linda Fetterling threw a chicken leg at me. She was standing in the front yard as Jon and I pulled into the driveway. It sailed right through my passenger side open window and hit me in the snoot. Other than that, Rothanbarger was a bullshit event. Twenty-one days later, on June 23 - 24, it was off to Lecompton, Kansas for the fight at Fort Titus and to ogle at big beefy girls at the annual coed softball tournament.

June 30-July 1, 1990 Carthage, MO

"By late June 1861, Brig. Gen. Nathaniel Lyon had chased Governor Claiborne Jackson and approximately 4,000 State Guard from the State Capital at Jefferson City and from Boonville, and pursued them until the Rebels found their backs up against Arkansas State line.

"Col. Franz Sigel led a detached force of about 1,000 into southwest Missouri in search of the governor and his loyal troops. Upon learning that Sigel had encamped

at Carthage, on the night of July 4, Jackson took command of the troops with him and formulated a plan to attack the much smaller Union force.

"The next morning, Jackson closed up to Sigel, established a battle line on a ridge ten miles north of Carthage, and induced Sigel to attack him. Opening with artillery fire, Sigel closed to the attack. Seeing a large Confederate forces—actually unarmed recruits—moving into the woods on his left, he feared that they would turn his flank. He withdrew. The Confederates pursued, but Sigel conducted a successful rearguard action. By evening, Sigel was inside Carthage and under cover of darkness; he retreated to Sarcoxie.

"The battle had little meaning, but the Pro-Southern elements in Missouri, anxious for any good news, championed their first victory. Losses on both sides were light, estimated at just fewer than 250 casualty's total."

The battle fought at Carthage has not received the attention it should. Two weeks later would be the terrible fight in Virginia, at Bull Run. On the 10th of August, near Springfield, Nathaniel Lyon would become the first Union general to die in battle when he lead a charge against these same Missouri State Guardsmen, supported by Arkansas Confederates, at Wilson's Creek.

Of the men that followed Sigel to Carthage was the 3rd and 5th Missouri Infantry. For the most part, these were immigrants from Germany who'd only been in America a short time and had been recruited by Sigel from St. Louis. With the rebellion only weeks old, most soldiers began the campaign with militia uniforms or something homemade by a local seamstress. These 3rd and 5th Missouri infantrymen found themselves adorned with a gray colored overshirt. Their foe, the Pro-Southern Missouri State Guard, came attired in whatever they normally wore at home. They would have no regulation uniform until early in 1862 when most of these men enlisted into the Confederacy and were sent east to fight Grant's army.

Sorry, got long winded. After all this is not a history book, but I think it's important to understand why we go to these reenactments. It's not always to drink beer! It's important to know something about the time you are recreating so you don't look like a dummy when a visitor comes with a question. There are times when you shouldn't say, "Go ask that guy," then crawl back in the fart sack to nap.

The reenactment at Carthage was not held on the original spot. It was in town on some property to the northeast near the public recreation spot, Kellogg Lake. At Kellogg Lake you could fish, swim, boat, or scoot around on a jet ski. I don't remember how big the lake was, but one narrow branch of the lake ran past the reenactment camp. At all times of the day, we could see bronzed young men and women shooting past on their very loud motorcycles on water. It was very distracting. More so because the bronzed women wore the skimpiest of bathing suits.

The other issue about Carthage was we were supposed to be portraying the St. Louis Dutchmen (German's) of Sigel's Union army. It had already been documented that the German infantry wore a gray overshirt. We had nary a one. Instead, it was requested we all wear our dress frock coats and Hardee hats, with brass pin decoration and an ostrich plume. If no plume available, one could be obtained by our friendly neighborhood sutler over at ZMART-John Zaharias.

Once again I found myself sharing a ride with Jon Isaacson. You may say to yourself, "Damn he's doing an awful lot of shit with Isaacson, what's the deal? Are they in love?" Consider this: Mona was out of the hobby, Hig was working most weekends at Missouri Town, and Maki was using his truck to take wooden boxes he'd built to sell at events. Plus, Don Whitson and Steve Hall were on the outs with their marriage, the Bagladies were on their way to college, and Pat McCarthy was busy most weekends in the police department. That left the only local guy to travel to events with being Jon Isaacson. Plus we shared a warped sense of humor.

After reaching the outskirts of Carthage, Jon decided he had to pull into an AMOCO station so he could take one of his famous half-hour shits. Afterwards we got onto Hwy 96 eastbound for a mile or two, then made a hard right turn through a cattle gate, past a registration tent (sign the papers), to orange vested volunteers who told us where to park. They must have run the cows off just a day or two earlier because there were fresh pies everywhere.

There were a couple new additions to Holmes Brigade. First, at Fort Scott I was introduced to Justin O'Rear, a slender, baby-faced teenager whose dad seemed more excited about the hobby than his son. Justin was quiet, hardly corruptible, and in school, I imagine he was an honor student. Justin seemed unfazed by his surroundings and did not quake in his shoes about sharing a weekend with coarse, uncouth, and profane old men. I'll never forget the time when Justin was dropped off at an event by his dad and left with these words of caution: *"Now mind Mr. Talbott and be on your best behavior and I'll see you Sunday afternoon."* I never felt more scared of responsibility in all my life. I could only imagine the stories Justin would tell his parents Sunday after the event-tales of vulgarity, profanity, drinking, and lewd behavior. Hardly material worthy of sharing with your classmates during a "what did you do over summer vacation" bull session. At Carthage, I introduced Justin to ZMART and he purchased several items including waistbelt, cartridge box, belt plates, canteen, and some mess gear.

Secondly, Carthage was the debut of the dancing stick dolls that Isaacson, Maki, and I created. Champion's Hill had been the previous May, yet the three of us had become so in awe of the Abraham Lincoln doll Tommy Rye operated, that in less than two months, we had our own dancing stick dolls. Instead of creating dancing Abe's, the three of us built Negro dolls.

I don't remember much about the doll Isaacson or Maki built, but mine had the look of a kindly old Negro with short white hair, white chin whiskers, short knee length britches, a long frock coat, and no shoes. I had carved and painted his torso from one piece of wood, his head from another. The hardest part of building the doll was the arm and leg action. They had to swing freely at the elbow, shoulder, hip, and knee. After some blood, sweat, and tears, I felt like Dr. Frankenstein. My creation was completed a week before Carthage. I called him Uncle Tom.

So the three dolls were introduced that first weekend night and we danced them together on a John Maki breadbox, but wouldn't you know it, our silly antics quickly turned obscene.

Finally a word on 'Boo' Hodges. I think his real name is Merle, so 'Boo" must have been a nickname he got as a little shaver, or maybe it was one he got in the medical profession as a doctor of gynecology. When he came to Carthage with 20 men, he already had them completely outfitted. The way I understood it, 'Boo' bought all the clothing, leathers, and weapons, and loaned or rented them out to his guys, and in return, he was elected as company commander. I'd call that "buying the vote," but politicians have been doing that for years.

'Boo' and the Eighth Kansas appeared at Fort Scott the previous May. Holmes Brigade was looking to grow, plus I suspect Don Strother had his eye on the higher rank of battalion commander. When 'Boo' asked if he and his boys could play with us, sponsor them in the MCWRA, and the Western Brigade, Don did not hesitate. Of course a vote had to be taken by all paid members. We all had our eye on the big picture of course, which was to field a battalion-sized unit to future events. We allowed them to keep their own rank structure. They would not be absorbed into Holmes Brigade, but would be joining as the stepchild who already brought his own toys to play with.

Along with an infantry company, 'Boo' promised at least one full-scale gun (he probably purchased it as well) operated by his daddy, Merle Senior. By a unanimous vote, the Eighth Kansas was welcomed with open arms. The first opportunity for Don to strut like a peacock would come at Carthage. I'll bet he was already placing an order for Colonel's bars.

So at Carthage, we had three full companies of infantry and at least three guns. I imagine Don was in 7th Heaven at the prospect of commanding source a task force. He probably puffed up like Douglas MacArthur. Unfortunately, Bill Fannin was still recovering from open-heart surgery and we were short one officer. John Maki would command 1st Company, 'Boo' would command the 3rd, but we had no one to command 2nd Company. Don Strother wanted to be battalion commander so bad. He had to find a replacement to fill Bill Fannin's shoes or forfeit his colonel's position.

We were all sitting around on our backsides after a hearty breakfast of bacon and eggs. Roll call had already been taken that Saturday morning and as First Sergeant, I had issued clean up, firewood and water details to a select number of men. At this time, I think our officers were attending the "big meeting" with officers of the Confederate forces to plan battle strategy for the upcoming reenactment. Of course I knew Bill Fannin wasn't here, but at this moment I wasn't privy to how complicated the situation was in terms of the battalion, nor how it would affect me.

A brief time later, I came to realize that our officers had returned by the most unusual of circumstances. Like I said, we were all at leisure after breakfast. I was sitting on a straw bale or a folding stool. I might have been playing with "Uncle Tom," my stick doll. Suddenly, I felt a dozen eyes on me. Looking up, I noticed a number of sly grins and smirks from the guys as they walked past me. Did I have my fly open or something? One or two guys actually saluted me as they passed. It was then that I realized that something wasn't right with my uniform. In a second I saw what it was. Someone had placed the bars of a 2nd Lieutenant on my shoulders. As if snake bitten, I jumped off my perch and hollered, "NO!"

During the meeting of minds, Don Strother and the others had come to the conclusion that they needed another officer and that officer should be me. For nearly an entire half-hour, I wailed and pleaded to the best of my ability, but as First Sergeant, I was the most logical candidate, so I reluctantly agreed.

I thought I would only have to serve as a platoon officer and merely have to stand behind the company as an extra file closer. When Don told me I would be commanding 2nd company, I nearly shit my pants. "NO!"

Another half-hour passed as I gnashed my teeth and pulled at my hair. I knew the school of the soldier, the manual of arms, and had had some minor experience drilling a small company at an earlier event. This time I was asked to be commander leading at least 25 men. Finally I bowed my head in submission. I would do it.

I retired to my A tent where I sewed the bars on my coat, changed into my dark blue trousers, and placed a forage cap atop my head. Don or one of the others loaned me a belt rigging with saber. I don't know if there was a pistol included or not. When I came out of the tent, I was greeted with catcalls, whistles, and other yelps of encouragement. I was looking for a rock to crawl under. After I'd pranced around the camp for awhile, I felt some sort of confidence. I was soon tested when Don Strother called the battalion to form up for drill.

If memory serves me, Saturday was a day filled with drill, which meant Sunday would be the actual battle reenactment. By this time, we had our new flags. The National colors were similar to the old one that got burned in the Glasgow fire, but it did not have gold painted stars, merely white. We also had a Regimental flag, which was simply a generic bald eagle on a blue background. With the colors snapping in the summer breeze, we marched out of camp, me leading 2nd company, alongside Randy Rogers who'd assumed my First Sergeants duties.

On a flat cow pasture Don took the battalion through a series of maneuvers (nothing too taxing for me to figure out I hoped). We practiced forming into a square using the three companies to form the box. How can you form a four-sided square with only three companies? I'm glad you asked. 1st company had the easy job, march straight-ahead then halt. It was 2nd company's duty to separate by platoons-first platoon would wheel to the right and second platoon would wheel to the left, then come to a halt once they were at right and left angles with 1st company. Sounds confusing don't it? Finally, 3rd company would march forward and close the door on the bottom end of the box.

We practiced this a couple of times, as it was my job to bark the appropriate orders to my lads in 2nd company. We also fired by company and by battalion. We may also have fired by the drum. Well done, I thought as I patted myself on the back. During the actual battle on Sunday, when it came time to form the square, we were taking fire from the Confederates from all sides, and I became rattled. Don hollered at me to move my men, but he ended up giving the commands himself. So much for my shining moment and my command indecision.

July 14-15, 1990, Macon, MO

Two weeks later, we attended an event in the north central part of Missouri. None other than our very own Jon Isaacson, hometown boy done well, organized the event at Macon. The Army National Guard was assisting in the support of this event. They provided water buffalos and few other amenities. It was a generic event with few outstanding moments. We were camped in a field on the outskirts of town. I think we were bused in for a parade.

The things I recall of Macon include riding on the back of a tractor with Isaacson, the appearance of Ray Woods drinking Wild Turkey for breakfast, and Scott White with his Colt Peacemaker. Scott had been hired as an extra for the TV movie Son of the Morning Star, another telling of Custer's Last Stand. In the afternoon, he spoke to a half-interested audience about his moment up on Greasy Grass when he dodged rubber tomahawks and arrows, and squibs that were rigged under the clothing to explode fake blood. He spoke of fighting the Sioux Indians alongside Custer until he was killed along with the rest and the director yelled, "CUT!" Scott demonstrated his heroics to us by rolling on the ground, as if avoiding the red savage, then leaping to one side with gun drawn and going "Bang Bang!" It's a good thing he didn't have the Peacemaker loaded.

August 4-5, 1990, Athens, MO

Same as it ever was. Holmes Brigade was the Home Guard up against the State Guard boys. By this time the motion picture, GLORY had made it to the big screen. A premiere had been held several months earlier at the Blue Ridge Cinema in Independence, MO. About 30 Kansas City area reenactors showed up for a matinee. Naturally we were all in uniform. I think we got a complimentary bag of popcorn.

During the battle reenactment at Athens, when the skirmish platoon was sent out, the rest of the battalion started shouting, *"Give 'em hell, 54th!"* For the next year or two, this would be used as a favorite call to any large group that passed by. When we had our end of the season toast, at Prairie Grove, we acted like the 54th around the campfire scene. *"Ah luvs de fitty-fouth....oh my lord, lord, lord, lord...em hmmm!"*

As this was the state event, we should have had Holmes Brigade elections, but we didn't. In elections past, you had to be present at the event to be considered eligible to vote or to be nominated. This was before the secret ballot and voting by proxy was initiated. There was no list of candidates prior to voting day. Although we pretty much knew who was running for Captain, the other positions most generally were up for grabs.

A typical election nomination would go this way: "We have six corporal positions available, who do you want to nominate?" Some boys would point out certain guys who would either say ok or decline. If more than six were nominated, they would stand, face away from the brigade, then the Captain would ask for a show of hands, "Who wants so an so?" It was a popularity contest, make no mistake. The top six became the corporals.

In 1990 the opinion was, and my memory may be a little unclear of this, Athens was too far to travel for most people, especially the Southern Missouri/ Oklahoma bunch (I think we had a light turnout this year). I don't know if some folks shied away from Athens because it was too hot (August), or if it was because it was in the extreme opposite corner of the state. Whatever factors contributed to the decision is debatable. What is clear is the brigade decided to cancel this year's officer and NCO elections until next year when we returned to Fort Scott, Kansas.

The annual encampment at Fort Scott had been attracting a number of boys since our first visit in '84. We began drawing as many as 60 men to the Kansas outpost. It was a short drive from anywhere in mid-Missouri and especially acceptable to our friends in Oklahoma. The only folks slighted by this change in venue, to hold the elections, were the St. Louis bunch. Athens was not that far of a drive for them, nor was Pilot Knob, the other location for our elections. However, numbers don't lie. More Holmes Brigade members were coming to Fort Scott than some of the state events.

It wasn't long before the St. Louis crowd stopped coming to events at all. With the exception of a few, like Gary Crane, we lost most of our eastern Missouri membership. Later we initiated absentee balloting and voting by proxy, but the die had been cast. Besides, no one from the St. Louis region was even being considered for a high level position in the brigade with the exception of Dan Krueger, our treasurer. I think Gary Crane was eventually elected to sergeant, but every other position was held by men from Kansas City, mid or southern Missouri, simply because these were the guys who always came to events.

Regarding the last statement, a contributing factor was the complete lack of events in the eastern part of Missouri. We no longer went to New Madrid or Jefferson Barracks. Most Civil War encampments/ reenactments have been held along the Missouri/Kansas/Arkansas corridor since the creation of the MCWRA. Lexington, Wilson's Creek, Carthage, Pea Ridge, Fort Scott, Prairie Grove, Bleeding Kansas Days, and Mine Creek, just to name a few. Once a year, an event **is** held in St. Charles (near St. Louis), but it is usually only to celebrate Robert E. Lee's birthday and to "wander around the old reconstructed village." With all due respect to my St. Louis pards, there is little to draw the membership to your region. From being rejected as a site for the military ball to having most of the Civil War events and the Holmes Brigade elections on the other side of the state into Kansas, I sympathize and understand the pain felt by the St. Louis boys. Be that as it may, the membership passed a unanimous vote to wait till 1991 to hold the elections, on the assumption that more boys would support Fort Scott rather than Athens.

After the weekend at Athens, my family and I took a vacation to Walt Disney World in Florida. I missed the Labor Day encampment at Pea Ridge, Arkansas. The autumn of 1990 was spent at a few mediocre places such as St. Joseph (a return to Players strip club?), Windsor (Kim McCall fell on his own musket), and Prairie Grove (another end of the season toast with large amounts of alcohol). Jon Isaacson and I even spent a Saturday afternoon at the old Rice-Tremonti home in nearby Raytown, MO. This house is one of the few still standing that was around during the Order No. 11days. The only highlight was I was only 5 minutes from home.

While doing research for the 1991 season I came across this letter to the editor of the Holmes Brigade Dispatch, regarding the October 20-21, 1990, event held at Windsor, Missouri. As I read the brief letter from Dave Kesinger and the episode he describes, a flood of memories came back, which prompts me to tell the tale as I remember it. I believe this incident, at the Windsor reenactment, happened before the Kim McCall pratfall onto his own musket.

The scene in the Federal camp was this: we had been waiting for the distribution of rations so we could eat lunch, I don't recall which day this was. At MCWRA events, the host was responsible for passing out the chow. I think a runner was then dispatched with the food on a wagon or a wheelbarrow. It was standard bill of fare including raw vegetables, bread, and stew meat. Once we got the stuff, it took some time to prepare, slice up the veggies, and get the meat to brown. My understanding was that the civilians and the Confederates had already been sent their parcels of food, but the runner was delayed in arriving in the Union camp for nearly an hour. As a result we ate late and missed the raffle.

Now call us ignorant, but we guys in the Union camp may not have been fully aware of the rules regarding the raffle. First of all everyone registered upon entering the reenactment site-no problem on that end. What we didn't know then and wouldn't know till after the fact was, **you had to be physically present if your name was called at the raffle in order to win a prize**. We were all finishing up our late lunch when Dave Kesinger came through and told us that Gary Crane's name had been called during the raffle.

"Gary Crane is still in camp," Kesinger had told the folks doing the raffle, "Holmes Brigade got their rations late so they are just now eating."

"That's too bad (translation: tough shit). The man must be present to win."

"Well I can go get him or take the prize to him," Dave pleaded.

"No, rules are rules. We'll draw another name."

So another name was drawn, despite the protest of Holmes Brigade representative Dave Kesinger, but that guy, a Confederate, was not in the audience either! However, a lady stepped forward and claimed the prize on his behalf.

"Boo, foul play," Kesinger was mortified. "Didn't you just tell me that the winner had to be physically present in order to win?"

"Well, I'm _____'s wife, so that's good enough."

The "johnnies" laughed it off, but when the rest of us got the news of how Gary Crane had been shafted, we all felt like rioting. The prize was a tent fly. Not that big of a deal, but it was the principal of the thing. This episode, though minor, was just another reason why we considered divorcing ourselves from the MCWRA.

Did we pout? Were our feathers ruffled? I suppose after ten years of "blue-belly bias" we had more than enough reasons to feel unloved. Take the Windsor event. Aside from the generic battle, the host of this event was planning on a number of five-minute scenarios depicting atrocities committed by the Federal's. There would be the raid on unarmed Confederate recruits, there would be the shooting of Southern sympathizers, there would be the hanging of a Confederate soldier on furlough, a captured Federal would be murdered in his underwear, and finally-the ultimate guilty pleasure-the Federal's would burn a widow from her cabin. Just imagine how we danced and clapped our hands in glee, given the chance to pillage and plunder. The only thing not offered was a chance to rape a gray-haired old granny. Thanks, but no thanks. None of us had any desire to look like fools. With that said, when a very large Andre the Giant looking confederate lumbered into our camp with a rope and a challenge for tug o' war, two men quickly volunteered. *"It was a hoot when our two smallest men, Andy Papen and Mark Strother, were jerked around like rag dolls,"* Gary Crane remembers.

By 1991, a very serious debate was raging on whether the Holmes Brigade should "quit" the MCWRA. There were many events listed in the Western Campaigner, voice of the MCWRA, which were considered of the "dog and pony show" variety. The Missouri Confederates seemed more interested in blowing cartridges and sitting in mountain man chairs in front of big wall tents than in conducting serious living history. Nothing is worse than being woken at 6 o'clock in the morning by a Confederate infantry battalion firing its guns into our tents. There was too much bullshit going on to suit us. What were once virtues were now vices. Holmes Brigade, I strongly believed, wanted to graduate from the "beer, balls, and battle" of so many early festivals of the 80's, to a higher level of reenacting.

What was decided at the start of 1991 was that Holmes Brigade would concentrate and encourage their membership to attend seven maximum effort events. These were the events that the membership thought were of the highest quality. If one or two of these happened to be MCWRA sanctioned events, so much the better.

After this announcement there was some alarm within the membership of MCWRA. Only support seven events? As newsletter editor Aaron Racine put it, *"by singling out these seven events, we are not excluding any other events from members' participation."* If the guys want to attend more than seven events, there's stuff out there to do. The focus beginning in 1991 was *"to get together as a battalion sized group for a smaller number of events rather than a small unit for a lot of events."* However, the writing was on the wall. We were seeing the last years of participation between Holmes Brigade and the MCWRA.

Meanwhile we were blazing new trails of higher authenticity, we hoped. The seven maximum Holmes Brigade events for 1991 included Fort Scott, Weston, Pea Ridge, Wilson's Creek, Lexington, Belmont, and an early March adventure with the Western Brigade. This would be our first exposure with the new Brigade commander, Dave Shackleford. The event was billed as a tactical war game exercise, held at Golden Pond, Kentucky otherwise known as the Land between the Lakes.

"Shebang City." Dave Bennett, Jack Williamson, Mark Gardner, Gregg Higginbotham, Don Whitson, and others at the 125th Anniversary Gettysburg-June 1988

"Retreat, boys, the Rebels have got us in a tight spot." Action photo from day two of the 125th Anniversary battle reenactment of Gettysburg-June 1988

Men of the "Iron Brigade" on Smokers Rock-Gettysburg.

During the evening, the play YIELD NOT TO TEMPTATION
was performed. In several acts, it tells the story of a young
soldier who was seduced by alcohol and its consequences.

Break time during filming of GLORY with Don Whitson and
Tim Moore. Tim seems to be saying, "Is it bullshit, or not?"

Having fun with one of the stunt men dressed as a horse.
Taxidermy prop from Hollywood for movie GLORY.
Tim Moore, Joe Covais, Don Whitson, and me.

During Ferris Bueller's Day off, Matthew Broderick poses with
Pat McCarthy, Tim Moore, Robert Talbott, and Don Whitson

It's the star of the PRINCESS BRIDE in yet another
swashbuckling adventure. Cary Elwes with motley
gang of reenactors on the set of GLORY.

The 125th anniversary of Franklin, Tennessee, December 1989. The only time I recall where we fought the battle wearing our greatcoats.

At Franklin, we were all huddled together like baby chickens trying to keep warm. It was colder than a landlord's heart.

Hillari Higginbotham and my own Katie Talbott. These girls began attending civil war reenactments since they could crawl. Camping outdoors was always an adventure to them.

A photo of the author just before the battle. Here I am in my home away from home, a common two man dog tent. A bed of straw and an army blanket.

The author with Jon Isaacson shortly after the Franklin, TN event. Pizza Hut was giving away sunglasses in sponsorship with Back To The Future II.

The author in line of battle at the 125th anniversary battle reenactment of Mine Creek, Kansas November 1989.

At the June 30-July 1, 1990 reenactment at Carthage, MO, I was reluctantly promoted to 2nd Lieutenant and given a command. Here I am posing with Sgt. Randy Rogers.

The 'belles of the ball.' Our better halves at the Capitol Rotunda in Jefferson City, MO. Once a year we put on our dancing shoes and waltzed the night away.

Steve Hall, Mark Olson, Robert Talbott, and Joe Hudgens at a Civil War Tactical Exercise event somewhere in the middle of Kentucky.

Some of the finest pards I've ever known. Don Whitson, Pat McCarthy, David Bennett, the author, Gregg Higginbotham, and John Maki at a Wilson's Creek living history weekend.

During a break during the Athens, MO reenactment posing for a group photo for wet plate artist Claude Levet. Pat McCarthy, Gregg Higginbotham, Ralph Monaco, Jon Isaacson, John Maki, the author, Don Whitson, and Steve Hall. Photo used by permission of Claude Levet.

Carpooling back from an event when the body is tired but the spirits are still high, the youngsters of the Holmes Brigade bidding the author a fond farewell with sights set on the next exciting adventure.

Chapter Nine

LBL

March 15-17, 1991 near Golden Pond, KY

"WARNING! THE EVENT YOU ARE ABOUT TO ATTEND MAY BE HAZARDOUS TO YOUR HEALTH! YOU WILL ENDURE FORCED MARCHES, NO SLEEP, AND VERY LITTLE FOOD! IF YOU WANT TO STAY WARM, COMFORTABLE, DRY, WELL-FED, AND AVOID STRENOUS DUTY, STAY AT HOME! ABSOLUTELY NO REFUNDS!"

This is the first event I think I've ever attended that had warning labels attached to it. It was like the warnings you used to get at those old cheesy horror movies of the early 1960's where they advise you that a "nurse will be in the lobby" in case you feel faint. Perhaps it was like going into a cheap carnival spook house with the cardboard monsters that pop up. All cheap thrills designed to make you wonder if you have the backbone to proceed into the dark unknown or turn tail.

LBL must have employed the greatest minds in advertising because the event had reenactors quaking in their boots even before it started. Would I get snake bit or lost in the woods? Would I get swallowed up by quicksand or kidnapped by Kentucky rednecks? It made Marine

Corps boot camp training sound like a Boy Scout camp out. This was billed as the "mother of all tacticals."

Prior to our departure to the Blue Grass State, we learned with some sadness that Bill Fannin was resigning as 1st Lieutenant. Since his by-pass surgery of a year earlier, his return to Holmes Brigade had been limited. In all fairness, he did not think his health would allow him to return with the same enthusiasm as before. He certainly could not "hoof it" in the wild terrain that LBL promised. We hoped he would somehow return to us in a limited capacity at a future event, but I never saw Bill again. Sometime after his resignation, he and Kathleen divorced. I could never figure that one out. Both of them made an impact on living history in Missouri-he with Holmes and her with the creation of the Ladies Union Aid Society. *"Both organizations suffered with the departure of these two figures from the hobby. The LUAS has never been the same and was quick to die, while in the year 2005, Holmes Brigade struggles to get 20 men on the field"-authors commentary.*

With the absence of Bill Fannin, Holmes Brigade was forced to promote someone from within the group in a temporary capacity until the elections in May. We'd been faced with the same problem at Carthage when I'd been "convinced" into taking the job as company commander and lieutenant's bars. I firmly believe I was being groomed for a permanent position as an officer at the next election, but I didn't feel worthy. I suffered from low self-esteem, plus I did not have the money to buy all the stuff required of an officer. With some reluctance, Pat McCarthy assumed the role as 2nd company commander. *"Bottom rail on top,"* Pat said of his promotion.

Once again we left home on a Thursday night and drove as far as Paducah, Kentucky, where we pulled into a rest stop for a few hours of sleep. Along on this trip there was Dave Bennett, Don Whitson, Jon Isaacson, Pat McCarthy, and myself that I'm sure of. Trying to sleep sitting up in that van was next to impossible-all our gear was in the back so we couldn't stretch out. Plus it was so cold that every hour Pat would start the engine for a few minutes so the heater would run. Finally we all went into the restroom and changed into our Civil War clothes. By this time it was sun-up, so we sought a hearty breakfast at a nearby restaurant called the Black Kettle where the motto was, **"Whole Lotta Eatin' Goin' On!"**

We ate our weight in eggs, bacon, grits, biscuits and gravy, and whatever else wasn't nailed down before heading to Golden Pond. I'm sure we all were acting a bit silly, but Isaacson claims, *"Whitson almost got us all killed at the Black Kettle with his "shit-eatin' dog joke."*

Land between the Lakes State Park is a narrow peninsula of land, 270 square miles, surrounded on three sides by water. Kentucky Lake on the west, Lake Barkley on the east, and a man-made waterway on the north connecting the two lakes like an upside down U. As you might imagine, this park is perfect for all sorts of water activities, plus its wooded trails are great for hiking. As this was off-season, the State Park people were allowing us on LBL to "fart around," but not for free. It cost each infantryman four dollars, mounted boys four fifty. I think the park was giving us free rein to do what we wanted, with 49 square miles as our playpen.

Once we'd arrived at reenactor parking, we saw quite a few Federals milling about by their cars getting their gear together and waiting for the official "go-ahead" to begin the hike to our first camp. This was a campaigner-style event with most of us carrying blanket rolls, although a few had knapsacks. I had removed the sling from my rifle and attached it to a short blanket roll that was slung behind my back. Inside the roll I had an extra pair of socks, an extra shirt, and 100 rounds. Randy Rogers had started rolling paper cartridges a year or two earlier. He claimed he made them while in front of the television watching porn. Higgy and some of the other lads of Holmes Brigade bought some of Randy's cartridges and claimed they were "top notch." I'd grown tired of rolling the rounds myself so I gave Randy 50 bucks for ten packets of ten.

We also had to provide our own rations. Holmes Brigade had spent so many years dependant on company mess, that most of us were all thumbs when it came to cooking individually. None of us owned a skillet that I recall. Most of us had muckets that we could boil rice, stew, coffee, or soup in. I'd say the majority of us brought cold food like jerky, salami snacks, summer sausage, cheese, sardines, hard bread, and stuff like that. I had some oatmeal that I cooked one morning and a hard-boiled egg, but it got smashed up in my haversack. Someone might have attempted boiling coffee, but for the majority of us, it was cold rations.

So we hung around the parking lot for a few minutes, shifting from one foot to the next, gassing about the latest gossip or just making chin music about nothing. When there were about two dozen of us, Don Strother led us up a trail to "Checkpoint Charlie." It was about a quarter-mile to the staging area where we 'loggy-gagged' on either side of the wooded path until more boys arrived.

From an after action report in the May 1991 Camp Chase Gazette; about 1200 boys had pre-registered for this grand tactical, with 350 Federals and 850 Confederates. Outnumbered three to one again! Since the weather had been lousy the past week, odds were that only 900 would show up.

I think we arrived at the event around 9am, and then spent an hour in the parking lot. After a short hike to the staging area, we sat in the dew soaked weeds, and ate a lunch from our haversack's (that's when I discovered my hard-boiled egg was smooshed). By the way, this was the Federal staging area. The 'johnnies" had their own rendezvous somewhere at the other end of the 49-square mile playground.

We waited till about 1pm until we had 125 infantry, 40 cavalry, and three artillery guns, then the call came to form up. Guys came out of hiding from nine different directions to form the battalions. Some of us had wet stains on our britches from lying in the weeds, and some were covered with "stick-tights." This type of thistle loved wool clothing. It had to be plucked off the fabric like a stubborn tick. If you had a real close pard, he might help you get them off your ass.

Now the command structure for the Federal Army was this: We had Dave Shackleford as the Brigadier, with the power of life and death over us all. We had three battalions. Don Strother commanded 2nd Battalion-Holmes Brigade and Logan's Brigade. *Holmes had two 20-man companies and Logan's about the same.*

Among the Illinois sucker boys of Logan's was my old grade school buddy, Ted Mueller. We gassed on throughout the entire weekend about the school days in Chester, and our families. Ted had a big German style tavern pipe, which he insisted on smoking even on the march. This annoyed Issacson, because the burnt offerings from the pipe sometimes drifted back into his face. Jon probably thought a Jew was being cremated in that German pipe for all the complaining I heard.

Did I mention that this was a judged tactical? Both Union and Confederate participants had goals that had to be reached or held within a time limit. There could be no night fighting. In fact, there could be no movement of troops until 6AM. Casualties would be judged and assigned dependent on how each army placed, deployed, and used its troops during the war game. At the end of the weekend, there would be a tally of points from all the objectives achieved. Whichever army had the highest points by the end of the weekend would receive an "atta-boy!" As far as I recollect there were no awards handed out. Perhaps Shackleford was hoping for an extra star on his collar or a ribbon to put on his brigade flag.

The first goals for Shackleford's army was to deploy each of his battalions at three different crossroads, set up a defensive perimeter at each, and hold those positions for twelve hours. Holy Jesus!

While one battalion advanced westward, another advanced north, 2nd battalion advanced one-third of a mile to the southeast to form a defense position on "Pike's Peak." This is how Steve Hall described the knob we were to secure. I think of it more from a flea's perspective trying to crawl up a fat woman's titty. *Where Logan's Brigade disappeared to, I don't know. Maybe they turned off another trail.*

About halfway up the mountain, John Maki and 1st company turned into a shallow ravine on the right. Pat led 2nd company another two hundred yards straight up till we halted at the edge of a tree lined clearing. Ahead of us the trees had been cleared to allow the growth of several electrical poles. These poles were stuck in the ground every one hundred yards from horizon to horizon till they looked like toothpicks in the distance. *Rednecks need electricity to run their satellite TV's.*

Once we stopped at what we assumed would be our home for the next twelve hours, the next order of business was to post pickets. I decided to place two men at each of three outposts and the fourth post would be a solo position. All posts' would be within one hundred yards of each other. Then I worked on a rotating schedule in my account book (*I still have it to this day*), figuring on a two-hour shift at each post. It was 3 o'clock in the afternoon once we arrived at our position, so I quickly hustled the men to their places. At Post One was Ray Woods and Phil Hamm, Post Two was Terry Forsyth and Joe Amos, Post Three was Jon Isaacson and Butch Wunderlich, and at Post Four was Bill Bartlett. After sunset, I was planning on making all of the picket posts a solo job. In my old account book, I'd already indicated who would go to which post from 3 to 5 PM, 5 to 7 PM, 7 to 9 PM, and so on. Once I'd placed the first set of pickets, as indicated, I went into the woods to take a crap. Along with rations, each man has to provide his own wiping material. I had my two front pockets bulging with Charmin bathroom tissue.

Once I'd finished my successful evacuation, I went over to talk to Pat McCarthy, when who should show up, but the brigadier himself. I suppose he was on a personal inspection and had visited all the camps to see how everyone was faring. Shackleford arrived on horseback because Generals never walk. I think Pat snapped off a crisp salute, but instead of returning it the brigadier began screaming.

"You all been sitting around here talking about women and fast cars and I'll wager you didn't even see that the enemy has crept up on you," he bellowed

About ten yards in the woods stood three harmless looking scarecrows. They'd obviously come the long way around through the woods and not past the pickets I'd posted. Shackleford was throwing a major shit-fit till the spittle flew onto his beard. Meanwhile Pat could only mumble a weak reply as he apologized for the carelessness of him and his men.

"Why I didn't pull him off that mule and punch his lights out is beyond me," Pat later confided to me. *"What a dick! I think I was so surprised by his verbal assault that I was stunned into silence. Besides, it was my first foray as an officer. I thought he was trying to stay in character, but later realized he was seriously chewing my ass. I should have had the patrol volley into him!"*

By this time, the rest of 2nd company had collected their weapons and gathered around. After the brigadier had finished spewing hurtful words, he was nearly purple with rage with a large vein throbbing on his forehead. I thought he might have a stroke right then. What if he fell and his foot was caught in the stirrup? What a picture! Finally Shackleford ordered us to fire at the three scarecrows. They had not moved one step. Perhaps they were enjoying the drama as an entertained audience. We weren't handing out free popcorn, so when we fired that volley the scarecrows walked off. The brigadier turned his nag about and he too disappeared.

During that lengthy tirade, the brigadier had also come to tell us all to move down to the base of the mountain. I called in all the pickets and we proceeded down the face of the ridge till we ran into Maki's company. They'd received the same orders as us, so we followed each other till we were back at the main intersection. I don't know where the Illinois sucker boys had been, but they were waiting for us upon our arrival. We'd barely formed the battalion, when we ran into a heated skirmish. We were just minding our own business, when we were ordered to load and fire a musket volley at some graybacks one hundred yards away.

LBL was John Peterson's first event and he describes the madness and confusion that followed:

"My first opportunity to fire my weapon **in anger** *came Friday night at dusk. I felt my chest literally* **"thump"** *when Pat was ordered to put us in line near a firing field gun. I was shaking in my brogans when the big gun fired a second round at a Johnny skirmish line about a hundred yards away* (shaking was easy to do since they were also brand new and not well broken-in). *I knew how to load the rifle having shot black powder guns before, but upon hearing the order to* **"load"** *I fumbled terribly and dropped my first cartridge. I picked it up awkwardly swinging my shinny new mucket and haversack into the side of my neighbor. I stood-up and tore open the paper, poured the powder down the barrel and immediately brought it to my shoulder to fire with the rest. I cocked the hammer and pulled the trigger upon hearing the order to* **"fire"** *and heard a disturbing* **"click!"** *You guessed it. I had forgotten to place a cap on the cone!"*

The order came to reload, but by the time the smoke from our first musket volley had drifted away, the Confederates were turning tail. Instead of being ordered to give chase, the army received a series of confusing orders to *"march, counter march, stand for a while, march, and counter march again."* Many of us were of the opinion that perhaps Brigadier Shackleford and his staff should ask our advice on where we should go. *"It is a good thing our officers are leading in the army where they can do no harm,"* pondered the philosophical Steve Hall," *instead of leading in civilian life where they would most certainly bring ruin to the economy."*

Near twilight, the army is halted. I think Shackleford was more concerned with wearing out his horse than in wearing us out. I'm a bit unclear how far we marched that Friday afternoon. Odds are we never moved more than a quarter-mile. Probably just ran around in circles wearing out shoe leather and patience. The next thing I knew was we were dropping knapsacks and blanket rolls near a dry riverbed. Steve dubbed it Stones River because it was filled *"with fist-sized rocks."*

With the fall of night came the fall of temperatures. We gathered around several small campfires that had been started in that dry river bed, in the hopes that they would knock some of the chill out of our bones. *"I remember freezing that night when we camped between those two high hills,"* said Pat McCarthy. *"Maki made his own camp about halfway up the side of a high hill, and I remember thinking-What the hell is he doing? Turns out he was smarter than the rest of us - he stayed warm knowing that the cold air would settle in the valley. I eventually gave up on sleep and sat by the fire with the other freezing pards."*

I recall little of that Friday night near "Stones River" except that I too had a hard time falling asleep. The ground was so uneven it was like trying to stretch out inside of a teacup. I might have managed an hour or two, but I woke up either because I got too cold or because my bones felt like they were being bent into a pretzel by the contours of the trench I was lying in.

At some point during the early morning hours, I felt a visit to the sinks was in order. It was pitch black with nary a star out. I didn't want to stumble around in the dark woods for a place to squat, plus I didn't want to wake a sleeping snake, so I walked the two hundred yards up the trail to the porta-potties. After the deed was done, I returned to my blanket and "catnapped" the rest of the night.

It was just before dawn when I was awakened by a babble of voices. Most of the boys had tossed and turned all night until finally they said, "to hell with it." I shucked off the blanket, staggered upright on my knees, and found the packet of oatmeal in my haversack. I had about half a canteen of water, which I thought was no big deal. I figured we'd have time to get our canteens filled before Shackleford took us on another adventure. I had just finished cooking the oatmeal and had eaten about half of it when all hell broke loose!

About 5:30 AM, Jon Isaacson had gone to the porta-potties in hopes for a famous half-hour shit. About fifteen minutes later he was literally blown off the crapper by enemy musket fire coming just outside the door. Jon barely had time to wipe and hitch his drawers, when he burst out of that porta-potty with two battalions of Confederate infantry less than 20 yards away. They'd come to give the Union Army a wake up call, but instead flushed Jon from the shit house.

Officers and NCO's shouted frantic orders to "strike the camp and quickly fall into line!" The Confederates had caught us with our pants down and were pouring it into us. Jon rejoined our lines, still half-dressed and cussing a blue streak.

After fifteen minutes, a truce was called to discuss an issue with the rules. According to the rules, there could be "no troop movement until after 6 AM". The Confederates clearly violated this by launching their attack at about 5:45 AM. After a lengthy discussion, all parties agreed that the Federals would get a 20-minute head start before pursued by the Confederates.

Given this head start, we had to get out of the area quick. This meant we wouldn't have time to refill our canteens or finish our breakfasts. We quickly rolled up our bedrolls and knapsacks, formed the battalions and marched away. Up the side of a mountain on our right we went. There was a trail, but it twisted and turned deep within a thick and dark forest. The sun was high enough, it was about 6:30, but the light didn't penetrate much into that forest. "*Nothing here but trees, thorn bushes, ups-and-downs, snags, ravines, and a heavy carpet of half rotted leaves that fell last autumn*," remembers the naturalist Steve Hall.

For the next several hours, Shackleford led us through the roughest terrain imaginable. Trees grew thick and close together making it hard to walk in a straight line, plus low hanging branches and creeping vines tried to snatch away our muskets, hats, and blanket rolls. Being confined within the dark forest made it impossible for any breeze to circulate. In no time at all, our faces were shiny with sweat and our breath was coming in gasps. Adding insult to injury was the fact that hardly anyone had a full canteen.

Brigadier Shackleford told us all not to worry. He would lead us out of the wilderness to a water buffalo that was parked only a few miles away. It might have helped if he'd had a working compass or the ability to read a map. As it was, we wandered around the forest like the lost children of Israel.

"Shackleford was mounted during our trek," whined first time reenactor John Peterson, *"I learned to hate mounted officers because they seemed to ignore the amount of walking we had to do"*.

Yes, our fearless leader remained ignorant of our suffering, perched as he was, on his throne of horseflesh, with a compass in one hand and map in the other. He was attended by several "paper collar" officers-his staff flunkies. These Majors and Colonels did not have horses so they had to trot to keep up with the boss.

Since everyone seemed to be unfamiliar with the terrain, scouts were sent out at least one hundred yards ahead of the main force. This twenty man patrol-dubbed "The Wombat Rangers"-included Don Whitson, Dave Bennett, Steve Hall, and Gary Gilbert. I distinctly remember seeing these lads gasping and panting one minute, then after a word from Shackleford, dashing off into the brush with all the agility of nimble-footed tree elves, leaping ravines and fallen trees with a single bound. The only thing they didn't do was take to the trees like squirrel monkeys. Of the four Olympians from 2nd Battalion, Gary Gilbert was the oldest, pushing sixty. However, Gary had had Marine Corp training, plus he was a long distance runner in his spare time. The other three boys were just insane.

"We continued to tramp around this part of Kentucky all morning and saw no Johnnies," John Peterson remembers. I don't know what happened to the enemy. I assumed they were hot on our tails, but obviously they zigged when they should have zagged and found themselves just as lost as us.

About mid-day *"we finally stumbled on a Johnny camp site. Success!"* Just as Peterson says, we literally stumbled on the second objective of this wargame. Our scouts had discovered the intersection of Casey Trail and the Trace. Not only was it a vital crossroad, but it had also served as a staging area for the Confederate General and his staff. Those fools left behind equipment that betrayed their identity, such as maps, written orders, signal equipment, plus the Confederate commander's dress kepi and a sash. The sash was tied to the National Colors as a trophy of war.

As outlined by the rules, we were supposed to hold this vital crossroad for two hours. That honor fell squarely on the shoulders of Don Strother and his men of the "fighting 2nd Battalion!" Not sure where the rest of the Grand Army wandered off to; perhaps they went into bivouac some distance to the rear. Anyhow, once given the order, the men of 2nd Battalion spread out in single rank till we covered an area one hundred yards long. From our position we could see into a valley where it was assumed the Confederates might approach. So with this important assignment, we made ourselves comfortable under the canopy of the trees and quickly fell asleep. If the enemy had suddenly appeared we'd all be dead. If Shackleford had caught us napping, he might have had us crucified. In all likelihood, he was probably stretched out as well. I'm sure his butt was sore from riding that nag all morning.

It seemed I had barely closed my eyes, when word came that we were moving out. The required two hours had passed, so the referee was able to put a big check mark next to "mission accomplished." Shackleford told us the Federal army was looking pretty and we should be proud of ourselves for accomplishing our goals. While he was occupied with patting his own back, we private soldiers were only concerned with finding water for our canteens. Once we reached the next intersection-we are promised-there would enough water to bathe in.

When we had started our little adventure, we were traveling northwest. Now we were veering back to the southeast. Our route of march from beginning to end resembled an odd looking triangle. We were doubling back to near our original position, but going about it by taking the scenic route or the long way around. We still had miles to go and still no sign of "Johnny Reb."

"Just a quarter-mile more, boys," was the refrain that passed over our cracked lips as we put one foot in front of the other. It was now the hottest part of the day and our supply of water was dangerously low. You would think that Shackleford's horse could sniff out some water, but his nostrils only puffed out dust. A few of the animal lovers in the Brigade offered to pool the remaining drops in their canteens for the old nag, but the wise brigadier declined the offer. He has faith that aid and comfort is *"just a quarter-mile more, boys!"*

We march, march, and march some more. The promise of cool water is like a dream that keeps each man moving another quarter-mile after another. Finally we break out of the dark forest into full daylight. We'd come out right next to a paved road. This is the Laura Furnace Road. Civilized people use paved roads and where there's civilization, there must be water!

Our excitement at reaching the road quickly sags like an old man's peter, when much to our surprise there is no water to greet us. There is immediate grumbling in the ranks, but in an attempt to avoid a mutiny, Shackleford orders the referee to summon an ambulance. Medical staff is only a phone call away. In this case, the referee used a walkie-talkie. Within a short time, the ambulance arrives and takes a few men, with a dozen canteens between them, to a water buffalo another mile or two down the road.

After about an hour, the ambulance returned. The men gather around the dripping canteens like a hungry pack of dogs. Ignoring words of caution we greedy bastards start gulping and slurping- which can be a sure recipe for a bellyache if not checked. Most of that water trickles past dry lips, soaking chin whiskers and wool jackets, but no one gives a damn. Some of the boys are too lame to continue the journey, so they are loaded in the ambulance. The rest of us seem well enough to continue on with the final leg of the march, so Shackleford gives us the old heave-ho.

It was mid-afternoon by now. To reach our camp for the night, we would now be traveling northeast (the final leg of that crazy triangle).

"*Everybody was pooped,*" remembers Pat McCarthy. *Ray Woods* (I think it was Ray) *fagged out from exhaustion, and I ended up carrying his rifle and gear along with my stuff. I found myself praying for a quick and painless death.*"

I believe we turned off the paved road and went a "quarter-mile more" up another trail. Finally the oasis is in site! It is nothing more than a dry creek bed, but to the worn and the weary it is the Garden of Eden. We are ordered to set up a defensive position, but everyone falls out exhausted. I find a small burrow near an outcropping of brush and quickly fall asleep. For the next several hours we do nothing, but eat, drink, and rest.

Just before dusk we learn that the Confederates are going to attack us. After all this time, they finally found us. Their infantry came from the north, while their horse soldiers attacked us from the south. "*Three battalions of rebels march down the road toward us,*" recalls Steve Hall. "*Our entire line is well positioned along the dry creek bed.*" Actually we were sandwiched in the middle of the two grayback forces. "*We have copious supplies of ammunition and are powerfully upset at these people for disturbing our siesta.*" Steve makes light of the situation, but that shows the grit of the common Western soldier who can laugh even in the face of death. With such men of firm backbone, the blue-clad warriors of Shackleford's little army were able to beat off the Rebel scarecrows of Doom.

After that minor annoyance, all of us prepare for a nice quiet evening under the stars. However, instead of stars, we instead begin to see black clouds boiling overhead. With the cloud formation there came a sudden drop in temperature and the wind began to pick up. Somebody came by a few minutes later with word of a storm headed our way. He'd been listening to an all weather radio and he came back to tell us about flash flooding, lightening, hail, and frogs falling out of the sky. Don Strother called 2nd battalion for a brief meeting and we discussed the situation. The consensus was that we should abandon ship. We'd gotten our four dollars worth of Kentucky excitement and we didn't want to tempt Mother Nature. Who knew what she would unleash on us?

Shackleford threw a shit-fit when he heard of our decision. One-third of his army was going to quit on him! Dammit it all! We continued to get updates on the weather and it was not looking good. Don simply threw his hands up in the air and told Shackleford it was the will of the people.

Our battalion was about half the size that we'd started with. Some had fallen out along the way with blisters, sprains, or heat exhaustion. For the survivors, we had had enough fun and were looking forward to a motel room and a hot shower. And so we turned our backs on Shackleford and his proud command and followed the trail "just a quarter-mile more" to reenactor parking and civilization.

CHAPTER TEN

Three Days in August

After the Grand Tactical at the Land between the Lakes Park in Kentucky, the next big thing was the 130th anniversary reenactment at Wilson's Creek. Up until this moment there had never been a big reenactment of any kind at this National Park. Other than a few park ranger supervised firing demonstrations, candlelight tours, and an encampment sometime around the anniversary date, the reenactors were not allowed to stomp and romp about in great numbers unless it was off site. That's just what we did in 1991. The 130th anniversary reenactment would be held approximately 3 miles northeast of the official National Park boundary line. It would be on private land. One interesting thing about this spot was the fact that Wilson's Creek ran through it. Before I begin my narrative into the three days of August, I should briefly mention a few things that happened in the spring of 1991.

During the weekend of April 20-21, Holmes attended the event at Weston, Missouri. Now called "Bee Creek," this event was not in town but some miles away in a park type area. This was the weekend were 'Zip Coon' made his appearance. During the generic battle, there was the cavalry boys doing there 'tink-tink-tink' with sabers. The Federals were put in a waist high trench line. Some straw had been scattered all along about the area, but the trench works were still as muddy as hell.

After a few rounds had been smoked, the Confederate infantry charged our lines and pushed us out of the trenches. A bullshit event made tolerable by the antics of Isaacson, Mark Strother, a human pyramid, and the 'soiled doves.'

For some unknown reason, I was unable to attend the spring muster at Fort Scott. Whether it was because I had to work Saturday I don't remember, but whatever the case, I missed the business meeting and elections. In a previous chapter I told you that Holmes Brigade had decided that from now on we would have all our future business meetings at Fort Scott. Remember I told you we skipped having our meeting at Athens in 1990, so all those boys elected to positions in 1989 would actually hold their positions for two years rather than one.

So the new and improved business meetings were held for the very first time at Fort Scott on the evening of May 4th, with the argument that more reenactors were coming here than attending many of the state events.

In my absence, the boys voted me out of office. I lost my position as First Sergeant to Randy Rogers. It's probably just as well; I was never really comfortable with that rank. There's more to being a First Sergeant than just taking roll call and Randy Rogers had some interesting ideas on how to run that office. I was, however, elected to the job of 2nd Sergeant. Meanwhile, Pat McCarthy accepted the office of 2nd Lieutenant, while Maki became first officer.

After the weekend at Fort Scott, Holmes Brigade was invited once again to Pea Ridge, Arkansas, for another encampment. This time our camps were located closer to the visitor's center. Better for the rangers to keep an eye on us I suspect. This would be the 1st and 2nd of June, the height of tick season.

You see there are hundreds of white tail deer that run all over Pea Ridge National Park. Their droppings are all over the place. There are also thousands of deer ticks in this area. Quite a number of the guys go home after a Pea Ridge weekend and pick ticks off themselves by the handful. I never found more than one or two around my waist. Some guys are mortally afraid of these little bastards. Well, the deer ticks can carry lime disease-which is no laughing matter. Phil Hamm always went into a panic about ticks. At this time, Phil was our company cook. He would nearly shit his pants if he thought a tick was in the area. Some of the wags used to throw twigs or pebbles at him and claim the ticks were falling from the trees.

Around this time, Holmes Brigade was introduced to Gonzales and Fontana, but I don't think they hung around for more than one season. Isaacson seems to recall them better than I do, although I seem to think one of them did a fair Mussolini impression. Both of them were at the June Pea Ridge encampment.

On July 13-14, we attended an MCWRA Maximum effort event at Cole Camp, Missouri (home of the plate-sized tenderloin). To their credit, the MCWRA had done some homework on the event.

In the early morning hours of June 20, 1861, a half-organized regiment of Union Home Guard, numbering about four hundred men, were surprised and routed by an equal number of Missouri State Guardsmen. The Unionists were quartered in two barns, fast asleep, and were completely unprepared for the rude awakening which came at about four in the morning. Although a few of the Home Guard boys were able to respond to the assault and put up a good defense, at least twenty-one boys were gunned down before they could get off their blankets. A few others were bayoneted or were executed like dogs.

The Home Guard was composed of many Germans, so they could not speak English too well. After capture, one German was interrogated, but he could only stammer in broken English, "Me cook," meaning he was the man who cooked the meals. However, the secessionists interpreted it that the man admitted to being Colonel Cook, the commander of the Union Home Guard. So they shot him down like a dog.

I don't know why we agreed to do this event. The scenario called for us to be massacred. It was a unique opportunity to dress out in civilian clothes, however. This was one of the first times, outside of the Bleeding Kansas or 1855 Missouri Town Days, where we could put on civilian clothes and interpret an event that happened during the early days of the Civil War.

Coming down from Iowa with Randy Rogers was a big boy named Jeff Baroom. Hell of a name! The two big-boned Io-weegins were decked out in civilian clothes the same as all of us, but because their bodies were so big and their heads were so little, I called the pair "Tweedledee" and "Tweedledum" after the <u>Alice in Wonderland</u> characters. Randy was not amused.

This was the event in which Robbie Piatt announced he was becoming a Jew! I think he made this decision based on his love life. I think he had girlfriend who was Jewish and she talked him into converting. We never saw Robbie again after Cole Camp, although we learned he had taken the Jewish name, Yakov.

It was at Cole Camp that Isaacson saw Dave Kesinger with painted toenails! Kesinger was going to soak in the horse trough, but when he pealed off those shoes and socks and those bright red tootsies popped out, Isaacson's eyes went cuckoo. Kesinger claimed one of his sons must have played a trick on him while he was asleep, but he did it himself, I hope, just to get a reaction from the Holmes Brigade boys. Dave Kesinger has always had a bizarre sense of humor.

That evening, some of the lads where invited to the local swimming pool, then later they met downtown at DER ESSEN PLATZ, or The Eating Place. This was a restaurant serving German cuisine. I'm not much for "schlong and kraut", so I had the plate-sized tenderloin at the Tastee Freeze up the street.

August 9-11, 1991 Wilson's Creek, MO

Most amateur scholars will tell you that Wilson's Creek was "a mighty mean fought fight." Although outnumbered two to one, the fiery Union commander, Nathaniel Lyon, led an early morning attack on southern forces camped along both sides of the creek. Once the shock of surprise wore off, the southerners, under Ben McCullough from Texas and Sterling Price of the Missouri State Guard, were able to turn the tide in their favor, due in part to a case of mistaken identity and the death of General Lyon. With the loss of the Federal commander and the rout of a portion of his army attacking from an opposite flank, the balance of the Union army had no recourse but to skedaddle back to Springfield.

Since Wilson's Creek 1991 was planned as a large scale reenactment with huge numbers of men, artillery, horses, and volunteers providing sanitary facilities, telephone service, potable water, and medical service, reenactors were asked to cough up a mere five dollars for registration. This event was held on private land, so I'm sure the owner was given a small percentage plus whatever the visiting spectator paid at the gate to view this circus act-$6 a day or $12 for all three days. The one thing the event sponsor could not supply was food. Holmes Brigade members were asked to cough up another eight dollars for grub. Once again we would pool all our resources into a company kitchen. The downside was Holmes Brigade had about ninety men divided into three companies. Hopefully, there would be enough food to last from Friday evening to Sunday noon.

With Wilson's Creek, we would finally have the Western Brigade on this side of the Mississippi River. Rumors indicated the Federals would have 13 guns, 70 cavalry, and 600-plus infantry divided into two battalions. Other than Pilot Knob, this was the only event where a large number of Federals was desired. Along with the Western Brigade came the brigadier, Dave Shackleford. I wonder if he was still pissed at us for leaving LBL during the middle of the night. Based on my observations and the comments I overheard during those three days in August, I'd say yes.

In recreating the 130th anniversary of the Battle of Wilson's Creek, the reenactors thought it important to remember the three most important phases of this fight-the fight in Ray's cornfield by the US Regulars, the rout of General Franz Sigel's German volunteers, and the climatic fight atop Bloody Hill. To do this event justice, we needed the three days.

The most unusual thing about this three-day event was we would have three different uniform impressions. On Friday, we would wear our dark blue frock coats and tall Hardee hats. On Saturday, we would be portraying Sigel's Third Missouri Infantry and would be wearing a gray overshirt, and on Sunday, we would be portraying the Second

Kansas Infantry, in which the uniform was sack coat with civilian trousers. This is the only time, with the exception of when we held this event again in 2000, where we would wear so many different sets of clothes.

In regards to the gray overshirt as used by the Third Missouri, research was done by several of our members to get the approximate look and construction of the thing. There are no photographs to speak of, but there are a number of descriptions from documents of said shirt as worn by members of the Third Missouri at Carthage as well as, Wilson' s Creek. The shirt was described as a simple pull-over gray shirt made from heavy cotton. In some instances, there was blue trimming around the cuffs, collar, or breast pocket. The ones Holmes Brigade would have made would be without the trimming or the breast pockets.

Ladies Union Aid Society member Ruth Hendy was commissioned to construct these shirts. Not sure when she actually began the work, but all orders had to be in by mid-July. By the time the Wilson's Creek event came in August, she had almost one hundred shirts finished. I think the price of each shirt was around $40. In order to get this cut-rate price, the shirts had to be a generic size. There was an order form included with an issue of the Holmes Brigade dispatch in which the interested party put down collar size, sleeve length, and preferred shirt size-medium, large, or extra large.

Before coming to Wilson's Creek, it was learned that Pat McCarthy would not be able to attend so that made it necessary to promote someone from the ranks to assume the role of 3rd company commander. Any guesses on who that sucker was? John Maki and Randy Rogers were chosen to be commanders of 1st and 2nd Company. Meanwhile, Don Strother would assume the role of staff flunky in Shackleford's little clique of paper pushers. He would get to be a bird colonel once again! Three companies of Holmes Brigade would merge with an assortment of lads from the First Minnesota, Fourteenth Indiana, Logan's Brigade (old buddy Ted Mueller), and the Mudsills, to form a battalion under Chuck Warnick. Remember this was the old sergeant from Gettysburg who I reminded about his bayonet? Chuck would command us, as a light colonel, during the first and third day of activities at Wilson's

Creek. On day two, Don Heitman would command our battalion. Who was Don Heitman?

Don Heitman was the cat from Indiana who dreamed up the idea of commanding us gray shirts while speaking only in German. During drill, he would 'sprectin ze deutsche,' and we would have to figure out what he was saying. Months earlier, when I realized I would have to be a company commander at Wilson's Creek, Don Heitman sent me a cassette tape with German commands and such so I had some idea what to expect. Some commands were easy to figure out. "Kompanie" for company, "Schulter-waffen" for shoulder arms, "rechts drehen" right face, "vorwarts marsch" for forward march, etc. Only Isaacson knew the words completely. When it came time for Heitman to bark the German command, Isaacson would lean back and whisper out the side of his mouth what the English version was. We didn't want to look like dummies if we all went huh? After all, we were supposed to be Germans!

I arrived at the event with Jon Isaacson, although I don't remember if we came Thursday night or early Friday morning. The Battle of Ray's Cornfield would not take place until Friday evening! The local weatherman was predicting mild weather with highs in the eighties. The camps were located on the other side of Wilson's Creek and fortunately there was a bridge to drive over and unload. Currently Wilson's Creek is much polluted and if one were to wade across it, you'd be covered in barnacles by the time you came up the other side. If you owned a horse, you avoided the creek. Drinking water, for man and beast, would be brought in 6000-gallon tanker trucks.

After registration, I drove my Mitsubishi to the campsite, which was no more than a couple hundred yards up a dirt road. As I've already hinted, I was temporarily promoted from 2nd Sergeant to 2nd Lieutenant and given command of 3rd company. I had my A frame tent, which I set up at the end of the company street on officers row. I had a rope bed, a folding table, a candle lantern, a folding stool, and a John Maki breadbox. I think I also had a small throw rug. All the creature comforts an officer needs. The only thing missing was a pair of carpet slippers and a chamber pot.

Within a short time, we had a row of tents all down the line as more and more of the Western Brigade boys arrived. No sooner had the guys settled in than the grayshirts arrived. Now, Ruth Hendy did not make these shirts all by herself. She was probably the main cog on the spinning wheel and had the ultimate say so on how they were made, but she had help from folks in Oklahoma including Holmes Brigade's own 'bobbin boy,' Scott White. Scott was on hand to help distribute these gray shirts to all the paying members of Holmes Brigade.

As mentioned there were no half sizes or form-fitting tailoring. There was one exception. Holmes Brigade member George 'Butch' Wunderlich is a big boy, almost seven feet tall I'll wager. He is also big-boned. He requested an xx large shirt. When the shirts arrived, Maki drew a huge laugh from the crowd when he put Butch's shirt on. Since John is so small, the shirt came all the way down to his toes and the sleeves hung several feet past his fingers.

So everyone was happy with the shirts, all except Mike Gosser. Mike is a little guy, probably 98 pounds soaking wet. One would assume a medium shirt would fit him just nicely, but for some odd reason, Mike filled out a form requesting a large shirt. Perhaps he thought the shirt would shrink after washing. When buying clothing from a department store, there is not much of a difference between one size and the next. A little more material perhaps. With the Ruth Hendy manufactured gray shirt, there <u>was</u> a radical difference and it became apparent once Mike put it on and found that the sleeves hung below his knees.

So Mike stood there in his "plus-size" shirt filling the air with venom against Ruth Hendy and her needlework. It was his own fault for adding the extra couple of inches on the form, but he did not see it that way. After some heated words had passed, Scott drew an 'Arkansas toothpick' and challenged Gosser to a knife fight. It was all theatrics and I don't think he would have actually stuck anybody, but then again Scott White has a history of bizarre behavior that he mixes sometimes with hard liquor and marijuana. Happily for all concerned, Mike backed down and Scott cooled down.

Looking back now, the event site was not that big. Everything was boxed into approximately one square mile. Remember, this was an area a few miles northeast of the National Park Battlefield site. The Federal camp was at one end of the box, while the Confederates were at another end. Ray's Cornfield fight and 'Bloody Hill' were both on the left-hand side of the 'box.' However, the area designated for Sigel's Retreat was about a quarter-mile beyond the right of the 'box' behind a wooded area. To get to these areas before the beginning of the battle, Shackleford would of course have us go the long way around to make it intriguing to the spectator and to us.

The dirt road, in which all traffic came through, was on this right hand side of this 'box.' Squeezed just off on the shoulder and right up against the bank of Wilson's Creek was sutler row. I seem to recall there were quite a number of merchants at this one. Not as many as some events out east, but a good number, including a photographer who made pictures using the old wet-plate process of 130 years earlier. Not to be confused with a paper print or CDV, this fellow made tintypes and ambrotypes (a small piece of glass treated with light sensitive emulsion). I don't remember what his prices were, but I think an ambro was $45.

By mid-morning on Friday, a line was already forming in front of the photographer where men were making appointments to have their images made. As I looked around, I realized that if I wanted to get my likeness made, it would have to be this day. I debated what set of clothes I wanted to wear for this likeness, but seeing that my appointment was at 5PM and the battle was a 7PM, I went with the uniform of the day which was the dark blues.

At some point Shackleford formed the Brigade so we could see how many boys he had to play with. In third company I had Terry Forsyth as my First Sergeant. I never had to worry one bit whether the boys were properly counted off or the fatigue details were properly assigned. As First Sergeant, Terry did an admirable job of taking care of everything, which left me more time to strut about like a peacock. *In less than ten years, Terry would become captain of the Holmes Brigade.*

Holmes had three thirty man companies. Among the heroes serving under me was Isaacson, Dave Bennett, Justin O'Rear and all the Bagladies. I distinctly remember Joe Anderson, Condra, A.J., and Charlie Pautler giving me grief the whole weekend, although in a playful way as only the Bagladies will do.

As newly appointed officer, I think I spent a lot of time over at Battalion headquarters with all the other company commanders, going over the plan of the day with Chuck Warnick. We most certainly went over the Cornfield fight and what was expected of us. Since most of us were new to our positions, especially Warnick himself, the plan for the battle was to 'keep it simple, stupid!' There would be no fancy wheels or breaking files to the rear in open order on the right by files into line or any of that other nonsense that we'd practiced out east. Frankly, there wasn't enough room on the drill field for all that trick stuff. The object would be just march in columns of fours then face front into a line of battle. 'Keep it simple, stupid!'

So Shackleford took us out on an early afternoon drill, just to see if we could march and form a battle line. The drill field was near the entrance into the event site, but not that big of an area to do too much. When forming from columns of four into a battle line, it was important that the line looked straight. A right and left guide stood at opposite ends of the Brigade and the men would align themselves between the two. These guides would hold little flags on a stick so they'd stand out.

We had marched in circles for several minutes. Finally, a halt was called and we were allowed to stand at ease for some time while a meeting of the minds was conducting by the brigadier and his staff flunkies. This went on for some minutes and the men were allowed to stack arms, refill our canteens from the water buffalo, and sit. After nearly a half-hour had passed, the recall was sounded and we all staggered to our feet and collected the weapons.

The Brigade was given the command to march, but wait! Where was the right guide? Don Whitson had volunteered to be the right guide, but he was not in line with his guidon. Less than thirty paces from the drill field, a flat bed trailer had been trucked in. Mounted on this trailer was a row of ten or twelve AT&T pay phones all connected to a satellite dish. Don Whitson was at one of these phones talking to his wife. The whole Federal army had to wait until Don finished his call. Don must have felt all the guys staring at him, because he quickly ended his call and rejoined the army; his face was red with embarrassment. Shackleford quietly steamed under his collar and gave Don a priceless look, while the rest of us just laughed.

The hours passed while we sat around and did nothing or ate supper. I had my likeness taken during this interlude. Meanwhile, the sun had slowly moved to the opposite horizon and soon it was time to form up for the battle. Most of us had on frock coats, although for a few, the sack coat was acceptable. For those that didn't have a Hardee hat, a slouch hat pinned up on one side was worn. Another anachronism was most men only had sky blue trousers to wear. The issue of sky blue trousers did not come into being until later in the year or early 1862. A pair of dark blue trousers to wear at one event was an investment most refused to make. This was not the time to worry about authenticity, only about having numbers of men.

Suddenly there came 'first call,' which meant the men of the Brigade had five minutes to get their weapons and accoutrements and fall into their respective company formations. This was followed minutes later by a bugle call and drum roll to move the individual companies into the Brigade line. As I already mentioned, First Sergeant Terry had the men all squared away and counted off. I didn't have to do anything but yell, "Forward March!"

Within moments the Brigade was formed, 600 men in two battalions, or 12 individual companies. Each company commander had to step to the front of the Brigade to get a final word from the adjutant, then the First Sergeant of each company came forward to report if his men were, 'all present and accounted for.' Following this ritual, the brigadier stepped forward to greet the men. One morning, Shackleford appeared before us in the uniform of a British soldier of the Zulu War. If you've seen the movie ZULU with Michael Caine, you can picture the red uniform jacket and white coal scuttle helmet. After some words of inspiration, Shackleford put us on the march.

As promised, Shackleford led us the long way through the woods on our left, about a quarter-mile, and then we doubled back or made a big circle till he brought us through the woods on the far or southern end of the 'box.' The cornfield was only about 100 yards in front of us. Our camps were about three hundred yards beyond that. I had to remind the reader, but every thing about the reenactment was contained in this small area, a one-square mile box or rectangle.

The 'cornfield' in question had been planted months earlier with the extreme purpose that we could plow through and trample it down. This was an area about one city block wide and another in depth. The corn stalks were about seven feet tall and had many ripe ears on them eager for the plucking.

We had formed a line of battle, or two ranks of men facing this wall of corn. The way our battalion was placed, it looked like we would strike it dead center. After we had formed our line of battle, it seemed we were waiting on the word to go. Finally the word came from Shackleford, who passed it to Chuck Warnick, who passed it down to the adjutant, who bellowed in a deep voice that we would prepare to advance. At this point someone in 3rd company asked the question, "Who all is advancing into the corn?" I responded in a voice loud enough to wake the heavenly host. I said, "EVERY SWINGING DICK!" The men cheered and tossed their hats in the air. After my proclamation of courage, every blue-clad warrior felt a deeper resolve to get 'kick ass and take names.'

Once the order was given to march, the blue line advanced down the slope one hundred yards until swallowed up by row after row of corn. The stalks grew so thick it was difficult to see the man next to you. Instead it was 'crash, crash, crash' as the corn stalks fell one by one as the human blue tidal wave pressed forward. As each stalk was pushed aside, corn dust was shaken loose until each man seemed covered in the stuff. It covered the uniforms, the weapons, and seeped into the nostrils, eyes, and throat.

After about five minutes tramping through this jungle vegetation, the blue line broke through to the clearing. In front of us was a split rail fence about waist high. Some men were already hunkered down behind it trading shots with the Rebel skirmishers. A few of their mountain howitzers opened up on us all well. Behind us our own artillery was talking back with its own dialogue of violence. To our extreme left, there was a line of spectators that I understand numbered 2,000. They were backed up along the road by sutler row and held back by yellow police tape.

I forgot to mention that I borrowed a sword from Gregg Higginbotham. It was a German saber that was about as tall and wide as John Maki. I exaggerate of course, but it was a good size hunk of steel that made me walk off balance whenever I wore it.

I had that saber drawn and was waving it at the enemy and saying some mighty hurtful words about their ancestry. We had not been given the order to fire yet and I was in front of the company waving that sword around like I was Conan the Barbarian. Maki and some of the guys in the battalion looked at me as if I had lost my mind. During my conniption fit, I almost decapitated Mike Gosser. I quickly apologized and gave him a smooch.

Finally, the battalions were given the order to fire and that gave me the excuse to hide behind the ranks. That's where all good officers go during the shooting match-to the rear to do a little 'coffee cooling' while the boys are getting shot at. Actually the officer stands behind the ranks and assists the file closers with discipline or helps a young private with his weapon, if it becomes fouled.

I don't know how many rounds the boys smoked, but the air was getting thick. We were surrounded by all that corn with no circulation coming through. We fired by battalion, by company, and we fired at will. As an officer, I was pretty much a non-factor. All I had to do was stand out of the way and try to keep my hair from getting mussed up while the boys did the devil's work of handing out punishment.

Finally there was a shout! The Rebel tyrants are pushing us, but we are in no hurry to give up ground. The blue lines slowly inch back through that forest tangle of corn. By this time, the stalks had been hacked or trampled to the ground till it looked like the aliens had left another crop circle in a farmer's field. We continued to ease our way to the rear even as the enemy hollers that dreaded Rebel Yell, a noise that sounds like someone is gargling with broken glass and razor blades.

So the losses began to mount in that terrible field of corn; the blue ranks are dissolving into a confused mob and dropping like horse flies. We fell back a full one hundred yards or more under the continual and relentless pressure of those unholy Missouri scarecrows. The survivors of the debacle formed some sort of line and marched off the field and into the sunset. That was the end of the Friday funfest!

At 6 AM, the event came to life with the flourish of drums and fifes. Reveille sounded, which was then followed by roll call. Breakfast had been started about an hour earlier as it took that long to get coffee to boil. Sometimes we had sausage and eggs scrambled together in one big 10-gallon pot. It's usually the same bill of fare every morning, then in the evening it's usually stew, or as I like to call it, 'leper in a hot tub.' For lunch we typically have cold cut sandwiches, usually ham and cheese. We eat cold on Sunday because all the pots and stuff have already put away in boxes in preparation for the 'big bug-out' following the afternoon battle.

Now the enlisted men always eat first. Probably because they have all the dirty details and labor to attend to. The officers are at the end of the chow line, because all they have to do is look pretty then bark like a puppy when giving orders.

On Saturday we all came out in the uniform of the day, the gray shirt. As far as headgear, anything other than a turban was appropriate. There were top hats, brown hats, bowlers, workman's caps, and Mexican War wheel hats. I wore a gray wide brimmed slouch hat that I got from Scott White for 'five dollah!' Trousers were another item open for options. Colored or checked wools, plaids, jean cloth, and cotton were acceptable, but most went back to the sky blue kersey. I don't recall what type of trousers I wore, but it was probably the drop front white canvas 1812 militia pants with my tall boots.

During officers meeting, we all went over the plan of the day with Brigadier Shackleford. Since half of his army would be on loan to Don Heitman, who wanted to do Sigel's Rout in gray shirts, Shackleford wanted to make sure we wouldn't have our head up our ass when he cut us loose. He had all the company commanders, including yours truly, in front of his tent, and then he proceeded to read the outline for the Saturday battle.

I believe Don Strother was the author of this outline, which basically spelled out the progression of events from the time the soldiers entered to field for the Saturday fight, until the very last shot was fired. I think Don wrote an outline for all three battles. With the Sigel scenario on Saturday, a number of episodes were to be played out which lead to the actual firing of muskets by both sides.

During the actual Battle of Wilson's Creek, specifically that part played by Franz Sigel and his men, a line of gray shirted men approached from out of the woods. The German's made the mistake of thinking them members of the 1ˢᵗ Iowa, who were also attired in a type of gray uniform. Unfortunately, these men were from Louisiana. The boys from the Bayou State opened up on the confused Germans and all hell broke loose. "They make mistake," one German officer proclaimed even as he tried to stop the fight. The boys from Louisiana were not confused and they chased the Unionists off the field.

In Don Strother's outline, he makes the written comment that Sigel's men "jacked-up." Shackleford got a big ha-ha out of that description. I could only shake my head and hide my embarrassment. Wilson's Creek '91 was essentially a Holmes Brigade sponsored event and since I was a member of Holmes Brigade, I felt Shackleford was looking his nose down on all of us. I'll admit Don could have chosen his words a little bit better when describing the Sigel's snafu.

Between 9 AM and 11 AM we had drill. This gave Don Heitman time to work with us. As I mentioned earlier in this chapter, he gave his commands in German. Our task was to translate that gibberish in our brains and then complete the maneuver like the good German soldiers we pretended to be. Thankfully, Don kept it simple. We went around in circles for about an hour, which included instruction in the manual of arms. During the actual battle, which would start at 2 PM, we would have little to worry about other than knowing when to run away in panic.

At the allotted hour, we marched from camp, took a right turn over Wilson's Creek, and passed through woods to a clearing a "quarter-mile" away. Even as we marched to the site, I seem to recall that the spectators followed right along side us, parallel to our line of march. Thankfully, they did not get in the way.

My memory may not be as sharp as it was in 1991, but I seem to recall that some of the "bagladies" were noticeably absent from

Saturday's fight. A number of them did not answer roll call, or if they did it was to say they were too tired, too sick, or too lazy. Some objected to the scenario, while others objected to the gray shirts themselves. I could never figure that out. The shirts were built on imperfect documentation, but it was the best we had. So based on one imperfection, some of the guys sat out Sigel's Rout.

Charlie Pautler sat out the fight because of a sprained wrist. It seems the "bagladies" went into Springfield to get some adult beverage. Once in the parking lot of a store, Charlie and one of the other "bags" started playing grab-ass and chased each other until Charlie slipped on the pavement and landed on his wrist. I was very disappointed in those guys that day.

This battle was mostly a stand-up affair with no highlights to speak of. Our lines were formed facing the woods even as our artillery support began barking. We could see nothing of the enemy, but assumed they would come streaming out of the woods in panic. *As in the original fight, Sigel's men thought they would mop up the Rebel refugee's fleeing from Lyon's fierce attack coming from the north.*

The field of battle was about the size of a football field. I think all of us grayshirts were on the fifty-yard line. On the far right hand side of this field was the spectators, once again held in check by a length of yellow police tape running from north to south. Directly in the right corner of the playing field was a fifty-foot tall scaffold or tower that had been built so a video crew could film from it and get an overhead shot of the action. An outfit out of Kansas City, MO., Video Post was putting together a documentary/reenactment video and they hoped it would be just as stylish as the Classic Images productions during the 125th anniversary battles.

So we were on the field in line of battle, waiting for the enemy, who was supposed to be running away from Lyon's men, and into our open arms. The grayshirts were in front, a battalion strength of about six companies. In reserve was the other battalion, led by Shackleford. In looking back at the old 1991 Video Post movie, it seems that battalion wore standard military attire, minus their jacket. They didn't want to spend their money on a gray shirt <u>and</u> dark blue trousers, to wear at only one event!

Getting back to the fight, here comes a body of soldiers, stepping from the woods, dressed in gray like us. Don Heitman detailed a horseman to go forward and ascertain the identity of this body of men. Some words were exchanged, and then a gunshot dropped the horseman. I think somebody advanced with the National Colors and he too was slain. It was scripted that the colors were supposed to just lie on the field next to the dead German, but I believe somebody ran out to retrieve them.

When Sigel saw those gray uniform's he assumed they were members of the First Iowa Infantry. Though attired in gray as the Germans, the boys of the Third Louisiana were not as confused as Sigel. Even as the bullets began to fly, Sigel and his men continued to protest and say, "They make mistake!" By the time Sigel realized he was facing southerners, many of his men had already panicked and were slipping to the rear.

So we had a stand up fight for nearly a half-hour, muskets roaring back and forth, all of us shouting gibberish in a quasi-German accent that only an imbecile could understand. Many of the officers in the rear of the line, including Don Heitman, ran around like chickens with their heads cut off and in their play acting they screamed, sobbed, and wrung their hands together still saying, "They make mistake!"

After a dozen or more rounds had been fired, the word came to my ears that we would abandon the field. We were being ordered to 'bug-out.' What started as an orderly withdrawal from the field, quickly dissolved into madness and pandemonium as the order came to scatter. "Every man for himself!"

Unit cohesion had evaporated. The battalion was wrecked. The gray shirts turned away from the fight with each man left to wander away from the field like refugees from a natural disaster. Some of the men went to the side of the road to sit, while others took to the woods as if the hounds were after them. Meanwhile, Shackleford's battalion of regulars stepped forward, blew a few more rounds of gunpowder, and in effect, covered the escape of Heitman's Germans.

Given the order to withdraw from my command, I turned away and entered the wooded trail back to camp. Within moments I found myself all alone, with only young Justin O'Rear as my traveling companion. Everyone else had vanished from the face of the earth, or so it seemed. Only the fading echoes of battle from far behind me reminded me of what I'd left.

There was supposed to be a pre-dawn tactical Sunday morning, but I don't recall anything about it. It's possible everyone was too fagged out from yesterday's adventure to muster up enough "give a shit" to get up at first light and run around. This lack of enthusiasm may have been tempered by a severe hangover many felt after a late night orgy of heavy drinking. I think there was a dance Saturday night and its possible many boys were dipping their tin cups in the firewater throughout the night. A tough looking hombre, who called himself *Gator*, offered me a taste of this rotgut. Luckily I did not spill any of it on my clothes.

On Sunday morning, we made our third and final uniform change, into the duds of the 2nd Kansas. As I mentioned earlier, the uniform would be civilian pants, civilian hat, and Federal issue fatigue coat, or as the soldiers called it, the sack coat. *The soldier's gave it that name because the coat hung on a man like a sack.*

One problem with a volunteer army, like the 2nd Kansas, was in the question of rank and how was it worn. In the early days of the Civil War, chevrons and officers shoulder boards were worn by the US Regular Army on regulation uniforms. For the volunteers who had no regulation uniforms to speak of at this early stage, they came up with other means of identification. For example, those elected as sergeants might wear a colored rag around one arm. Before coming to Wilson's Creek, researchers said that some officers wore a thin piece of tin on their coat as their badge of rank. Don Strother worked at a Tool and Die factory in Purdy, MO and promised he would try to bring some tin foil pieces for us officers to wear, if we wanted. Not knowing any better, I sewed a couple of pieces of Reynolds Wrap aluminum foil to my coat. From a distance it was hard to tell that I'd committed a farbism of the highest order.

The Battle of Bloody Hill, or Lyon's Last Stand, would be at 1 PM. We had a morning formation, but I doubt if we did any drilling. There was church service offered to those that needed it. I'm sure the pastor was ready with a sermon on "demon rum" and it's possible he had many converts the day that swore that they'd never touch another drop to their lips. Yeah, sure!

We had a problem with drinking water, but not sure what day this dilemma reared its ugly head; probably Sunday morning. As I mentioned long ago in this chapter, water had to be trucked in. In two days, 3,000 reenactors, plus nearly 200 horses, had used up 6,000 gallons of water. Take away the water used for cooking, washing dishes, and what the horses drank, and you have about a gallon per man, woman, and child. Not that big a deal you say, but since this was the hot month of August, the reenactors sucked down a lot of water.

In his morning speech before the Brigade, brigadier Shackleford mentioned the water issue. He seemed to insinuate that the event sponsor/ host was falling asleep on the job and doing the event a great disservice by not keeping up with the demands of the reenactors. As a member of Holmes Brigade, I felt Wilson's Creek was our backyard baby, so for Shackleford to make those comments was like a slap in our face. God knows that not every Civil War event is perfect, even the ones out east. When you get thousands of reenactors in one place, not everyone is going to be happy. Some snafus are bound to take place. It's best to just go with the flow and don't sweat the small stuff. By the way, the Western Brigade only comes to Missouri maybe once a decade.

In order to get back on our good side, to be a pal to all of us, Shackleford promised he would not let any of us drill hard until we had water. He was lodging a formal complaint and he would not play ball until the water came. Just as he finished his remarks, Isaacson said, "We don't want another LBL on our hands," or words to that effect. I gave Jon an elbow, but he was voicing the same disgust we all felt. Here was Shackleford, bitching about water when only five months ago, at Land Between the Lakes, we were in exactly the same situation with supply problems and lack of available drinking water.

We had one final lunch before our date with destiny up on Bloody Hill. I invited John Maki and Randy Rogers over to sup with me at my tent. Not sure if it was this meal or one earlier. Whatever the case, at one meal they agreed to break bread with me. And so it was, the three of us at my folding table, eating cold cut sandwiches smeared with a generous portion of Grey Poupon and gassing about the latest fashions from New York or if the upcoming battle would award any of us a medal.

Right after lunch, and just before First Call, I wandered past the company street and saw Charlie Pautler lounging inside his A tent in a state of melancholy. He'd been noticeably absent during most of the day on Saturday, especially during the battle. He'd complained of a sore wrist, brought about by his own foolishness outside a liquor store, which I've already talked about. When I asked Charlie if he was going to participate in the battle today, he said he didn't feel like it. At first I didn't understand the severity of his wrist injury. I thought it only a minor sprain, but I guess after he got home and had it examined and he'd actually chipped a bone.

I'll admit I wasn't very sympathetic. I told him he would be letting me down if he didn't come out with us. I said, "It's Bloody Hill, for God's sake!" Charlie continued to whine and I continued to plead until finally he reluctantly said, 'OK." He agreed to play with us, but I doubt if he did much shooting, probably none at all. I didn't want him to sit in his tent and pout. Once again, I didn't understand the severity of his wrist injury till much later.

A little while later we were up on Bloody Hill, actually about fifty yards back or so from the crest. Shackleford had marched us the long way around and had us halted along the trail so he could deliver a pep talk. Once our columns had halted, he wanted us to us to undouble our lines. Normally, when marching in column, we are in ranks of four men abreast. When the order to face FRONT is given, the men turn left, undouble, and present a line of battle of two ranks. What the brigadier was asking was that the men turn into column, but only with two men abreast.

I was new at this game and in the past, Holmes Brigade officers would shout, "Without doubling, right face," if they wanted the men to turn into columns of two. There is a specific order for this and it is simply to order "Right Face." If you say, "Company, Right Face," then the fours will develop. Being new to command, I was ignorant of the nuances of this particular facing movement and Shackleford was there to ream my ass in front of the entire battalion. I felt the heat rise to my face as he sat there on his horse talking down to me as if I were a child. I never thought about this possibility before now, but maybe it was payback for the LBL comment Isaacson had made that morning. A general would never verbally abuse a common soldier, but he could give the man's commanding officer, me, an earful. All Shackleford needed was some minor excuse to go off. This was his chance to be the big man on campus, in my biased opinion.

After the tirade was complete, we were ordered forward to the brow of the hill where we wheeled into a line of battle stretching nearly "a quarter-mile," but I exaggerate of course. 1st Battalion was on the left of the line and 2nd Battalion was on the right. Facing us, down a gentle slope about one hundred yards away, were the massed ranks of our foe. Within moments of forming our lines, the enemy opened the ballgame by throwing out the first pitch. Their artillery guns spat out clouds of smoke, but it took about a full second for the sound to reach our ears. Human scarecrows toting squirrel guns, shotguns, or captured Federal rifles added to the noise and smoke of the general mayhem of the moment. The gentle summer breeze was throwing that sulfur smoke, that "rotten egg smell," back on the foe or drifting to the spectator lines to the rear. The Federal artillery guns were located between the battalions and on either flank. As soon as the Confederate guns began barking, our own guns started answering back. Our lines were partially hidden within a tree line while the scarecrows were parked on open ground.

Battalion commander Chuck Warnick was giving the command to fire by companies. With this method, each company would volley fire from right to left. However, 1st Company would fire first, followed by 3rd, the 5th, then 2nd, 4th, and finally 6th. This way one flank would not be totally exposed. If the firing went 1-2-3, and so on down the line, one flank would be exposed and susceptible to attack by the enemy. By volley firing by every other company, at least one company in that flank would have loaded muskets in case of surprise.

So I was in the rear, with all the other officers. I had to watch for Maki, who as 1st Company commander fired his guns first. Then I had to repeat the order to fire to my men in 3rd Company. I had to be ever watchful if the men needed help or if the Battlion Commander had something to say, because he was losing his voice. Chuck Warnick had been croaking all weekend and now his voice sounded like Granny's old rocking chair. I knew the men would not be able to hear him. So when Chuck announced we would fire by battalion, meaning "every swinging dick" would shoot at once, I had to watch him and as his lips moved, I added my own gruff voice like a ventriloquist to its dummy. **"FIRE!"** We fired by battalion at least a dozen times and each time I helped Chuck Warnick by adding my own voice to the chorus.

After nearly three-quarters of an hour, it was time for the final tragic act of this melodrama-the death of Lyon. Old buddy, Chuck Counts, from the 1st Colorado, agreed to enact this sorrowful moment of the Battle of Wilson's Creek. Chuck looks so much like the fiery Union general it's almost scary. He already has the fiery red beard and when he gets mad, or has had too much popskull; his face has a tendency to get as flushed as a lobster. I've known Chuck Counts since 1981 and I can attest to some of his famous bouts with the bottle or a can of Schaeffers lager.

At a designated cue, Chuck Counts came out on a fine stallion, rode between the two battalions of infantrymen, brandished his gleaming saber in a posture of defiance, then promptly tumbled from the saddle as an "enemy ball struck him dead."

The horror! Nathaniel Lyon struck down before our very eyes!

With that act, we Union boys slowly drifted to the rear. The enemy pressed forward and began coming up the slope towards us. Finally, the order was given for us to shoulder arms, form column, and march off the field. But when we left Bloody Hill, were we feeling depressed and sad? Not a bit! In fact we felt gay and happy. The last visible memory I have is when our battalion led the march back to camp with a rousing chorus of Gay and Happy Still, a song popular among Union troops at the time of Wilson's Creek:

We are the boys so gay and happy, wheresoe'r we may be, if at home, or on camp duty, 'tis the same, we're always free.

So let the wide world wag as it will, we'll be gay and happy still, gay and happy, gay and happy, we'll be gay and happy still!

CHAPTER ELEVEN

The Muddiest Event

Even as I compose this memoir, I find it hard to believe that I've been in this hobby 25 years. Two and a half decades running around in wool, blowing cartridges, eating poorly cooked food, and sleeping out of doors. During those years, which began in 1980, I have been to all four corners of Missouri, eastern Kansas, northern Arkansas, plus I've been to Mississippi, Louisiana, Tennessee, Kentucky, Virginia, Pennsylvania, and Georgia. While attending Civil War reenactments within these states, I've suffered through the strangest weather conditions from extreme heat at Mansassas, Virginia, to extreme cold at Franklin, Tennessee.

While in Jefferson City, MO, during a 1984 Civil War encampment, I experienced the wettest weather possible when the camps were bombarded with rain for nearly 24 hours straight. The only saving grace was we were located within a grassy park area and not in a muddy field.

Speaking of muddy fields, which is the subject of this chapter, some chaps will proudly proclaim the honor of the muddiest event in history rests with a 1997 Shiloh, Tennessee event. I was unable to attend that early April event, but I have heard the horror stories from those that went. No sir, my first experience with an ocean of mud came a few short weeks after the reenactment at Wilson's Creek in August.

After the Lexington reenactment of mid-September, Holmes Brigade was invited to participate in a MCWRA maximum effort event, in the boot heel of Missouri, where the November 7, 1861, battle of Belmont was fought.

Belmont was the first engagement for a new brigadier general named Ulysses S. Grant. He'd been given his star in July and had spent the interim, prior to Belmont, in whipping his brigade in combat readiness.

During the late summer and autumn of 1861, the state of Missouri was being threatened in the south and west by Confederate general Sterling Price (Carthage, Wilson's Creek, and Lexington); while in the southeast another threat was taking shape in the form of several thousand confederates under Leonidas Polk. General Polk and his men were just across the Mississippi River on the heights above Columbus, Kentucky, seemingly just waiting on the word to invade Missouri.

The commander of Union forces in the Department of Missouri at this time was John C. Fremont, the great pathfinder himself. He sent Grant and his brigade to Belmont. Grant's job was to be seen by the enemy, a "demonstration of force" if you will. If Polk saw a strong Union force in the area, he would think twice about sending his people across the river.

Polk thought Grant's brigade only a decoy, perhaps bait for a much larger Union force. Under this assumption, Polk dispatched Gideon Pillow to "brush aside this minor annoyance."

What began as minor skirmishing soon evolved into a four-hour engagement with both sides giving and taking their best shots. Grant had a horse shot out from under him, but remained cool and calm throughout the ordeal. Pillow's Confederates yielded ground first, but the Union soldiers made the mistake of celebrating too soon. Shells from Columbus soon came across the river and turned these jubilant Yankee soldiers into frightened children.

Subordinate officers under Grant suggested surrender, but he quickly "pooh-poohed" that idea. Instead the brigade fought their way to the river and effected a brilliant escape aboard waiting transport vessels.

Though Grant's retreat from Belmont was considered a Confederate victory, the ground was considered worthless by the victors. It did put Grant in the public eye as a general who was not afraid to take risks or fight.

Once again, another bastardized version of a history. There are several books on U.S. Grant, many which talk about the battle of Belmont in better detail that my meager attempt. My brief sketch was edited from an old Holmes Brigade Dispatch.

No trip through the boot heel of Missouri is complete unless you stop for dinner at LAMBERT'S FAMILY RESTUARANT in the town of Sikeston. This eatery is famous for laying out the grub in mass quantities and I think one of the signs out front states that "if you go home hungry, it's your own fault." Lambert's is best known for throwing dinner rolls at you. They're constantly running the oven to bake dozens upon dozens of heavenly dinner rolls and every few minutes, one of the employees will pitch one at you if you call for one. You better have good hands because they'll toss them clear across the room.

On this trip, I believe I rode with Pat McCarthy, Jon Isaacson, and Don Whitson in Pat's van. We had a hearty meal at Lambert's that included playing catch with the aforementioned dinner rolls.

The October 26-27 reenactment of Belmont was held on the original site, which meant it was on a flood plain next to the Mississippi River. I'll wager that during the spring and summer months most of the land is under water. From the look of the property, it appeared as if the tide had just receded. A narrow gravel road bisected an ocean of mud. There was a bit of vegetation, some trees, and one or two areas of high ground, but where the camp was set up that weekend, was on a quivering quagmire of brown ooze.

It was a real challenge setting up the tents in the mud. It was like asking a toothless man to bite and hold onto a turkey leg. The ankle deep mud did not have much of a bite and after a short time the tent stakes would pop out. The sponsor did provide tons of straw, but most of it was wet. Nevertheless, several bales were busted, with the loose straw scattered about so we'd have some sort of carpet to walk on. However, it was not a good idea to stand in one place too long otherwise you might sink.

A smarter man would have laid wooden slats or branches around the camp to walk on, which in Civil War jargon is referred to "corduroying."

But we did not have the time to scour the woods for planking material, nor were we smart, so we made due with the straw. After about an hour, the straw sank into the mud and we'd have to put down even more.

I think we had to provide our own rations so it's likely the guys coughed up a few bucks for beans, bacon, and coffee. The sponsor did provide an all-you-can-eat fish fry one night. Don't know if this was Friday or Saturday night. But with the ground wet and a constant drizzle in the air, I don't know whether the boys had the stomach to eat more than two or three plates apiece.

The skies dried up long enough for us to march around and burn powder, but the clouds remained dirty all weekend. Rain fell off and on in annoying drizzle. Just enough to rewet the ankle deep mud that was our constant enemy. I don't know how the Confederates fared, but they must have been going through the same trials with Mother Nature as we were.

Damp weather is no friend to the rifled musket, because when they are outside in the elements, they become rust magnets. Unless the gun parts are quickly wiped free of moisture, orange-red boils will develop overnight. Then you must find a way to get the rust off. Nothing will incur the wrath of an inspecting officer more than spying a musket with rust on it.

Saturday morning, after the skies had dried up, First Sergeant Randy Rogers took the company up on some high ground where he proceeded to demonstrate how to get the rust off muskets by using ashes from a dead campfire.

With a dampened rag, Randy picked up a small bit of blackened ash and rubbed it into a spot of rust on a musket. In moments, the rust disappeared! WOW! The rest of us quickly went to work dipping into the ashes and rubbing at all the orange spots we found. For about a half-hour we labored, till Randy finally inspected everyone and declared to Captain Don that everyone's musket looked ship-shape. This was the first school of instruction as taught by Randy Rogers.

At one point during the weekend, about fifty of us reenactors went across the river into Columbus, Kentucky. We boarded a square-shaped barge pusher. I had a flashback to my Navy days when I was boatswain's mate third class and driving the Captain's gig around Tokyo Bay. I had also spent many a watch on the bridge of the USS Oklahoma City, spinning the big wheel that drove the huge cruiser through the Taiwan Straits. During a run from Japan to the Philippine Islands, I was called upon to work the engine order telegraph, an apparatus that sends signals to the engine room, so the speed of the propellers can be increased or decreased.

As the barge pusher putt-putt-putted across the Mississippi, I got all glassy-eyed and went into a hypnotic trance. I began shouting: "All ahead two-thirds, right standard rudder," or I acted like I had a Boatswain's pipe screeching out commands to "All hands on deck, set the special sea and anchor detail," or "contact off the starboard bow, bearing 035 degrees, hull down!'"

Everyone must have thought I was nuts, but for a brief time I thought I was back aboard the 'Okie boat,' in my white jumper, bell-bottom pants, and my white Dixie cup hat. I could almost feel the sting of salt coming off those waves. My illusion was shattered when I realized the salt was coming off the sweaty and pudgy face of Randy Rogers.

We left the shores of Missouri still under a storm cloud. As I had mentioned, it had rained off and on the whole time. Mud was everywhere and in everyone's pores. Once we stepped ashore into Kentucky, it was like entering the Garden of Eden. The heavens seemed to open up, the sun came from behind the clouds, birds sang, flowers opened up, and young girls frolicked on the green grass like nymphs.

Our stay was to be a brief one as we had come over to inspect the old Confederate earthworks. This was where artillery shells had been fired and went all the way across the mile wide expanse of dirty water to strike at Grant and his lads over on the Missouri side. I believe this portion of Columbus had been made into a State Park. I remember it was well manicured and the leaves of the trees were already turning lovely shades of orange, yellow, and red. There was also one or two very pretty Kentucky lasses who smiled our way.

After about an hour, we had to go back aboard the barge boat. No sooner had the barge touched back down on the Missouri side then the sun went back into hiding and the drizzle began anew. I swear it was like stepping through a door from sunshine and warmth to mud and misery (get it, Missouri ha-ha). That trip across the river to Kentucky was like stepping into the Garden of Eden. We had sampled the Food of the Gods, now we were back in reality with the bitter fruit that Missouri had vomited out for us. I sighed like a man who has loved and lost.

Just because we didn't like our surroundings was no excuse not to support the event. In the actual Civil War, do you think the soldiers fought in perfect weather all the time? Hell, no! So we got rained on a little bit! So we got our feet muddied up, too! The MCWRA and the powers that ran Belmont behind the scenes had banked on a battle reenactment. Unless the rain was coming down like Noah's flood or we were carried away by a mudslide, we were obligated to fulfill our contract as "actors." A wise man once said, "The show must go on."

The reason I mention this or act like it was a Holy Crusade to reenact the battle in the mud was because two of our members staged a "sit-in." Jon Isaacson and Don Whitson thought it ridiculous to tramp around in ankle deep mud just to blow cartridges back and forth just so a few people under umbrellas could get a little amusement. Don especially complained the loudest by stating that he had just bought some new duds from Joe Covais and he was damned if he wanted them soiled. Jesus Christmas!

Don had lately become concerned with his appearance as a Civil War soldier. He had been buying a lot of original stuff, as well as, the top grade in reproduction merchandise. Don spent a lot of money of this stuff, which is one of the reasons why his marriage became strained. His wife couldn't understand his obsession. Quite frankly, I couldn't understand it either. It's only a damn hobby!

Anyway, when it came time to go out for the afternoon battle, both Jon and Don complained and whined until Captain Don said "to hell with them." Of course I knew in my heart that the weather was too lousy to play around in, but I went out anyway. I knew it was the right thing to do.

I think a light drizzle was falling. The only time we didn't feel water falling from the heavens was for a few brief moments, plus when we went to Kentucky. Many reenactors assume that rain follows reenactors. We have been rained on many times- Champions Hill, Fort Scott, Jefferson City, etc. But at Belmont, it was more about the mud.

We began a march on a gravel road, and then peeled off into a sodden cornfield. Some artillery pieces belched close by and a few rounds of musket fire sounded. As at Champions Hill 1983, the drizzle held the gun smoke low to the ground like a fog. Instead of dissipating, the smoke seemed to be sucked down into the mud.

The artillery pieces had not arrived on the field drawn by horse. Tractors had ferried them to their present location and tractors would have to pull them out once the reenactment was concluded. Crisscrossing the field were stretches of tractor tracks, some leaving trenches nearly a foot deep.

Mud was thrown up by cavalry as they trotted past. The hooves from these horses threw up huge globs of the putrid brown stuff the size of cantaloupes. One group of Federal horsemen that we saw riding past was none other than "US GRANT" and his staff. *I don't believe Marty Brazil played "Grant" at this event. Marty Brazil had played the general at the Champions Hill and Shiloh events during the 1980's. He might have hung up his beard and cigar by the 1990's.*

During the trek through the mud, several boys thought they might drown or have the shoes sucked right off their feet. John Maki told me that the bottom of his boot came right off. The sole of John's boot had been pegged and sewn, but the mud was like wet concrete or glue. *"Next second,"* John says, *"it was like walking with a leather sleeve around my leg. My stocking foot stuck right out of the bottom."* John further states that he rooted around in the goo to find the lost sole, but his hands came up brown and empty. His sock became so caked with mud that it was as thick as his boot had been.

I don't think anybody took a hit during this fight. Who would want to lie in the mud? A fellow might have gotten swallowed up, never to be seen again!

After a little more than half an hour, the game was called. The few spectators who had braved this foul weather had already begun to limp to the warm confines of their cars. We crawled out of the muck up to the gravel road where we paused to shake the stuff off our lower legs as best we could, and then we stomped and shivered our way back to camp, our cars, and dry clothes.

This event was replayed in 1993, but for some reason I did not return. Maybe I had grown tired of the long drive through the boot heel of Missouri or maybe I had had enough of wallowing in the mud like a hog. Those that went in '93 complained of similar muddy conditions so I didn't miss much.

So this chapter concludes on what many consider the muddiest event in Holmes Brigade history. No longer is this event called by its correct name. Whenever it is spoken of, the event in southern Missouri is called, "BEL-MUD!"

CHAPTER TWELVE

We Fight Under the Flag

In hindsight, 1992, was not that special of a year. There were only a couple outstanding moments at a few events, including two changes within Holmes Brigade, a near riot at Fort Scott, a near knife fight in Kentucky, and a brief shining moment under stadium lights. Nineteen ninety-two got off on a sour note right off the bat with the arrival of the January Holmes Brigade Dispatch.

It should be noted that Aaron Racine had been editing the Dispatch for nearly two years, from his dorm room in Stanford University. He was working on a degree in law (I may have mentioned that in a much earlier chapter). Despite the fact he was over burdened with a mountain of legal textbooks and fraternity parties, Aaron volunteered to assume newsletter duties after Bill Fannin retired. Regardless of these good intentions, Aaron was plagued by the ineptness of the US Postal Service. In an explanatory note he attached to the January newsletter, he said that the post office lost 170 newsletters. He further explained that the amount of money *that went down the drain*, due to this SNAFU, was about $90.

In the three years Dave Bennett and I edited the Western Campaigner, I had similar problems with lost newsletters. Ours were sent by bulk mail, or at a fourth class rate, while Aaron mailed the Holmes Brigade Dispatch at First Class rates. Losing 170 newsletters in the mail was not what got Aaron in hot water with the membership of Holmes Brigade. What got everybody's panties in a bunch was Aaron's use of a four-letter word in the newsletter.

I told you about Randy Rogers and how he reminded every one of "Mongo," from the movie <u>Blazing Saddles</u>. In one scene from that movie, local townsmen are in the saloon talking about Louis Pasteur and his cure for anthrax, when one of the men interrupts the other by saying, "*Never mind that shit, it's Mongo!*" We did the same thing whenever we spied Randy Rogers lumbering towards us. He usually had just come out of a porta-john, no coat on, suspenders hanging loose, and a white shirt plastered wet with sweat. Randy is the only man I've ever known who can sweat in the winter. One of Bag Ladies would interrupt the conversation by saying, "*Never mind that shit, it's Randy.*" He would just smile that crooked broke tooth smile of his just before swallowing you in his beefy arms.

So we used that tired phrase over and over until one day, in the January 1992 newsletter, Aaron used it in the opening article of the newsletter. "*Never mind that shit, its a few words from Captain Don*". Yes, this was Captain Don Strother's monthly report on previous and upcoming events and Aaron soured things by using a four-letter word.

Most of the old grannies in the Holmes Brigade (mostly those from St. Louis) were shocked by Aaron's use of profanity in their sacred newsletter. You'd think someone had just farted in church or waved their nuts at a nun. At the Fort Scott spring muster in May, the public outcry rose to a fever pitch. It was like a scene from a Frankenstein movie just before the villagers stormed the castle. Aaron, thankfully, was absent from this abuse. He was still at Stanford, but I'm sure he felt the shock waves that came his way from the Holmes Brigade earthquake. Whether it was because of his "slip of the pen" or his college workload, Aaron soon resigned as newsletter editor and the task fell on Jon Isaacson.

It recently came to light and unbeknownst by me, that Jon Isaacson himself had been the author of this coup to upset AJ from his editorial throne. This revelation does not surprise me, as Jon always seemed more than casually motivated by the politics within the hobby.

It was at Fort Scott that I came to the conclusion that I would turn my stripes in. I had been a sergeant for exactly ten years, beginning way back in 1982 when I 'banged my own drum' to get myself elected to 3rd Sergeant. This was followed by a couple of years as 2nd Sergeant and two years as 1st Sergeant. Back in '82 I think I was power hungry and viewed the extra stripe as a badge of honor. I also thought the boys would respect me more if I wore those stripes. As time went along, I think the boys showed a margin of tolerance toward me and I didn't try to step on anyone's toes by being too pushy or being a martinet.

As time went along, and especially during the two years as 1st Sergeant, I discovered there was more to being a noncom that just taking roll and standing next to the captain during formation. I began to doubt myself. Perhaps I was not the only one getting tired of the same old same old. That's why I didn't put up much of a fuss when I was pushed aside by Randy Rogers in 1991.

Ten years is a long time for any one person to occupy a ranking position in Holmes Brigade. Dick Stauffer was aware of that when he stepped aside as captain in '87. I remember once telling Dick that I was considering stepping down as a NCO. This may have been right after Dick resigned. Dick told me that Holmes Brigade needed stability and that I was one of the vital cogs in the organization. He said never to doubt I; that's a job for the boys to do on Election Day.

On the tenth anniversary of my ascension to sergeant, I thought the time was right to step aside and rejoin the ranks as a private. Holmes Brigade was continuing to grow with many capable lads with fresh ideas. Plus, I found it hard to get enough time off from work to participate in many of the fine events that were scheduled.

During the Holmes Brigade business meeting, I calmly announced that after ten proud years, I would step aside and allow another to assume the rank of sergeant. I was slightly embarrassed that at the conclusion of my speech, the boys all stood up and gave me a rousing ovation followed by a firm handclasp and well wishes. Following my announcement, I took the back stairs out of the barracks, and hid my mixed emotions in the privacy of my dog tent.

The very next afternoon, right after the last drill of the day, I requested a ceremony in front of the entire company in which my stripes were cut from my jacket. In a scene that reminded one of a court-martial, I faced the company while John Maki and another soldier (Steve Hall?) sliced those chevrons off with a pocketknife. Another bitter sweat moment that left me misty eyed. Three months later, I was once again overwhelmed with emotion when I was presented with a plaque which complimented me on ten years of outstanding service with Holmes Brigade. If the boys didn't respect me, at least they liked me a lot.

Going back to Saturday night, after I left the Holmes Brigade election/ business meeting to do my own meditating, it is my understanding that a near riot took place. The topic of discussion concerned the recent Butler event that we'd had in April. This was an MCWRA affair and similar to one we'd had in 1986. However, this year we were camped within a stone's throw from the county rodeo.

To say this was a dog and pony show would be an understatement. The highlight of the weekend was the brother and sister musical act known as Frank and Mean Mary James. This duo could pluck guitar strings and belt out folk songs, but it was Mean Mary's singing talent that drew the crowd. That and her D cups. Mean Mary was supposedly twelve years old, but she had a rack on her that rivaled Jayne Mansfield. At the advice of her mother/manager, Mean Mary sometimes wore a heavy greatcoat, but it did little to disguise her ballistics and only made the dirty old men in Holmes Brigade (Jon Isaacson) drool even more.

I'm making a long story longer, but getting back to the heated argument regarding Butler, I had vacated the infantry barracks after my resignation as sergeant, but I heard later that a discussion was brought up about the Confederates shooting their guns in the Union camp. I told you about this episode in an earlier chapter; when we were rudely awakened by this Confederate alarm clock at about 6 AM. I guess this was only one of several complaints the boys of Holmes had about the Confederates and the MCWRA in general.

I think David Kesinger was one of the sponsors of the Butler event or at least he was on the MCWRA board at this time. While many in Holmes Brigade were thinking of distancing themselves from the MCWRA, Kesinger was like an unofficial salesman for the association and kept saying they weren't all that bad. As for the unsafe episodes at Butler, Kesinger is quoted as saying, *"It was all in fun and nobody got hurt."*

From what Isaacson later told me, he said after Kesinger made that glib remark, Dave Bennett just about went berserk and threatened Kesinger with bodily harm. I think Dave was able to restrain his emotions otherwise he might have faced manslaughter charges. Remember that I heard this after the fact, but I believe this was another straw that was pushing Holmes Brigade further and further away from future dealings with the MCWRA. We were just tired of the bullshit and unsafe silliness. This is just further conformation on why we decided early on to limit ourselves to only a few maximum events. We would support the state of Missouri whenever possible, but we were no longer going to attend every 'sock washing' event as in years past. In all honesty, we were better than that and we felt the citizens of Missouri deserved a quality showing of dedicated living historians and not a bunch of gun-toting yahoos!

A week after Fort Scott there was a big Western Brigade event in Georgia, but because of my vacation restraints, I was unable to go. In mid-August, there was the motion picture *Gettysburg*, which drew several thousand reenactors to play as extras. Unfortunately, one had to commit to one full week of being on the set. Again, I did not have enough vacation time available to "throw away" on yet another movie. In 1992, there were events from Fort Riley, Kansas, to Glorietta Pass, New Mexico, and from Gettysburg to Langley, Oklahoma. As much as I desired to attend some of these events, I just could not justify taking the time off from work to go.

In the meantime, I attended a few events including Glasgow, MO, on the weekend of August 1-2, 1992. This was Ralph Monaco's first event (mentioned in greater detail in the chapter, Fresh Fish). This was where I received the plaque honoring me on ten years and it's also where Jon Isaacson got ripped for individual cooking (also in the chapter Fresh Fish).

This year, we were camped in a pasture outside of town. The generic three-ring circus occurred between the Blue and the Gray forces as Ringmaster Sonny Wells provided an unwelcome narrative over a bullhorn. *"Ladies, Gentleman, and children of all ages! If I can direct your attention to the Union soldiers marching through the cow pies."* When the artillery starting banging away, Sonny told the audience to look for the "big donut holes", or the smoke rings coming from the guns. Throughout the half-hour duel, Sonny attempted to wow the crowd like some kind of snake oil salesman. To give Sonny credit, he is passionate about the Civil War, but he could have done without the soapbox and the play-by-play with the bullhorn.

In late September, we returned again to another exciting Pilot Knob. This may have been the one in which Ralph nearly burned himself alive when he fell asleep next to the fire pit.

Oct 11-13, 1992, Perryville, KY

Here was one event I wanted to return to, so I took a four-day weekend and traveled back to the Blue Grass State with Isaacson and Steve Hall; the three of us were traveling with Pat McCarthy in his van.

This was one of those 'you have to provide your own rations and do your own cooking' events. I was still unused to cooking, so I asked Steve to pick me up some salami snacks and jerky from FRITZ'S MEAT MARKET. I included some odd stuff from the grocery store like a round loaf of sourdough bread and some 'dead things from the sea.' The sourdough bread was a little bit bigger than a grapefruit, but I got it squeezed into my Mexican War knapsack along with everything else. I may have had some cocoa mix and maybe some instant oatmeal, as well. Really eating authentic, wasn't I? I just wasn't comfortable with frying salt pork or using a skillet at all. Come to think of it, I don't believe I owned a skillet until 1994.

I believe we left Friday morning and drove till darkness settled over us. Pat drove all the way and we parked in a fenced-in lot about three miles from the park. All the Western Brigade boys had decided to park for the night in this lot and we would all march, come sunup, the three miles to the battlefield site.

I remember Isaacson and I tried to sleep in the back of Pat's SUV. We had to sleep in a fetal position, as there just wasn't enough room to fully stretch out. I think Pat slept in his driver's seat and Steve might have slept outdoors. Quite a number of the Western Brigade boys slept on the ground that Friday night, right next to their parked cars. It was too dark to see much other than the headlights of other cars coming through. I didn't want to get run over during the night and I was in no hurry to get bit by chiggers.

After wolfing down a few breakfast bars and a variety of other cold substitutes, the Western Brigade was finally assembled for the early morning stroll along the paved road to the park. It took us the better part of an hour to cover the three miles. To say that many of the lads spent a restless night and started out with less than fresh spirits would be an understatement. Everyone was weighted down with knapsacks or blanket rolls, bulging haversacks, and twelve-pound muskets. By the time we arrived at the battlefield site, we were worn out.

We'd barely set foot on the Perryville State Battlefield, when what should come to our ears, but the sound of a brass band. Yes, we had arrived just in time to take part in a Union memorial service. All the Union reenactors, save for us Western boys, had camped inside the park. These lads were already in place at parade rest and looked at us late arrivals like we were tardy little schoolchildren. This memorial service would have been more enjoyable if we hadn't just finished a three-mile hike, still had our knapsacks on, and the speechifying hadn't lasted the better part of a full hour. By the time the political 'windbags' had finished wagging their tongues, most of us Western Brigade boys were bent over like old men.

After this episode, we were allowed to drop our packs and ease our aching shoulders for a spell. We were in an area we incorrectly assumed was our bivouac for the night. Once given the order to rest, we flopped down on our backsides and started looking for something to nibble on. I tore into a couple of salami snacks and bit a hunk out of the sourdough bread. The rest of the two hundred or so Western Brigade boys were in a state of repose, when we received word that a photographer wanted to capture our image. This was the same fellow who took our photo five years ago at the 125th anniversary Shiloh reenactment. He stood atop a thirty-foot stepladder and used a camera that took a wrap-around photograph. It was like the camera was mechanized with the shutter remaining open while it pivoted in an arc and took a panoramic picture. For a small fee, we each could own a copy of the picture. I have one here around the house somewhere. It arrived in the mailbox rolled in a tube and measured about 12" x 36". One can clearly see that Randy Rogers and I were doing obscene things with the salami.

While we lolly-gagged and got grass stains on our butts, the officers had themselves a meeting with the result being we should drill some. So we worked the kinks out our legs for the better part of an hour. This was followed by a brisk jaunt into the woods to take part in a hot powder-burning contest with Johnny Reb. This was one of several scripted skirmishes in which we formed lines in the dense woods and shot back and forth at shadows. I don't think artillery was used in this fight. I recall we did a lot of firing and then we were obligated to fall back.

By this time, it was mid-afternoon. We were told Holmes Brigade would occupy a length of ground on either side of a wooden rail fence. Some guys had brought dog tents, while most of us made due with ground cloths and gum blankets. I was planning on sharing a piece of real estate with Isaacson, so the two of us combined our gum blankets, making a lean-to. Another couple of gum blankets were spread inside. A light mist/rain was starting to fall, so we placed our lean-to as close to the ground as possible, leaving only two inches of open space to crawl under.

Once our temporary refugee camp was set up to some satisfaction, it was discovered there was no firewood close at hand. Lieutenant John Maki ordered a detail to go forage for some wood and I quickly became part of this detail. Here is where the story gets interesting.

No firewood was left for the 5th Battalion, and foragers were sent to procure some. A detail went in one direction, when suddenly, coming up the trail, was a wagon loaded with wood. A swarm of blue bellies converged on that wagon like hungry locust. However, on the wagon seat sat two Rebel scarecrows, one old fellow and a younger one. When they saw the blue tidal wave coming at them, the scarecrows got alarmed and looked as if they were going to wet themselves. The old fellow said the firewood was already claimed for the Confederate camp and we Yankees had best not bother it. The younger fellow also had hurtful words for us, plus he made the mistake of waving a boot knife our way. Did he think he could take all of us with his pig sticker?

Terry Forsyth, Jack Williamson, and I were so hot about the whole business, we went back to camp, got our bayonets, and followed the young pup and the wagon nearly all the way to the Confederate camp. About half way down the hill, we thought we'd better about face and return to our own lines. The Confederate camp had a strength of about three thousand and we didn't think they'd take too kindly to three Yankees chasing a kinsman with bayonets. Instead, the incident was reported to the Park Ranger and Mr. Bowie Knife spent the night in jail. Eventually we found some firewood somewhere and I had my hot cocoa.

Sunday started with a Grand Review, followed by a knapsack inspection, and then, after the noon meal, we had the all-important battle. I don't remember the first two activities, although I'll not deny they probably took place. I do remember the last activity, because it's where I handed out free safety instructions.

During the Sunday afternoon battle, I was on the far left of the Holmes Brigade company, as a corporal. I don't know why I stitched on the two stripes for this Perryville event, although at the time I probably had a reason. Actually, I was nothing more than a private, having returned to the ranks after Fort Scott. Whatever reason compelled me to slap on those stripes, I was a corporal right then and there with my place in line on the far left.

In the winter issue of the Holmes Brigade Dispatch, Steve Hall wrote an after action report of the Sunday afternoon episode. It pretty much sums up the highlights of my tirade to a better degree than any humble explanation I could muster.

"It seems that when the right division of the battalion adjusted the battle line to angle to the right, one of the companies obliqued toward the right, but did not come into line with the others."

What Steve is saying is, the company to our left did not move up and align themselves shoulder to shoulder with us. They were about ten yards to our left rear.

Because this other company was not perfectly aligned with ours, it seemed as if their guns were going off right in my ear.

Again, I was on the far left on the line. Just behind me, at an angle only a few yards away, was the other company. What got me riled was the first corporal, of this other company, seemed to be firing rounds that had 120 grains of black powder. Every time he fired that gun, I thought my left eardrum would burst.

"Whatcha shootin' over thar, Whitson torpedoes?"

Don Whitson was notorious for over stuffing his paper cartridges with as much black powder as he could squeeze into it. When Don fired his gun, it usually sounded like thunder and made the other boys curse him. Here, in this other company, we had found Don's twin. This was a fellow who also liked a loud bang. Problem was most of that bang was going off in my ear.

I turned around and screamed obscenities at this guy, but he did not react or perhaps he was already deaf. I remember begging, pleading, and cursing to the company officers that they'd be better served if they aligned themselves with us. But those pleas drew no response. In the meantime, the man continued to BANG away like the dull clod he appeared to be and my left eardrum continued to ache.

Steve says it was interesting to note *"the spit shooting from his* [Bob's] *powder blackened lips, the twisted, contorted, angry face, the foam drooling from one side of his mouth. It reminded me when we had to shoot that one pard after he got bit by a mad dog* [a joke no doubt].

After a spell, I seriously thought about butt stroking the bastard, until much to my relief, the fellow drew a cartridge marked with black paint *(indicating he was to take a casualty)*. The fellow did a swan dive to Mother Earth and my eardrums were allowed to heal.

Right after the battle, the Western Brigade boys decided to march off the field directly for the parking lot-three miles away. We'd barely had time to catch our breaths after the hot, ear-shattering escapade with Johnny Reb, when the commander (Dave Shackleford) ordered us out on the road.

After a sleepless night under less than ideal conditions, bad and poorly cooked food, several drills, and a run through the forest blowing cartridges, Shackleford expected us "dogfaces" to still have a little spring in our step. About "a quarter mile" from the parking lot, it was suggested that the rest of the distance could best be covered if we all ran at the double quick. I said, *"Screw that!"* A few of the sad sacks took off at a trot, but I knew Pat McCarthy was not going to drive off with out me. As a matter of fact, Pat was just as tired as the rest of us and was in no mood to go into cardiac arrest just to prove he was a "macho man".

Dec 13, 1992, Kansas City, MO

Two years earlier, my family and I thought it would be a cool idea if we supported the local football team, the Kansas City Chiefs. In 1989, after nearly twenty years of mediocrity, the team owner, Lamar Hunt, hired a gung-ho general manager, who in turn hired an equally gung-ho and compassionate head coach. The combination of these two determined individuals, it was hoped, could return the Kansas City Chiefs football club to those glory years of the 1960's and quite possibly, a repeat of Super Bowl glory of 1969.

Football tickets were not easy to sell back in the seventies and eighties. Most fans in Kansas City were infatuated with the baseball team, the Royals. In a ten year period from about 1976 to 1986, the Kansas City Royals won several division titles and made two trips to the World Series, winning one out of two.

Mona and I attended many baseball games during this time period, but I can only remember attended a football game once. Despite the fact Arrowhead stadium was in the same complex and just across the parking lot, I hardly knew it existed. Arrowhead could hold nearly 78,000 people, but it rarely drew more than 20,000 a game. The team rarely finished better than last in its division. A couple of years it went 2-12, another year 4-10. Generally, it finished 8-8.

A series of inept roster moves, poor drafting, and five different head coaches in less than fifteen years, was one reason why fans shied away from football. The other reason was the Royals were just so damn good, plus they had a future Baseball Hall of Famer on its team by the name of George Brett.

But by 1989, the Royals were beginning to struggle. The manager who had guided them to the World Series prize in 1985 had died of cancer. A player was promoted from within the ranks to assume the job, some high profile trades were made, but the Royals were never able to recapture the magic of the seventies and early eighties. Meanwhile, the Chiefs were rebuilding their fan base.

As Aaron Racine would say, "*Never mind that shit, what's all that local sports trivia got to do with Civil War Reenacting and Holmes Brigade?*"

Out of a sense of morbid curiosity, Mona and I attended a November 1989 Chiefs football game, and then the following year we invested in season tickets. I think back in 1990, the price of tickets was about twenty bucks apiece. A season was ten games including two pre-season games. We bought three seats because we wanted to take Katie along. We had season tickets for ten years and witnessed some exciting, as well as, many heart-breaking contests.

Before each game started, there was the National Anthem complete with a color guard detail that marched to the center of the field. It was usually the United States military or local police or firemen who carried out these honors. However, one afternoon, I saw eight men wearing colonial dress of the Revolutionary War period, march up the 50-yard line. They carried flintlock muskets and the "Betsy Ross flag". The PA announcer said this group was from Fort Osage. I nearly soiled my MC HAMMER style baggy red sweatpants!

I was surprised to see they were using some local historical reenactors for this ceremony and at the same time, I was imagining the Holmes Brigade Color Guard in front of those 78,000 screaming Chiefs fans!

I wrote a letter to Carl Peterson, the President and General Manager of the Chiefs, who referred me to the Game Production Coordinator. I believe I wrote a passionate letter explaining our outfit and even included a recent photo of the Color Guard. I even left phone messages. Just before the spring muster at Fort Scott, I received a letter of acceptance for our group to appear at the December 13th home game against the New England Patriots.

I was dancing on tiptoes and was full of electricity as I made this announcement during the Fort Scott business meeting (*this was before the elections, my resignation, and the following blowout*). Naturally, this appearance would only benefit eight men, but it would allow those men, representatives of Holmes Brigade, to be seen by 78,000 people. Maybe one of those people at the game would become curious and possibly join the hobby? Who could tell?

I planned on using only the local guys from Kansas City, but since Terry Forsyth and Jack Williamson were the elected Color Sergeants for 1992, I invited them. They had the flags in their possession anyway, so it was the least I could do.

After months of pleading I got the nod from Terry, Jack, Ralph Monaco, Jon Isaacson, Steve Hall, Don Whitson, and Tim Moore. I was the eighth man. This was my affair so I'm damned if I was going to miss out!

A month before the game, I received another letter from the Game Production Coordinator. The letter instructed us where to assemble, what time to arrive, and so on. Enclosed were eight game day tickets, a parking pass, and eight vouchers for free chow!

On the big day, I woke up at 6 AM, took a hot shower, put on my uniform (sack coat w/forage cap) and walked out of the house into the rain! Yes, it was raining! It was not a frog strangler and it did not come down like Noah's flood, but it was annoying none-the-less. The cold drizzle would not stop the ballgame from being played, but it would put somewhat of a damper on us, as we would have to stand in the rain in wet wool and 12-pound rust magnets. Oh well!

I arranged to meet all the guys at Shoney's (I-70 and Noland Road) for breakfast at 8 AM. The guys were right on time, all except Ralph. While the rest of the guys were sucking up scrambled eggs and biscuits and gravy at the all-you-can-eat buffet, I was sweating bullets waiting for Ralph. About forty-five minutes passed before Ralph pulled into the parking lot. Whew!

We continued to feed our faces until about 10 AM or a little after. According to the letter I got from the Chiefs, we were supposed to be inside the stadium at 11:15 PM so I hustled the boys along.

Terry and Jack were not going to stay for the ballgame. They planned on returning to Springfield right after the ceremony. Jack brought his wife and a couple of his kids up from Springfield to Kansas City. They were seated at another table away from us heathens. When we got ready to go, Ginny (Jack's wife) would follow and park just outside the stadium. But first we would all move our cars to Blue Ridge Mall and all the guys would climb in the van with me.

I told Ginny to follow me to Blue Ridge Mall; it was only two miles up I-70 and not hard to find. Perhaps I was too keyed-up to think clearly, but as soon as I hit the interstate, I zoomed off like I was on a Jet Ski and left her picking raindrops out of her teeth. Luckily, she has smarts to match her good looks. She found us at Blue Ridge Mall in a matter of a few minutes. I remember she gave me a look of venom.

The boys piled into my Ford Aerostar for the brief two additional miles to the stadium. I think Don Whitson might have taken his own car. I don't think we could have <u>squeezed</u> eight of us, traps, muskets, and two flags in my van. I had one parking pass, so who ever took their personal car had to pay.

It was close to 11 o'clock by the time we squeezed into Arrowhead parking. We had to be <u>inside</u> the stadium within 15 minutes. We were already dressed out, thank God, so it was a matter of moments to slip on traps, etc, and head for the stadium entrance.

We had to enter by the South 'elephant' tunnel. This is where all the players, television equipment, trucks, and other maintenance vehicles come through. The tunnel is about forty feet wide by thirty feet high and is big enough for two jumbo elephant's to pass through side by side. The 'elephant' tunnel extends way down into the bowels of the stadium for almost a quarter-mile.

Once we got to the end of the tunnel, we stopped and gazed out into that painted field of Astro-turf. Miles and miles of television cable snaked out of the tunnel behind us and on either side of that field. Civilians wearing badges were walking or going past in golf cart type vehicles taking equipment out onto the sidelines. We saw shapely looking cheerleaders, executives in business suits, and working stiffs in coveralls and rain slickers scurrying about like mice in a cage. It was a regular Chinese fire drill, but it seemed everyone had a purpose and knew what they were doing.

The Game Production Coordinator found us. We had about thirty minutes to kill and he told us if we needed to us the toilet, we could go through the fifty-yard line entrance on the Chiefs side. We all nodded like "bobble-heads' as we were led down a small flight of stairs, behind the Chiefs bench, to a small hallway where a restroom was.

As we waited, in out of the rain, for a few moments, a few of the Chiefs football players came out of a side room (*their locker room no doubt*) and headed out the side door to the field so they could go through some warm-up exercises. I remember standing out of the way as these lads in tight britches and shoulder pads came striding past. One of these athletes was Chief's quarterback Dave Krieg. Ralph Monaco said a few encouraging words to the quarterback as we watched his tight buttocks go past us.

By now, everyone had emptied their bladders, so it was back out in the rain. The football players of both teams were throwing the pigskin around or doing sprints and other activities to get the blood going. Meanwhile the drizzle was beginning to wash away some of the white paint that was on this Astro-turf. There were little pools of water about an inch deep here and there. Walking on the field was like walking on a wet squishy sponge.

After a bit, all the players left the field and the mascot, KC WOLF came out in a go-cart to perform some antics. This was a guy in a silly, fat wolf suit, but he always played to the audience and got a rousing ovation. His 'schtick' involved pouncing on some hapless fool dressed in the uniform of the opposing team.

By this time, the eight of us had moved to the visitor's side of the field, right at the fifty-yard line. We formed two lines, four in front, four in back. Jack and Terry were in front with the colors (naturally).

Steve Hall was the only one of us who wore rank, so he would lead us up the fifty-yard line to the center for the National Anthem ceremony.

As we received our final instructions from the Game Production Coordinator, the visiting team was announced. The New England Patriots were a much different team back in 1992 than they are today. They weren't that good, but they still had some big looking boys. The Pats came charging out of the 'elephant' tunnel like freight trains and lined up near us. Damn, these pups were tall and each looked to be about 300 pounds dripping wet.

Then after the home team was announced, it was show time for us!

Steve ordered us to shoulder arms and we marched straight as judge's right up that fifty-yard line and halted dead center. Then we went to present arms while the anthem was sung. Of course, the PA announcer said the colors were presented by 'the Holmes Brigade Civil War Reenactors Color Guard!' I felt so proud and under the microscope at the same time.

So we stood there, at present arms, with the rain coming down and turning our muskets into rust magnets while, Kansas City's own version of Kate Smith warbled and wailed like a lounge singer. Of course she was under an umbrella! After what seemed like five minutes, the lady concluded her soulful rendition and we were allowed to exit the field.

Steve commanded us to turn at a 'left half wheel' and we marched back to the corner of the field, right at the entrance to the tunnel. Just as we reached the end zone, I heard a tiny voice calling my name. It was my ten-year-old daughter, Katie.

My family and I had our tickets in this part of the stadium, about midway up the aisle. Katie had walked down and was standing on the other side of the stadium railing and had hollered my name. *Mona had let one of her co-workers from the hospital use my ticket.* I waved at them all and gave Katie a smooch and told her to tell mom that I'd come by to visit in a little bit, after we got rid of our stuff.

So it was back up the 'elephant' tunnel for us. The kickoff had just begun and the game was in its first few minutes as we walked back toward the cars. Don Whitson wanted to change into 20th century clothes, but the rest of us just slipped a poncho over our heads and went back in with our CW clothes still on.

I had the fist full of tickets and food vouchers, so we went in through the turnstile and walked up to the nearest food vendor. The stadium food is pretty generic, mostly hog dogs and burgers. Our vouchers got each of us a box lunch with one dog, one bag of LAY'S potato chips, and one small PEPSI! Better than a poke in the eye with a sharp stick. The boys wolfed the chow down and we went to find our seats. Terry and Jack announced they were going to leave. Ginny was still waiting up the street in the car and wanted to get back to Springfield. The boys had left the colors with me in the mini-van. They didn't want to pack 'em in Ginny's car all dripping wet. I told them I would hang the flags in my garage to dry and would get them back to them at the next event, which wouldn't be till March.

Our complimentary tickets were near the west end zone, near the ten-yard line. I had the tickets in my pants pocket, but when I went to dig them out, they looked like wet mush with the seat numbers barely readable. Fortunately, there were several empty seats to choose from; some of the fans deciding they could watch the game just as well from the warm, dry comfort of their living rooms. A fan in a red rain slicker told us to find a seat anywhere. We arrived at our seats just in time to see Chiefs running back, Christian Okoye, run into the end zone from the five-yard line.

After a few moments, I got up and found Mona and Katie in the opposite end zone area. It took about fifteen minutes to walk all the way around the concourse to the other end of the stadium. The problem is there was so many people that just lolly-gag around, either standing in line to go to the restroom, standing in line at the beer or food vendor, or just standing about smoking. Trying to get through a mob of fans during game day can be very trying. It seems there are just as many folks standing in the concourse as there are sitting in their seats. The main reason for this congestion is no smoking is allowed in the seating area itself.

Anyway, I gabbed to the girls for a spell. I think Ralph was with me. I don't remember who the other lady was, that Mona brought to the game to use my ticket, but she was very grateful. By the way, our seats are just under the Club level overhang, so the girls did not get rained on. They were thankful for that as well.

I don't remember how long we all stayed at the game. Did we watch the whole shebang or did we leave early? Mona and the girls would take the Metro bus back to town. *Early on we bought a bus pass that was good all football season. I think it cost us ten bucks apiece, which is about one dollar per home game to take the bus. We drove ourselves a couple of years in a row, but we found it much more convenient to take the bus.*

Anyway, the brief moment under the eye of all those Chiefs fans was over. Whether it was because of the football game or what, we did get some new recruits over the next couple of years. It's too bad the weather was so lousy, but it was fun.

We kept our season tickets ten years. It seemed each year the organization raised ticket prices. Finally, Katie got tired of going and Mona and I wanted to take a vacation. Kansas City Chiefs season tickets were costing us almost $1500, which we thought we could better spend on a vacation. So after the 2000 season, we said farewell to Arrowhead and went to the Grand Canyon.

Surprisingly, after the spotlight performance of December 13th, 1992, and despite my best efforts, Holmes Brigade was never invited back to Arrowhead for the flag ceremony. This was around the time of Desert Storm, so from then on; it was all military people during the National Anthem. Perhaps Holmes Brigade closed the door on reenactors at ballgames or perhaps we can blame it on a real shooting war, which made 'make-believe' play soldiering seem insignificant and silly.

Chapter Thirteen

Changes

In February 1993, Mona and I bought a new house. We had lived in the same single-level 'cracker box' house in south Independence for twelve years. Katie had been raised in that house, but we had outgrown it.

The other concern was with Mona's mother. Corrine Ross was over 70 years old, a widow, and lived by herself in Windsor, Missouri. She had diabetes, but otherwise her health was okay. However, the house in Windsor was just too much for one lady to care for alone. So she agreed to sell it and move in with us.

During the late summer, fall, and early winter of 1992, we looked at a several homes in the area. We wanted to stay in the Raytown School District, plus we wanted to stay within a certain price. It also had to pass the mother-in-law seal of approval as she was fronting about half the money for the new digs.

In late January 1993, we signed the papers on a split-level home that was located about one mile south of our old home. This new place was still in the Raytown School District, but it had a Kansas City address. The home cost us about 120 grand, but it was plenty big for all of us.

It had four bedrooms and four bathrooms including a completely finished living area in one half of the basement. The basement living area was big enough for a king-size bed, was carpeted, had a big closet, and its own private bathroom and shower. It was the perfect place to put mother-in-law, as she would have her own space, but still be a part of the house.

I had to take some time off from work to move all our stuff. We rented a U-Haul truck and over the course of four or five days, with the help of Gregg Higginbotham and some others, we moved all our memories from one house to the other. Personally speaking, it was quite sad to leave that old house after twelve years. Despite the fact we had been robbed twice, the house still held many fond memories. I admit to weeping like a baby as I took one last look at the empty house we were leaving.

We were completely moved into the new digs by February 1993. The following March, I celebrated my 40th birthday. Some of my reenactment friends came over to eat, drink, and make merry. Mona hired a singing telegram. A gal in a silly outfit danced, sang, and made me toot my own horn. She said something about 'I heard you was full of hot air,' so I pretended to toot the horn by using ass gas.

Our new home was in an edition known as Glen Lakes. Right behind our house was a small lake. It was about an eighth of a mile long by a hundred yards wide (at its widest point). Some people fish its muddy waters and have pulled up catfish. I've seen frogs, snakes, and rats infest the area, as well. The edition is near a thick forest, so at times we've seen white tail deer run about. The most common residents of Glen Lake are the Canadian Geese. It seems like all season these honkers are either swimming in the water or flying overhead. Most of them stay around during the winter months. Sometimes they can be seen walking around in people's yards, looking for chow and leaving green turds all over the place.

Moving into this neighborhood, we had to join the Home Owners Association. This outfit dictates what you can or can't do with your own property. As long as you keep up the maintenance on your home or lawn, they won't bother you too much.

Right after we moved into the new house, I had deadbolts put in all the doors, then we hired a security company to hot wire all the windows and doors. In this day and age, I'm ashamed to admit, you can't trust anybody. After the experiences we'd had at the old house and with my mother-in-law taking permanent residence here, we wanted added protection from any possible danger or break-in.

Meanwhile, I was still attending a few events-very few. Of course, I attended the living history encampment at Pea Ridge in early March and the annual encampment at Fort Scott the following May. Nineteen ninety-three was not that special of a year for me. Even though there seemed to be some quality events planned, I just didn't get out to more than a small handful. Maybe it had to do with new house phobia.

In late May 1993, a bunch of us went west to Fort Larned, Kansas, to attend the nuptials of our own John Maki to Teresa Cowen. This was the same lady he met at Fort Scott and had been sweet on for almost two years. Teresa had been married before and had about five or six daughters, but that didn't matter to John. She was a swell gal with a great sense of humor, but the most important feature was John was head over heels in love. After the last ten bitter years, John deserved some happiness and I was more than happy to attend the union.

I neglected to mention that this was my second visit to the old frontier fort. An earlier visit was made on Labor Day weekend 1986 and I apologize for not telling that story in Chin Music Volume One.

Suffice to say Fort Larned is located in south central Kansas-about 3 hours from Kansas City. The fort was built about 1866, but was only occupied for a brief number of years. The fort lacks a stockade wall; it is open on all four sides to the elements, but otherwise the buildings are laid out in a square similar to Fort Scott.

While most of Fort Scott's buildings have been rebuilt, the buildings of Fort Larned have stood the test of time because they are constructed of sandstone. Over the decades, passing visitors and soldiers have scratched names and dates on the walls of these old buildings. Some etchings date before the turn of the 20th century.

The year I first visited the fort, we stayed in the completely restored infantry barracks, stood sentry duty, and did work details (such as sweeping the porch, policing the area and kitchen cleanup). Don Whitson had the distinct honor, that year, to volunteer to be an officer's 'striker.' This was a soldier who, for the lack of a better word, was an officer's personal valet. The 'striker' was responsible for maintaining the cleanliness of the officer's living quarters (*these buildings had been rebuilt because they had been made of wood*). The 'striker' could also be called upon to mend the officer's uniform, shine his boots, or other personal needs the officer thought up.

By volunteering to be a 'striker', the soldier was exempt from any other duties of the post. He was also excused from drill.

My first experience as to the seriousness of the living historians at Fort Larned came by way of reveille. Instead of the traditional bugle call, a very loud cannon erupted in the middle of the drill field. Next second, the post sergeant major barged into the room, shouting, "Get outta them bunks!" Damn, I thought I was back in boot camp! All weekend it was 100% dead serious. There was no goofing off allowed or any slipping back into 20th century mode.

After that trip to south central Kansas, I had wanted to return to the old fort several times, but something always got in the way. Part of it was the long drive through half of flat Kansas out in the middle of nowhere. Fort Larned is out in the middle of nowhere. It is many miles off a county road. At night you can see nothing, but an ocean of stars in the heavens. Quite breath-taking!

Anyway, in 1993, we had come down for the John Maki wedding.

Gregg Higginbotham could not make the trip. I think he was tied down to activities going on at Missouri Town. Either that or he was involved in another History Channel documentary. Whitson, Isaacson, Steve Hall, and some other reenactor pals were driving down on their own, so I was obligated to share the three hour drive through Kansas with five females-Mona, Katie, Gail, Hillari, and Shelby Higginbotham. I was the only guy in the van and it was all I could do to tune out the hen chattering going on between those gals the entire way. At one gas station, I considered picking up a cheap bottle of whiskey to dull my senses or perhaps lull me into a coma. Instead I buried myself in a Louis L'amour western novel and a Mountain Dew soda.

If memory serves me, this was Memorial Day weekend. We may have driven down that Friday evening after I got off work. *This was probably the reason why I rode with the women folk. All the other guys took Friday off.* After one or two piss stops, we arrived at Fort Larned just as the sun was beginning to drop. The girls had a motel room already reserved at the Best Western in the town of Larned-only ten miles away. The girls dropped me off at the fort, and then took the van to the motel.

By this time, all my Holmes Brigade amigos were on site, including Charlie Pautler and Aaron Racine. I convinced the boys we should go into town for a cold brew (*one of the bagladies drove*) and then I bluffed our way into the local VFW by flashing an old membership card from the Sedalia, Missouri chapter. When we got back to the fort it was late and I convinced the boys to find an empty bunk in the barracks, rather than pay for a room at the motel.

I think we reenactors did some dirty work around the fort and quite possibly some drill using the tactics of 1869. By this time, the long awaited stockade was complete, but I think it was closed or something. I never got a chance to visit it.

Over the years, John Maki and Steve Hall have become quite close to the people at Fort Larned. I think they go out to the old fort at least once a year. John has even made some boxes for the folks here and I believe he also donated or sold a .45-.70 trapdoor Springfield musket that is documented as having been issued from Fort Larned. So when John expressed his desire to have a wedding ceremony at the fort, the superintendent fell all over himself to fulfill John's wishes.

The exchanging of the wedding vows was to be held on the front porch of one of the rebuilt officer's homes. A reception, complete with snacks and punch, was to be held in an adjacent building big enough to hold all of us. I believe this was the quartermaster's building.

Bride and groom were decked out in attire appropriate for 1869 and were attended by a parson who was also dressed in 19th century garb. At the bride's side were all her daughters, while at John's side stood several of us Holmes Brigade boys. Because Gregg could not be here, John asked me to be his best man. In all honesty and no offense taken, John would have preferred Gregg at his side, but since he couldn't be here, I was chosen as his substitute.

At the conclusion of the sacred ceremony, we all adjourned to the quartermaster building for a joyful party complete with wedding gifts. Since this was supposed to be a period wedding, gifts like blenders, waffle irons, and toaster ovens would be inappropriate. Instead the happy couple probably received stuff like quilts and candleholders. The girls came up from the motel earlier in the day all decked out in their finery, just to socialize and be an audience at the happy union.

I spent Sunday night at the Larned motel with the girls, then the very next morning we drove directly east for about an hour to the town of Hutchinson. Once a year, this little burg plays host to the Kansas State Fair. It is also home to the Kansas Cosmosphere and Space Center. The Center had some moon rocks, an Apollo capsule, and some other odds and ends of space junk. At the time, Hillari Higginbotham was considering a career with NASA, so a trip to Hutchinson was made to order.

This was one of the last times the Whitsons were together. They might have got divorced the following year. Anyway, Don, his wife Susan, and daughter Emily all wanted to see the space stuff also, so we all left together.

After a couple of hours looking at space stuff, which included a 30-minute movie inside a dome, we headed north toward I-70. We stopped at the old Brookville Hotel restaurant for a fried chicken dinner. Located in the tiny burg of Brookville, population 50, this hotel was built about 1870. Sometime during the middle part of the 20th century, the hotel was converted into a family style restaurant serving mammoth chicken dinners. The popularity of the place was so great that people would come from miles around to eat the stuff that you had to wait a couple hours to get a seat.

Upstairs at the old hotel, the rooms had been restored to look just like they did around 1870. Some people thought ghosts still wandered the halls and rooms of the place, but no spook bothered my chicken dinner or me while I was there. In the year 2000, the Brookville Hotel Restaurant was closed down, but a similar one was built closer to Salina on I-70. I've never been to the new place. I suppose they trucked over all the memorabilia and knick-knacks from the original hotel, but I doubt you'd get the same feeling you got from being on the original property. It would be like moving Lincoln's boyhood home closer to the interstate so that more people could see it. I haven't been back to Brookville since 1993, so I can't speak for sure.

During the last weekend of June, we returned to Lecompton for the Battle of Fort Titus "Bleeding Kansas Days" and in August we returned to Athens, MO. Same goings on as in years past, but with one minor <u>change</u>.

For over ten years, I had worn a goatee. I started growing the tufts of chin whiskers in 1980 while still at CMSU in Warrensburg, MO. As much as I tried I could never grow a full beard. The stuff would only grow on my upper lip and on my chin. But during the summer of 1993, I decided to try a change. Maybe it had something to do with resigning as sergeant and wanting a fresh start. I'm not sure what my reasons were at the time, but whatever the case, off came the chin whiskers!

You can see me on the front cover of this book with a completely nude chin.

My extreme make over was short lived, however. Once I got a real good look at my double chin, I started to grow the stuff out again. As of this writing, I continue to sport a goatee. It is more gray than brown and my attempt to grow a full beard is just as fruitless today as it was those many years ago.

After a year and a half as newsletter editor, Jon Isaacson announced his resignation. I'm not aware of the particulars regarding his decision, but in the Sep/Oct 1993 issue of the Holmes Brigade Dispatch, he claimed he had run out of source ideas. I find that hard to believe, for someone as opinionated as he was, he would be at a loss for words. Perhaps he had issues with the direction of Holmes Brigade or of some of its membership. *Roger Forsyth became the next editor.*

Jon would stick with Holmes Brigade about one more year and then he would make a permanent move to Harper's Ferry where he would marry and open a business as a 19th Century clothier. About every other year, Jon comes back to Missouri to see his mother and would take an extra day or two out of his schedule to visit some of us in Kansas City. Jon is he still involved in living history, but he is also an accomplished musician in a country and western swing band in Nashville.

The final change occurred in February 1994. After ten years, I decided to turn in the old Mitsubishi truck. During the last six months or so, it had been leaking oil at the rate of one quart a week, but otherwise it did not have any other mechanical breakdowns. The original spare tire was still chained to the undercarriage. I never suffered a blow out on any of the tires, while on the highway, to force me to put on that spare tire. Over the course of ten years, I had hauled everything in the back of that truck from drunken reenactors, children, camp equipment, tents and tent poles, muskets, and cases of cold beer. It was with mixed emotions that I sold it.

I'd always had my eye on an SUV, especially the FORD BRONCO. My brother Bill worked at the FORD dealership in Sedalia and he got me a deal on an EXPLORER. It is also a SUV and just as good as the BRONCO.

In February, I signed the papers to lease the vehicle for three years. After three years, I had the option to buy the vehicle or turn it in and lease something else. I think when you lease a car you don't have to pay sales tax or some shit. Can't recall, but it saved me a few dollars at the time.

Just like the van, the SUV had power everything including cruise control. One thing it did not have was automatic transmission. I was so used to driving a stick (*in the Mitsubishi*) that I insisted on manual transmission. Bill was able to find just the right SUV that fit all the criteria I wanted.

Just two months later, I took the EXPLORER on its first real acid test when I went down south to Louisiana and the event at Red River.

CHAPTER FOURTEEN

Red River

April 2-10, 1984, somewhere in west central Louisiana

A couple of things excited me about Red River, once I got wind of this event.

This was not a typical weekend blowout with battle, beer, and a ball. This would be 7 days in the backwoods of central Louisiana, "marching, foraging in villages, camping in churchyards, sleeping on arms, and moving several miles each day". The object of this event, the 130th anniversary of the Red River Campaign, was to spend an entire week campaign style, cut-off from civilization and comfort. We would march 5-10 miles per day over rough country and dirt roads, going miles without seeing anything at all, only to be suddenly surprised by a few enemy skirmishers just around the bend. This would be similar to LBL, but on a much grander scale.

Roughly following in the footsteps of the soldiers of the original 1864 campaign, the reenactors would walk from Natchitoches (Nak-a-tosh) to Pleasant Hill, a distance of roughly 30 minutes by automobile. But since we weren't traveling by automobile, walking the scenic route instead, the distance over back trails and farm roads doubled the journey to about 70 miles. Meanwhile, the Confederates would follow on a parallel course with the two sides separated by at least ten miles.

Both sides would have cavalry scouts out and occasionally we might bump heads, but for the most part it would be a long lonesome quiet hike.

With this being similar to the LBL tactical, each man was responsible for his own comfort. It was stressed that no man should carry any more than was absolutely necessary. Of course that meant bedding, rations, and ammunition, plus the ten-pound musket. *Could we go seven days without a bath?*

Rations would be distributed on the march. They would be issued from a horse drawn wagon each day beginning on day three. So for the first two days, we had to provide our own mess. That meant summer sausage, jerky, hardtack, etc. I still did not own a skillet, but I had a coffee boiler to cook soup in.

Following the foot soldiers would be several horse drawn wagons, at least one with the daily rations and probably one or two carrying extra ammunition and forage for the horses. There would also be the United States National Guard. These khaki clad lads would follow a short distance behind us, in military ambulances, and offer medical assistance to any who might need it. It was probably a good thing because there'd be plenty of blisters and sprains before the week was out.

Because of the seriousness of the event, the sponsors demanded a registration fee of 50 bucks! This fee not only covered the cost of food, transportation, and protected the sponsor against liability; it also provided insurance, up to $5,000 apiece, in case someone was injured in an accident. If a man received an injury that required a trip to the hospital, he wouldn't have to root around for his insurance card (which he probably left in his car some twenty miles away).

The second reason I got excited about Red River was because this was the area my great-great grandfather, John R. Hodges, was in while a member of the 33rd Missouri Infantry. His unit was in this entire Red River campaign from start to finish under the generalship of Andrew Jackson Smith. This was probably the only time in my reenactment years that I could walk in the same footsteps as great-great granddad in virtually the same terrain as 130 years earlier.

What the hell was the Red River Campaign? You "axed" for it. Here then is a brief, but informative run down of what happened and why. Excerpts taken from THE CIVIL WAR IN THE AMERICAN WEST, by Alvin M. Josephy, Jr.

For months, the Federal blockade of Southern ports had been ruining the textile industry in the Northeast, shutting down mills and factories because of a lack of cotton. Most of Louisiana's great cotton plantations lay beyond the Union lines. A delegation of New York and New England businessmen and political leaders pleaded with Lincoln to launch an expedition to seize the huge cotton growing areas.

Lincoln was more concerned with opening up the Mississippi River and told lobbyists he could not spare troops for an invasion, but he promised to consider the subject at a later date. After Vicksburg's fall, Lincoln's thoughts returned to the western situation. Not only would Louisiana need to be liberated, but a greater concern was manifesting itself it the form of a foreign presence in nearby Mexico, which threatened the state of Texas.

While Americans were locked in Civil War, the French Emperor, Napoleon III, under the pretext of providing a stable central government in Mexico, had been attempting to overthrow its President, Benito Juarez. On June 7, 1863, some 40,000 troops, ignoring the Monroe Doctrine, occupied Mexico City and ousted Juarez from power.

This move filled Washington with a fear of Southern intrigue with Napoleon. The French, it was rumored, would occupy the Mexican border states, provide assistance to the South, and possibly annex Texas, Louisiana, and Arizona. Lincoln decided that "in view of recent events in Mexico, I am greatly impressed with re-establishing the national authority in Western Texas as soon as possible."

On March 10, after months of preparation, nearly 10,000 western troops of Sherman's veteran Army of the Tennessee, boarded a fleet of 26 transports and steamed for the entrance of Red River. Somewhere near Alexandria, Louisiana, these troops would rendezvous with 17,000 men under Nathaniel Banks and another 15,000 under Frederick Steele arriving from Little Rock, Arkansas. Opposing this force was 30,000 Confederates under Kirby Smith who were strung out in various outposts and hastily constructed forts along the banks of the river.

Over the next month and a half, nearly a dozen skirmishes would erupt all up and down the Red River on fields with such colorless names as Fort De Russey, Hendersons Hill, Piney Woods, Wilson's Plantation, Monett's Ferry, Grand Ecore, Sabine Crossroads, and Pleasant Hill.

It was at Sabine Crossroads, or Mansfield, merely a short distance from the Texas state line, that the Federals got a terrible spanking, which began the long retreat back down river. By late April, the water level had gone down to such an alarming degree, that the naval transports were in danger of grounding. In one of the most imaginative engineering feats of military history, Colonel Joseph Bailey, using a lumberman's technique, raised the water level by a series of wing dams, and the fleet completed its passage of the obstacle on 13 May.

In conclusion, the expedition was a failure. The federal support from Little Rock never arrived in time to assist the effort, Texas remained in Confederate hands, the suspicion of French involvement did not happen, and most of the prized cotton, some 150,000 bales, was ordered put to the torch by Kirby Smith, rather than have it fall into Union hands.

Sorry I got so long winded. This was another poor attempt at providing the reader with a history lesson. As mentioned at the start of this segment, most of this information was taken from THE CIVIL WAR IN THE AMERICAN WEST. There are probably only a handful of books that cover the war in the Louisiana region and this is one of the best as it also covers the Civil War in New Mexico, Minnesota, Colorado, California, Missouri, Arkansas, and Kansas. Anything military happening that occurred during the war years, 1861-1865, is covered in this book.

And now boys and girls, its time to get back to our show! The real reason you bought this book and are stuck here in these pages is to read about me! Without any more fanfare, here is the Red River as I saw it during the week of April 2-10, 1994.

Hig, Maki, and Jon Isaacson were not making the event. Ralph Monaco had to see the Easter Bunny (April 3rd), but would come down a day or two later with his brother-in-law Mike, a cat named Jeff Pearman, and new recruit Mark Olson. I wanted to leave Saturday morning and the only dude I could convince to make the journey with me, in my brand new SUV, was old reliable Steve Hall.

Steve and I arrived in Shreveport, Louisiana after a drive of about 10 hours. It was probably about 7PM when I pulled into the local

Shoney's restaurant and I made a call home. I had one of these new-fangled cell phones, but it was contained in a leather bag, looking like a ladies handbag. To get it to work, one had to plug one end in the cigarette lighter. The hand held receiver part was almost as big as a loaf of bread, with an antenna a yard long. After some moments, I talked to the wife and told her we made it alive, and then I placed a call to Ralph. I'd promised to give him a call, as well. He asked me to call him back after we pulled into the event site and let him know if there were any sutlers. He wanted to buy a Hardee hat or some shit.

Either before or after I made the call, Steve and I went into the Shoney's to eat. The only other meal we'd had on the way down was a hastily devoured drive-thru grease burger. We both felt we should chow down one last time on a restaurant meal before entering the seven-day wilderness journey with nothing but poorly cooked bacon, beans, and burnt coffee to sustain us.

Walking into the Shoney's, I immediately noticed that at nearly every table was a one-gallon plastic tub for the diners to throw bits of garbage into. I couldn't figure out what the deal was, until Steve and I walked up to the buffet table.

At one end of the steam table, next to the fried chicken, meat loaf, mashed potatoes and gravy, was a 3-foot square metal tub of boiled Cajun style crawfish. This is the only place and the only restaurant in America where I saw an entire section of a buffet table set-aside for these miniature lobsters. Now I understood what the one-gallon plastic tubs were for. They were for the crawdad skins after you ate the little spoonful of meat out of the ass end. I'd eaten some of these bastards before, at Natchez, Mississippi, during the NORTH AND SOUTH miniseries, so I knew what to expect.

Even as I stood around in wonderment, little kids as young as five years old were elbowing me out of the way, just to spoon big piles of those creatures on their plates. Oh, well, when in Rome! Without hesitation, I spooned some crawdads on my plate and was soon burning my lips on the cayenne pepper seasoning. Steve Hall is a slight fellow; not weighing more than 98 pounds soaking wet. I think he passed on the crawdads and confined himself to the salad bar and Jell-O.

After this hearty meal, it was probably after nine, Steve and I decided we should head on down the road and look for the event. My gas tank was about empty, but I figured there'd be a station outside the city limits. Once we got going however, it was like stepping out the door into the dark. Where the city ended, there was nothing on the other side. In most towns, you figure you'd see a few motels and a convenience store, setting on the fringe of the city limits! We drove a good ten miles or more, on the other side of Shreveport, but there was nothing in sight!

The needle on my gas tank was in the red and I was afraid the SUV would die somewhere in the middle of the boondocks, with nobody around but the inbreds of the bayou. I remember seeing a movie called SOUTHERN COMFORT where these National Guardsmen were terrorized by angry Cajuns, and that's what I feared.

A few miles down the road was an exit ramp, but there was nothing there! Just a road going off into the woods. So I turned around and drove all the way back to Shreveport. Thank God we made it back! By this time the SUV was probably running on fumes, but the vehicle did not let me down. *Come to find out, we still had another 60 miles to go before reaching the event, and just as I suspected, there wasn't another gas station between here and there.*

With a full tank of gas, Steve and I headed back down the highway again. Some months earlier, after sending in the $50 registration, I received a "confirmation package," which included a Provost Pass, ration pass, a validity slip for muster rolls, a pass into camp, and a parking pass.

Most of that paper crap was just that, crap! It was just to prove that you were you. The most important piece of paper was the one that told you how to "get into the damn event site." After finding the correct turn-off spot, we followed a one-lane gravel road to the town of Pleasant Hill. This was near the site of the 1864 battle of the same name, but the town itself couldn't have been bigger than a football field! There were only about a half dozen buildings on Main Street (that I saw at this late hour), not including the local one room firehouse. The town supposedly has a population of 200, but I couldn't see where they hid them all. There was one building which was pretty empty except there was an old geezer still awake inside who claimed to be a member of the local historical society. He took our signatures on a sign-in sheet and tried to sell us a T-shirt and other 130th anniversary trinkets out of cardboard boxes. Against my better judgement, I bought a <u>I SURVIVED THE RED RIVER EVENT</u> T-shirt and a Battle of Pleasant Hill 30-page booklet.

The old boy, with a heavy southern drawl as thick as lumpy gravy, informed us that all the "Yankee" boys had already been bused to 'Nak-a-tosh' and we'd have to wait till the morning for a bus ride. Just across the narrow one-way street, was a big green Army tent. Inside this tent were about a dozen folding cots. The old southern gentleman told us that the National Guard had set that up and we were welcome to bed there till daybreak-which we did.

Before going to bed, I told Steve that I was going to use my car phone, but here in this part of Louisiana, I couldn't get a clear signal. The old geezer said there was a pay phone a few miles up the street. I drove to a general store that looked right out of Petticoat Junction. Inside, I met Ma and Pa Kettle and three barefoot brats who were baby-sitting a rack of potato chips, a cooler full of beer, videotapes for rent, and scratch off lottery tickets.

There was a pay phone on the porch, next to the coin operated VENDO-BAIT machine, so I placed a call to Ralph and told him there weren't any sutlers and not to bother bringing any folding money, unless he wanted to buy a T-shirt or some 'shine.

Come sunup, Steve and I changed into our civil war duds and I moved my Explorer about a quarter-mile to the parking lot (just an old cow pasture). We nibbled on donuts and coffee, which I think was provided by the historical society (might have been the same old geezer from last night). A short time later the school bus came around the corner.

Steve and I were not the only passengers at this hour. I think we picked up four other "Yankees" who were coming from the parking lot, plus we had two Confederate lads already seated in the rear of the bus when it first arrived. These boys were going to be dropped off some way up the road, about ten miles or so from the Federal position.

We had all our stuff, knapsacks, traps, and muskets trying to navigate up the narrow school bus aisle, but we managed to get comfortable for the bouncy ride. This bus was not overly crowded, only the eight of us, so each man could stretch out a bit. I might have snoozed.

After a drive of unknown length, up gravel roads, onto pavement, then back on gravel roads, the bus stopped to let the graybacks off. Some 30 minutes later, the bus entered the city limits of Natchitoches.

We were supposed to meet the Federal army at a roadside park near Lake Sibley, but when the bus pulled into the parking area, there was no one to be found-with the exception of a few reenactor ladies. Included in this bunch was Ladies Union Aid Society member, Michelle Yipe!

Steve and I hopped off the bus and gave Michelle a big old hug. After the pleasantries had passed, we inquired as to the whereabouts of all the blue boys. Michelle told us that they'd left about an hour ago, but she didn't think they'd gone too far yet. There were wagons, cavalry, and horse drawn artillery and she didn't expect they'd make progress better than a snail's pace. She thought they'd probably be somewhere alongside the levee about now and nearly ready to cross.

Back aboard the school bus, we told the driver to head back out of town to the highway. On the lake side of the highway was a levee. The boys would have to crawl up out of the flood plain, up and over the levee onto the highway.

On reaching the intersection, we bailed out because here were about one hundred late arrivals, milling about on both sides of the two-lane blacktop. These were some "Yankee" boys, who had overslept, missed the bus, or just arrived in town. Steve and I dropped our packs at our feet and waited, with the rest of the mob.

I was puffing on my cherry wood pipe and had smoked about half a bowl, when someone spotted something on the other side of the levee. All that could be seen were the tops of regimental flags and the tops of rifles as the boys walked parallel with the levee. Finally, the boys marched out through a natural break in the levee and poured out onto the highway like water from a bucket. *Now the horse drawn stuff, including the artillery had taken the roadway all this time. They would have gotten stuck in the bog-like conditions. Coming up out of the ground was all the infantry boys.*

Steve and I shouted a hearty HUZZAH as we spotted the Holmes Brigade boys, then we shouldered our stuff and fell into step. Everyone was marching at the route step, as if it was nothing more than an early Easter Sunday stroll-which it was!

There were about thirty Holmes Brigade lads that were here this day, including Mike Gosser, Phil Curran, Gary Crane, Joe Amos, John Peterson, a cat named Kirk Freeman, Roger Forsyth, Captain Don Strother, Mark Strother, and Kyle Bean. These are the only names I recall after 12 years. There was also one guy, whose name I've forgotten, who did a dead-on impression of Jimmy Stewart. At any given moment, he'd bust out with some Jimmy Stewart dialogue from the movie, SHENANDOAH. He had everybody rolling with laughter. He had a buddy with him, some sort of weasel-looking guy. I don't recall either of their names.

As can be expected, we laughed, giggled, and told stories throughout the entire morning as the miles disappeared under our feet. After Steve and I joined the party, the army marched up the paved highway for about a mile or two, and then went up a country trail that cut through a deep wooded forest. The local police were on hand to block traffic while we plodded along.

Whenever stuff like this happens, i.e., a reenactment group passes over public roads, some type of highway patrol or police department follows alongside us with flashing lights or stops traffic at a road block so we can pass unmolested. We appreciate that courtesy, as we don't want to get run over by an 18-wheeler or a family car. This inconvenience to the motorists only lasts a few minutes with only a few catcalls along the lines of "Yankee Go Home!" or "The South Will Rise Again!"

Roger Forsyth kept a small diary, and then later he wrote an after action report based on what he observed at the Red River event. On Easter Sunday, Roger states, *"we marched 14 miles-half of which was on asphalt-giving the Johnnies a 10-mile head start. Straggling was a problem, many of the horses came up lame, and there were reports of 20 soldiers being taken to the hospital.*" I can't confirm or deny the distance covered that first day, but Roger may be about right.

After leaving civilization and striking off into the woods, it was if we'd been swallowed up. I'll not attempt to explain the wild haunted forests we navigated ourselves through or the crooked country roads that caused blisters and ankle twists. Suffice to say the National Guard Medical people worked overtime on mostly minor foot ailments. By the time the event ended, six days later, most of us had developed a fond relationship for Dr. Scholl and his many foot remedies. A personal favorite for many was 'mole skin'; a wafer-thin piece of padding that protected open blisters.

That first night, we camped in a wooded area. The ground was fairly flat all around and most of the trees were only saplings, growing about a foot apart from one another. Some areas were thick with poison ivy and poison oak, so we had to be aware where we sat. I don't remember being bothered by bugs, with the exception of the 'chigger in the waistband.' We were too far away from open water to be bothered by 'skeeters.'

With that said, John Peterson recalls an episode in which "*the battalion came to a halt and we were allowed to plop down on either side of the road. Roger Forsyth sat down, then just as quickly jumped up to discover his whole right side, from hip to knee was covered with red fire ants.*" The National Guard came to the rescue, but I don't remember if they used a broom, insect spray or gasoline to get the monsters off Roger. Needless to say, he probably carried a few hundred tiny bite marks for many days.

That same day there was another bizarre incident, but it happened between a man and his horse. "*As I remember it,*" Peterson says, "*the rider was having difficulty controlling his rented animal so he punched the animal in the face. One of our boys* (Gary Crane) *threatened to pistol wipe him if he did that again.*"

Upon reaching our camp for the night, some people were commissioned to dig a slit trench to poop in. It might have been the National Guard who went to work with the pick and shovel and opened up a trench about six foot long by three foot wide and three foot deep. Upon completing the excavation, some brush was drug over to act as a screen to give the user some privacy. Why would a bunch of infantry soldiers need privacy? Because we had some reenactor women who were following the army. I could never figure out what role these females had in this tactical, but here they were; at least a couple that we saw. Michelle Yipe might have been one of these 'tag-along' refugees, but I don't recall for sure. Its possible these females rode in one or more of the horse drawn wagons or maybe their role was as laundresses, or 'soiled doves.'

The brush arbor around the slit trench was so the ladies could squat with some privacy without displaying their muff for the entire world to see. The embarrassing thing about it was the outdoor toilet was right next to a walking trail. Anybody who walked by could hear the 'toot toot' of escaping gas and the tinkle of pee hitting the dirt and know what was going on. I was just as embare-assed, so I waited till it was after dark before I straddled the trench and deposited my Easter egg.

According to Roger Forsyth's after action report for the next day, *"Monday's march totaled about 12 miles. Skirmishing erupted early and continued throughout the day with Holmes serving as the lead element. At one point, along a wood-lined road, Confederate artillery and obstructions blocked our path... temporarily."*

After a hasty breakfast on Monday morning, we resumed our wayward travel through the wilds of central Louisiana. As Roger expertly implies, Holmes Brigade was the lead company on this day march. The day before, we had been the tail end.

I neglected to mention that our army was divided into two battalions for a total strength of about four hundred. This was a Western Brigade function, but not sure who commanded the entire shooting match. I'm pretty sure Dave Shackleford was out by this time. All I know for sure was 2nd Battalion, that which had Holmes Brigade, the Mudsills, and the 1st Colorado, was led by the tubby twat inspector, Merle 'Boo' Hodges.

"I knew a man who was looking for work as a gynecologist, but he couldn't find an opening"- George Carlin.

In his early days of reenacting, Boo Hodges, OB/GYN, had been the redheaded stepchild of the Holmes Brigade, with his fledging unit the Eighth Kansas. A few years and a fistful of dollars later, Boo had promoted himself to Colonel leading a battalion. He even had his own horse, which I'm sure protested having this fat ass on his back. At least the horse was not female otherwise Boo might have been tempted to practice his craft.

Nevertheless, Boo was a happy go lucky sort of fellow and never allowed his rank to get in the way of sharing a joke with the common private. For the most part he was like one of the guys, as if being a full colonel was no big deal. I always found him to be very approachable and ready to hear a word from anybody. He reminded me of Ralph Monaco, a man who <u>always</u> sought the center of attention.

On this day, 2nd Battalion led the advance. I distinctly remember we went up one-lane dirt roads, with maybe one or two mailboxes every other mile. There was very little to break the monotony of the walk, except for the squeak of thousands of crickets as they hopped back and forth in the tall weeds.

Suddenly, from a bend in the road about fifty to one hundred yards away, there appeared a small mountain howitzer. Manning the piece were three ragged looking Rebel scarecrows. There might have been a company of Confederates in support of the gun. Anyway, both gun and Rebel infantrymen fired, and then they high-tailed it at a trot. I think Holmes Brigade might have smoked their retreating backsides before they disappeared. I don't think the three ragged looking scarecrows could have manhandled the mountain howitzer by themselves so that leads me to believe that the gun was towed away by a horse.

We followed the timid graybacks about another quarter-mile or more, and we may have exchanged volleys for a few minutes, but they seemed to have no desire to linger or to show us their entire battalion. This had only been an annoyance on their part and once they had bitten at us, like so many chiggers, they were content to melt into the brush, bothering us no more that day.

About noon, we halted on some rough looking land that looked like a plow had <u>tried</u> to work its magic, but failed. The field looked as if it'd been used as a playground for angry gophers. For several hundred yards nothing seemed to grow in this field but rocks, dirt clods, empty beer cans, and old automobile parts.

Standing on some cinder blocks was a trailer home. Word came back to us that the old hillbilly had several cases of cold beer sitting in iced wash tubs, which he was willing to sell to us 'Yankees' for a dollar a can. Do you think that maybe he was waiting for us all along? I'm sure he knew the route of this campaign, went to the Piggly-Wiggly, bought a supply of popskull, and was ready for any sucker that passed by, whether he be Blue or Gray.

Though tempted, I declined the cold brew. Despite better judgment, many of the fellows traded a greenback for Budweiser. Alcohol is not the best tonic for long marching in arid temperatures as it will only make you thirstier, but it was out of my hands. I was concerned at that moment with finding a place to squat.

The hillbilly would not let me use his trailer home toilet, so I crawled under a split rail fence, walked a little way below a hill, and found a natural depression where I could squat and the turd could tumble down hill. Thankfully, there were no four-legged animals about. I had seen a video where a lustful donkey tried to hump a man and I wanted no business with that!

After the better part of an hour, which many of the guys spent under closed eyelids, it was time to put another six miles under our feet. We had to get to our bivouac before nightfall so we could receive our first ration issue.

A couple of hours later, we stopped at an old cornfield. It was a horrible looking place with many of the stubs sticking about a foot out of the ground. At first it was thought we'd be forced to camp here for the night, but after a few moments, we moved on about another quarter-mile to a lush field surrounded by full trees.

It was here that we received our ration issue. I seem to recall that the men of the battalion had to buddy up in a group of four and receive the rations accordingly. Steve Hall, two other lads, and I agreed to 'mess together.' When it came time for the issue, we went up to the supply wagon, where food was being divided up on a rubber blanket.

According to the information packet we received before Red River, it was announced that the ration issue would consist of dried and fresh beef, bacon, sausage, potatoes, onions, yams, carrots, cabbage, cheese, apples, and hardtack. We also were to receive little muslin poke bags that would contain peas, rice, grits, beans, peanuts, parched corn, dried fruit, raisins, and coffee.

I don't remember how much we actually received, from that grocery list, but I do recall one of those cloth bags contained lentils! Now lentils were some kind of mixed beans, good for nothing, but making soup. The sad part about lentils was you had to soak them overnight before you could cook them. I think most of us ate the other stuff and threw the lentils away.

I recall little of the Tuesday morning or afternoon march. Roger says "*a nice breeze, moderate temperatures and an Arkansas championship made Tuesday a great day to march 8 miles.*" Roger is alluding to the Arkansas Razorback basketball team, which won the NCAA Final Four tournament. Obviously, someone had an ear to a radio.

The forecast for Tuesday evening called for thunderstorms and no sooner had we got into camp for the night, than the skies opened up. Within moments everything and everyone was soaked.

Steve and I tried to make ourselves comfortable by setting up a gum blanket shebang under the limbs of some thick trees, but the rain dripped off those low hanging branches and nearly drowned us.

It was well past sundown when word came that a citizen was offering shelter in his garage. Any man, who feared for his health, could escape the elements and hide in this man's garage.

Steve and I, along with several others, gathered our belongings and tramped about a quarter-mile across a swampy, muddy bog to an area where there were modern homes. Inside the open garage of one of these new homes was about fifty 'Yankee' boys lying or standing about in various stages of misery.

After a short time, a National Guard 'deuce and a half' came roaring out of the darkness and stopped in front of the house. Some bigwig officer said if any of us wished, we could take the truck and go back to the Pleasant Hill firehouse to sleep. This option, he said, was open only for those who were over forty years old.

I was 41 and I didn't relish lying out in the cold, wet rain, so I 'wussed-out' and left the event. Steve and I, along with about twenty other 'old farts,' climbed over the tailgate into the dark interior of the Army truck and away we went.

It seemed like we were on the road all night. The 'deuce and a half' went several miles on the highway, then off onto muddy roads, then back onto pavement. It seemed like hours had passed before we pulled up in front of the old firehouse. We were back at our point of origin, when Steve and I first arrived on Saturday night. It was now Tuesday night, it was still raining like the dickens, plus the temperature was falling into the lower 30's.

We slithered like wet snakes over the tailgate, (it was about a six-foot drop to the ground) then we shuffled into the firehouse.

About a couple dozen other wet 'Yankees" were already inside the place, all spread out on the flat concrete of the garage. The emergency vehicles had been parked outside, so the reenactors could flop down as best we could.

Inside the firehouse, we were no longer bothered by the falling rain, but someone forgot to light the furnace, because it was colder than a landlord's heart lying on that cold concrete. We'd tried to hang our wet clothes on a line to dry, but they only got colder and stayed wet.

While many of us were bitching and moaning about this new predicament, a couple of jokers, hidden in an upstairs loft (and off the concrete) were hollering at us to turn off the "fucking light and get the fuck to sleep." Well, the very next morning, all us 'Yankees' were all still wet and cold. The two sons-of-bitches who'd hollered at us (and stayed dry by lying all night on top of a closet) turned out to be the two Confederate reenactor's Steve and I had shared a school bus with on Sunday. Seems they weren't as dumb as they looked. At least they looked somewhat refreshed. I should also note that they quickly dressed and got the hell out of the building. Maybe they were afraid that one of us cold, wet 'Yankees' would still be offended.

Later on we discovered the firehouse thermostat could have been turned on if we'd only asked someone. Maybe they forgot to tell us on purpose.

It was Wednesday morning. I doubt if anyone got any sleep; it was so cold lying on that concrete, with nothing on but wet clothes. The sun was out, but it was still cold from last night's rain. It was at that moment, Steve and I decided to abandon the event.

Steve told me he had an uncle who lived in Shreveport, who would probably let us come by for a visit and allow us to dry our clothes. We hauled our stuff down the short quarter-mile to the Explorer, I let Steve make his phone call, and then we pulled away. Needless to say, I had the heater turned on for quite a long time. As the warm air began to thaw us out, it also caused our wet wool uniforms to smell horribly. One is reminded of the foul odor of wet dog on a hot summer day inside a hot car.

Another hour back up the highway until we ran into Shreveport and then another short drive found us at the home of Steve's aunt and uncle. *"Actually, they were recently married and I had never met her before,"* Steve says. I think Uncle Bill had been a widower or divorcee, but whatever the case, he must have gotten the itch to remarry. Steve remembers that *"Elane seemed like a proper southern lady and I joked about her home being invaded by Yankees."* They didn't seem to mind the intrusion; in fact they insisted we make ourselves at home.

After Steve and I had each used the shower, we changed into our civilian clothes and then were invited to sit down to a hearty breakfast. While our Civil War shirts and drawers were in the wash, Uncle Bill took us outside to show us his RV. It was the first time I been inside one of these recreational vehicles and it was fully loaded. I think it cost about as much as a new home! It had a kitchen, dining area, bedroom, and a bathroom. He told us they go on trips all over the country, now that he's retired from his profession. I couldn't imagine driving that great big sucker!

After a bit, Steve and I announced that we were going up to Mansfield to site-see, and then we'd probably check into a motel for the evening. Uncle Bill said we could stay the night in a spare room, but we respectfully declined. We wanted to clean our muskets and didn't want to dirty up his house even more than we already had.

So Steve and I spent an afternoon at Mansfield Battlefield State Park, and then swung back by Uncle Bill's house to get our white clothing. It was late afternoon, when we checked into the Motel 6, spent an evening at a Pizza Hut, watched the local weather forecast, then an hour or two cleaning our muskets in the motel shower. I'll bet the cleaning woman was pissed when she cleaned up our room the next morning and found all the towels and the shower stall was dirty with black powder residue.

It was about 7 AM Thursday morning when Steve and I crawled out of the clean, dry motel room sheets. The sun was up, the clouds had moved away, and it looked like the rest of the weekend would be nice. We had not washed our wool uniform coat and pants, merely allowed them to air dry. It was simply a matter of brushing off the dried mud. Our white undergarments were clean; that's all that mattered.

After a quick breakfast at a drive-thru, we set our sights on a return to the event. The sun was definitely in our faces and the warmth was very uplifting for our spirits as well. The day off had been what Steve and I needed to restore our souls.

Once more we found ourselves at the Pleasant Hill parking area, but were at a loss trying to figure out where the Union army was. I think we asked some of the people standing around the historical society area or maybe some National Guard soldiers who were around and found out the boys were three miles up the road at a living history village.

I can't remember exactly how we got from the parking area to the new Union camp, but I think Steve and I crawled in the back of someone's pickup truck.

Whatever the case, Steve remembers, *"it was still early morning and there was heavy dew on the grass. It was very obvious where the columns had marched and we just followed the trail* (of beaten down grass) *to where they were now stopped."*

We found the Union army lounging in a field of green grass right alongside the reconstructed village. The village reminded me of Missouri Town, but if memory serves me, there might have only been a few buildings. The boys had she-bangs and blankets laid out near a tree line, with a couple of roaring fires to cook lunch.

Roger Forsyth states that after Tuesday evening's rainstorm, there were many *"bail-outs on both sides of the march."* Steve and I weren't the only ones to go AWOL. I personally heard many that drove one hundred miles to spend the day in Vicksburg. John Peterson remembers that a few of the boys went to a local Shreveport laundry mat *"stripped off their wet uniforms to dry them and sat around in their drawers?"* Much like gazing at a Medusa, John Peterson says, *"it was not a very pretty site! I'm sure the locals were traumatized".*

As far as I can decipher, there wasn't anything going on Wednesday. The roads had turned into a muddy bog and reenactors were in a cold, damp mood. The weather was so bad many of the boys had to be trucked to Pleasant Hill by the National Guard. The Union army stayed right around the Pleasant Hill Fire Station, regrouped, and headed out early Thursday morning, hours before Steve and I arrived.

When Steve and I arrived at the village and helloed at all the boys lounging in the yard, we were met by Ralph, his brother-in-law Mike, Jeff Perriman, and Mark Olson. These boys had arrived at Pleasant Hill on Wednesday morning. The first thing they heard was that the event had been canceled. Naturally, they were shocked, but quickly learned that the event was NOT canceled, but merely set back by one day, due to the weather.

Ralph and the boys spent Wednesday night in the cold firehouse (*I bet they wondered what the hell happened to Steve Hall and me*). On Thursday morning, they marched out, with the rest of the reorganized army, to the village. And that's where Steve and I met them.

Ralph and the rest of the Holmes Brigade boys thought we'd gone home. They certainly didn't expect to see us tramping up across the field like two wandering vagabonds with shit eating grins! When we told them we'd spent Wednesday night under clean sheets, and ate at a Pizza Hut, they gave us the raspberry noise. Steve and I were given the business and we took the light-hearted verbal abuse in the spirit it was dished out. All kidding aside, and in a perverted sort of way, Holmes Brigade was glad to see the return of two of its prodigal sons.

There wasn't anything going on at this time when Steve and I arrived. I think the army was still reorganizing, so instead of a lot of marching and shooting, a liberty was granted. The guys were allowed to kick back and do whatever they pleased. At one of the old buildings, there was a medical display. As a doctor himself, Mike Monaco was very interested in old Civil War Medicine. At home, he owns a few original surgical tools and accessories.

Across the street from the village were several food vendors, a T-shirt peddler and (I think) one or two authentic sutlers. Ralph may have found his Hardee hat after all. One of the food vendors was selling steam boiled crawdad in Cajun spices. Ralph, on a dare, bought a two-pound serving of the miniature lobsters. They were ladled into a Styrofoam box. The big-boned gal who ran the operation actually showed Ralph the proper way to eat crawdad, from the ass out. No extra charge for instructions.

Meanwhile, several hard-looking 'southern' women had set up a refugee camp in the village itself. These creatures of the fairer sex glared daggers at us 'Yankee' trespassers the whole time we were in the area. *Michelle Yipe was not with this bunch. This might have been a local group of southern belles.*

About late afternoon, it was announced that the battalion was going to leave the area and march to a new site for the night. Before vacating, we were ordered to police the area and return the site as we had found it. We had several cords of firewood stacked nearby and we were ordered to burn them.

As John Peterson recalls, *"We were burning the extra wood to keep it from being used by the 'Johnnies'. Not a very Christian action, but in keeping with our general attitude at the time, we'd collected it and we were damned if we were going to give it to the 'Johnnies' in a nice neat pile"*.

It was while in the performance of the last detail; one of the ladies from the refugee camp came stalking over. With one hand on her hip and the other waving a large wooden spoon, she declared that that firewood belonged to her and her 'gallant heroes in gray' and we had best not burn it up.

After twelve years, I don't recall all the details of the dialogue, but Steve claims the lady was using language that would make a sailor blush and called Boo Hodges, *"an a**hole"*, with Boo replying, *"That's Colonel A**hole to you!"* The one thing I do remember hearing, and it's forever tattooed on my brain, is our Sergeant Major stepping forward and shouting, "*Woman, hold your tongue!*" The woman rocked back on her heels like she'd been slapped.

"*After the heifer about-faced and waddled back to her tent,*" Peterson remembers with sadistic fondness, "*the Col. ordered everyone to gather a single stick for deposit in the refugee camp. We were ordered into line preparing to march past single-file when someone, I'm not sure who, started the Zulu war chant* (associated with the famous movie of that name. I'm not sure why re-enactors love this 1960s vintage flick so much).

"Anyway, *whoever did the chant knew what he was doing and somehow most of us got into the mood and rhythm of the chant gesturing and grunting when the time was right with our wooden spears. Very impressive! I'm sure our southern bells were frightened for their collective virtues. A slave insurrection would sound no less threatening. I could just see them swooning en mass only to be savaged by these smelly aboriginal creatures dressed in blue!*"

After a moment of absurd behavior, the Colonel and the Sergeant Major told us to say nothing to the ladies. So we marched in silence and deposited the firewood right at their feet. Naturally, these hard-hearted southern belles did not bother to say thank you. Instead they gave us the old fashioned cold shoulder and turned their backs to us.

The last full day of the event remains somewhat of a blur. Roger writes "*the final four-mile march was through a marsh, over vines, and sections of a corduroy road. We went into bivouac outside Mansfield along a hillside, threw up cotton bale barricades, and gathered firewood before the battle of Sabine Crossroads*".

Of Friday's battle, I do recall our company sat in reserve. There might have been a couple of companies with Holmes Brigade, who also sat in reserve. The rest of the grand Union army was on the other side of a tree line, which was about two hundred yards wide. They were busy giving battle with the Confederate foe.

One trail went around the tree line from the northwest with another trail going around the northeast. The northeast trail was much narrower, barely wide enough for two men side by side. On the other side of the woods were several gray-clad horsemen. I tried to suggest to Captain Don or Colonel Boo that if we send a few guys around the northeast trail, as bait, we could lure the Confederate cavalry into giving chase and draw them into our waiting arms. The two or three companies we had in reserve could surely smoke a few of those scarecrows as they came riding around the bend.

However, my suggestion fell on deaf ears. We remained in seclusion and away from the action for the balance of the fight. *"Overall, it was a lackluster battle,"* Roger observed. *"We retreated* (as per the scenario) *without being nudged by our worn-out enemy."* It seems the Confederates *"were so worn out they could barely stay on their feet."* Apparently, seven days of campaigning had been a much rougher journey for the scarecrows than the seven days us Union boys endured.

By Friday evening, about half of the original 900 registrants had bailed out. About a third of those who fell out did so because of foot injuries-blisters, sprains, ankle twists, etc. Holmes Brigade's own Kyle Bean suffered a knee injury and Mark Strother left because of a pulled groin muscle.

The others who left the event early probably did so around Tuesday or Wednesday-about the time of the rainstorm. I thought about driving back to Kansas City that Wednesday morning, but Steve talked me out of it.

The event wasn't quite the same after the mid-week rainstorm. It was kind of like a football game where you play real good one half, but come back later and play poorly the second half of the game.

There wasn't much of anything planned for Saturday, with the exception of the Battle of Pleasant Hill (the fight my great great granddad was in). However, the fight wasn't scheduled to start until 4 PM! I didn't want to loaf around all day doing nothing but fanning my balls. If the fight had been at 1PM, it might've been a different story. I convinced Steve that we should head out.

Ralph and the bunch he rode down with were disappointed. They didn't arrive at the event until Wednesday, and then they sat in a firehouse all night, and didn't really begin the campaign till Thursday morning. They didn't get the full $50 tour like Steve and I did. After some cussing and discussing, all six of us voted to take off. Imagine my joy when I discovered the parking lot was less than a 'quarter-mile' from where the "Battle of Pleasant Hill" would take place.

While the ragged remnants of 'Boo' Hodges little army scurried about like soldier ants, building hay bale breastworks for the 4 PM fight, I went to get the Explorer. I drove right through the middle of camp, with my tape deck playing YMCA, by the Village People. I got some cold looks from some of the weary boys in blue, but I thought, to hell with 'em.

Mark Olson asked if he could share the ride back to Kansas City with Steve and me. The Monaco vehicle had been a bit overcrowded on the trip down, four guys and all the stuff. I didn't mind one bit. It would give me a chance over the next ten hours to get to know the guy better, plus I could use his gas money. So Mark, Steve, and I hopped aboard my SUV and followed the Monaco three-some back to civilization.

At some point, after we crossed into Arkansas, we found a motel and a restaurant. We might have stopped in Texarkana. It's likely all six of us dined and lodged together, and then all headed out come Sunday morning. We all had to be at work Monday, so we wanted to get as many miles behind us as possible.

In hindsight, the Red River event was fun while it lasted. It certainly was a test for all of us who are used to only doing mainstream events, otherwise known as 9 to 5 reenactments (public comes through about 9 AM, then the camps close about 5 PM). All of us who participated in Red River are, of course, too old and too fat, when compared to the average Civil War soldier. I don't know how those young pups of 130 years earlier managed to overcome all the obstacles that we seemed to take so lightly during those seven days. Neither great great granddad Hodges nor any of A J Smith's boys had the luxury of quitting the army or taking a day off because of rain.

But we all have real jobs and only do this as a hobby. It is no better or worse than playing golf on your day off or going sailing or dirt biking. If you like doing something, you'll invest the time and money to do it. I thought Red River was a challenging experiment for me and I would consider attending another campaign event in the future.

Postscript: At the next event, Roger got hold of several dozen wooden ice cream spoons, "*which we carried for the rest of the year in commemoration of the confrontation with the sweet-talking southern <u>spoon woman</u>.*"

CHAPTER FIFTEEN

A Minor Annoyance and
other Amusements

A funny thing happened to me when I returned to work the very next Monday morning after the Red River event. I got fired!

I was off work one day. That evening, I received a phone call from an ex-Missouri Poster employee. He told me that a screen printing company in Kansas City, Kansas was looking for a screen maker. The next day I journeyed to Graphic Communications, INC and was hired immediately.

I had been an employee at GCI less than two months when I experienced car trouble. I should mention that within three years of ownership, the mini van began to act up. We had problems with the brakes, the cruise control went out, and the front-end alignment went haywire. Seems like we had a number of issues with the van that suddenly developed once the warranty ran out.

One day, I decided to drive the mini van to work. This was barely two months after my hire at GCI. Mona was using the Explorer for something, so I was driving the van towards Kansas when all of a sudden the engine conked out right on the Lewis and Clark viaduct over the Kansas River.

I called work to say I'd be late, and then I waited for Mona to show up. She didn't get off work till 7 AM and it was almost 8 AM when she arrived to rescue me. After she dropped me off at work, she called a tow truck for the mini van.

To make a long story short, the mechanic said the engine was shot and it would take a couple grand to get things right. As I'd stated earlier, the mini van had already had more than its share of mechanical problems in its brief six-year life. We sold it on the spot and Mona bought herself a small economy car from my brother, the used car salesman, at the Ford dealership in Sedalia, MO.

That mini van had taken us to Gettysburg and back during the summer of 1988. We put a lot of miles of it, but it should have lasted longer than six years.

I wouldn't allow these two minor annoyances to dampen my enthusiasm for Civil War reenacting, so in May, I attended yet another Fort Scott encampment, then on June 11-12, I returned to Weston, MO.

It was at Weston, or Bee Creek, that the reenactment resembled something from the siege of Petersburg or perhaps the trench works of World War One.

There were two lines of trenches, which faced each other about one hundred yards apart. In about three of four key areas within each trench, ramparts had been built to accommodate artillery guns. The guns could be wheeled down into the trench with only the muzzle poking out exposed. The ground in front of the cannon was shoveled away to allow a clear field of fire.

I believe the trenches had been dug with a backhoe. The Confederate trench works looked magnificent. They had even constructed a brush arbor over the gun emplacements like some sort of camouflage. Meanwhile, the trenches on the Union side looked half-assed and were only about seven inches deep. The trenches were muddy and had about six inches of water in them. Union volunteers worked throughout the day with picks and shovels to make the trench line a tad more presentable. Fortune smiled upon me, as I would not have to slog in the mud that weekend.

Ralph Monaco was toying with the idea of purchasing a mountain howitzer. One was available for a couple grand, but instead of buying it himself, Ralph suggested that five of us so go in on the purchase. *I'll bet Ralph's wife would have thrown a fit if he'd come home with that thing hitched to his sport's car.* I think Ralph's brother-in-law, Mike, was one of the conspirators along with Jeff Perriman. Not sure who else was involved in the scheme for the Monaco gun, but Ralph gently elbowed me into considering going in on the deal. It would be a couple hundred dollars apiece, but I was reluctant to throw my hat in the ring. I said I'd think about it.

Meanwhile, the gun was available for us to play with. It was positioned on the far left of the Union line, on high ground and away from the mud. A paper collar artillery officer taught us the drill so we wouldn't blow ourselves up. I explained that I had served as an artilleryman in 1980 and could handle the loader's job. I bragged that Gregg Higginbotham and I had manhandled a 7/8 scale Napoleon during the October 1980 Battle of Trading Post, Kansas. I boasted that we'd fired cow pies and hornet's nest from the muzzle, but the ninety-day wonder was not impressed. He was dressed in a crisp artillery shell jacket with shiny brass buttons while the rest of us manhandled the gun in our shirtsleeves. Throughout the battle, the officer kept an eye on us. I think he was as nervous as a mother hen.

About the only other thing I can recall from this Weston event, I introduced Ralph to the all-female vaudeville troupe, the 'Soiled Doves.' One of the 'doves' was attracted to Ralph and showed him some 'cheesecake' pictures of herself in various stages of undress. Later that evening, she shared small talk and a bottle of wine with Ralph. Three is a crowd, so I retired to my fart sack under the moonlight.

July 23-24 Windsor, MO

During the early summer of 1994, I was invited to Mark Olson's house and I met his wife Diane and their two children. I think the daughter was about twenty and worked at Price Chopper. Their son was maybe seventeen and member of a local rock band trying to make the big time.

I brought Katie and one of her girlfriends along, because Mark said he had a pool we could frolic in. Not much of an Esther Williams myself, I sat on the patio, sipped cold beer, and showed Mark my reenactment photo albums. I visited the Olson house on several occasions after that, sometimes with Jon Isaacson in tow.

In July, the three of us went down to the Windsor event.

Aside from the Saturday afternoon battle, the only thing that I recall was Isaacson was playing his banjo and I had my Uncle Tom stick doll. It was so hot we'd set up our dog tents shebang style, but there was nary a breeze that day.

I don't remember the particulars of the afternoon battle. It was another one of those generic 'blow powder back and forth for the amusement of a picnic audience.' It was hot! We might have worn our jackets unbuttoned, with the accoutrements worn under the coat.

At the conclusion of the fight, I noticed a small group of people standing off to the left, near a stand of trees. Someone shouted that Mark Olson had passed out. A bunch of us started to walk over that way, when Mark Strother came running past with a first aid kit and shouted, "Everyone, get out of the way!" I stepped aside and wandered back to my own tent and sucked down water. I couldn't see what was going on, but at a distance of almost one hundred yards, I could see that Mark Olson had been stripped of all his clothes except his briefs. After a few tense minutes, an ambulance came through and took him to the hospital.

I had only known Mark Olson a few short months, since the Red River event. However, as I got to know him with each passing month, I sort of took him under my wing. You could never count on Ralph or Mike Monaco to show up at an event, plus Jeff Perriman was on the outs with his marriage. Meanwhile, Jon Isaacson was only coming to events to play his banjo, therefore I felt it was my duty to be Mark's big brother and help integrate him into the hobby as best I could.

With him being carted off to the hospital, I was visibly nervous. What would I tell his wife? I began to imagine a scenario where I would have Mark's dead body in the back of my Explorer on the drive home. His body would be covered with a gum blanket and wedged between all the rifles, dirty uniforms, and tent poles.

Many hours passed. It was late afternoon, close to sundown, when Mark Olson returned. Not only was he wearing his 20th Century clothes, he also wore a sheepish, somewhat embarrassed grin.

As some of the boys gathered around to hear the tale, Mark explained that near the conclusion of the fight, he felt somewhat fatigued.

"As I got to the grove of trees," he recalled, *"I sat down for I was getting dizzy. Randy Rogers and others immediately started stripping me down and pouring canteen water on me from my head to my crotch. I was actually feeling better when from behind and unexpected by all, I was baptized with a large bucket of ice water* (this from an overly concerned reenactor woman). *The needles that went through me were indescribable, but it only lasted for a few seconds.*

"Things went black after that, until I woke up in a Clinton, Missouri Hospital. I remember waking up lying buck-naked on a "cooling bed". As my eyes began to focus, I recognized one of my pards, Mark Strother, standing next to the bed holding my wallet and keys. He looked down at me and asked, 'How come you don't bring any cash to reenactments?'

"After I was released from the Hospital and we went back to Windsor. It was good to be reunited with the group. Randy Rogers took me aside and apologized for what had happened. As First Sergeant, he said he was responsible for us and was sorry he couldn't stop the ice water lady. I told him everything was fine and there was no reason to apologize. After finding all my clothes that were stripped from me, I was able to continue the event and participated in Sunday's battle without a repeat performance of Saturday."

On the way home Sunday afternoon, Jon Isaacson and I vowed not to say anything to Mark's wife about his 'near death' experience or his stay in the hospital. For the ride home, Jon decided to wrap himself up in a bed sheet. Where Jon got the bed sheet is anybody's guess, but Jon had it around him and off one shoulder like a Roman toga. He even had a sprig of green in his hair. Andy Fulks, over at Fall Creek Sutlery, said Jon looked like *Edwin Booth* (John Wilkes' brother). The heat must have affected Jon just as much as it had Mark.

Sept 17-18, 1994, Lexington, MO

This was the first time doing Missouri State Guard at Lexington. Dave Bennett organized the Macon County Silver Grays, and had a company strength of about 30 guys including Hig, Isaacson, and myself. I was reluctant to abandon my Holmes Brigade pards; I felt like a traitor for switching sides, but I vowed I would dress in the Federal blue on Sunday.

On Friday night the Macon County Silver Grays set up camp on the front lawn on the Amy Heaven-Greg Hildreth home. In 1994, they were living in a small Victorian house near the center of town. Within six years they would move south to another Victorian home, with more acreage, near the edge of the city limits.

As all Missouri State Guardsmen, in the autumn of 1861, wore only civilian clothing, carried civilian accoutrements and weapons from home, I had to modify my impression. One of the most important changes involved finding different bedding.

Gum blankets were out! Plus no gray army issue blankets! It was suggested to me earlier in the year that I bring a painted ground cloth and a quilt. Well, I have several old quilts at home, but for a ground cloth, I bought a piece of canvas from the fabric store, about 6 foot by 4 foot, then I painted a pattern on it using plain ordinary enamel paint. After the paint dried, the cloth was heavy, but it was moisture-proof.

The early fight on Saturday had the Missouri State Guardsmen in line of battle right in the middle of a residential street with a mountain howitzer to keep us company. In a prelude to the original battle and siege alongside the Anderson House, a brisk skirmish took place in the local cemetery, followed by street fighting right through the town.

The residential streets of Lexington are barely wide enough for two cars to pass side by side, much less thirty men elbow to elbow. However, here we were, in line of battle, facing five companies of good Union men. We glared at each other from a distance of 50 yards and then we commenced to fire away.

Only about an arm's length away, on either side of us, was the city sidewalk, packed with men, women, and kids. A patrolman had the unpleasant duty of keeping the people from wandering in the path of gunplay, while a squad car blocked the intersection. This reminded me of the street fighting in Ironton (on the path back to Fort Davidson in Pilot Knob), but the streets of Lexington were not wide enough to break ranks in the center and fall back to the rear. Instead, we were obligated to 'about face and fall back' a few dozen yards.

This side show only lasted a short time, then the Federals walked away, via a side street, presumably to their own camp, about two hundred yards east of the Anderson House.

Don't know what all transpired over the course of this weekend, other than the fact we probably downed a far amount of 'popskull'. I may have slept with the MSG that Saturday night near the Anderson House in an area that once was a garden.

Saturday evening, John and Teresa Maki invited all the Holmes Brigade boys, (including us *redheaded step children*, the Macon County Silver Grays) for a whole hog feast in the backyard of his home on Franklin Street. The Maki's live in a three-story turn of the century home only a few blocks from the battlefield. The dinner made gluttons of us all because John laid out quite a spread of breads, roasting ears, salads, baked beans, and especially beer. John and Teresa had only been living here a few months, if memory serves me, so this was considered a house warming party. I believe Mona, Katie, Gail, and Hillari came by that day and they were also invited to 'break bread.' I think thirteen year old Katie and Hillari were a little timid of seeing a butchered hog laid out on the table, complete with the apple in its mouth.

On Sunday, I changed into my Federal duds, and served alongside the boys of Holmes Brigade during the Battle of the Hemp Bales. I fought against the same Macon County Silver Grays that I'd served with the day before. What a paradox!

Following the shindig at Lexington, Holmes Brigade was invited to attend a living history event at Mine Creek, Oct 29-30. This was then followed by the 'every other year' event at Prairie Grove, Arkansas. I can recall nothing of Mine Creek, which was merely an encampment near the same spot as in 1989. I don't have any specific memories of Prairie Grove either. Any recollections I have or care to say about this event I've already said in Volume One of Chin Music.

This concludes my observations on the year 1994. In the next chapter, I'm going to discuss the change of command, a battle reenactment near Pea Ridge, a return to Tennessee, a war-game in Kentucky, and stuff. Over time, we would return to the same events over and over again, so it is my intention to combine several episodes, from 1995 to 1997, which is the legacy of John Maki.

Chapter Sixteen

The Chronicles of Maki

It came as no surprise to us when Don Strother decided to resign as Captain of Holmes Brigade. He had made this announcement many months earlier. Don cited personal reasons and claimed it was time to allow someone else the chance. Holmes Brigade had a large membership and seemed to be operating on remote control. At several events, when we had large numbers, Don would assume the role of battalion commander and wear the insignia of a bird colonel. If given the chance, I think Don would have liked to remain in the background in a staff position and shuffle papers when called upon.

As I've mentioned earlier, Don seemed to prefer his own company. With the exception of the drill field or the battlefield, Don seemed to spend many hours in his tent hunched over his camp desk going over paperwork. He rarely socialized with the guys, with the exception of the 'end of season toasts.'

There was a mystery about Don Strother that I couldn't find figure out. In the fifteen years that I knew him, I never really 'knew' him outside his role as an officer. I didn't know him as a person. The most I knew about Don was he was married and worked in a Tool and Die plant in Purdy, MO. He never brought his wife to events. In later years, Michelle Yipe and he would travel to events together. Many of us began to wonder about this relationship.

Don was an officer for nearly thirteen years, from September 1982 to April 1995. As a member of Holmes Brigade he never had to stand in the ranks as a common private with the only exception (*that I recall*) being Lone Jack, August 1982. For thirteen years, Don had wrapped himself up in the illusion that he was an officer and a gentleman. Maybe the weight of all those years was too much.

After thirteen years as an officer, Don decided to step aside. In the immortal words of Douglas MacArthur, he vowed, "I shall return!" Don promised that in future events, he would fall in the ranks as a private. But as of this writing, I have yet to see that return. Though he still receives the newsletter, he has never once attended an event, either as a participant or a spectator. Like Bill Fannin before him, it's as if Don Strother simply fell off the face of the earth.

At the annual encampment at Fort Scott, during the business meeting held on the evening of April 8, 1995, Don Strother resigned as captain and the job was offered to John Maki. As our 1st Lieutenant and next in command, John was the natural choice for captain and he was offered first crack at the job. Within moments of the end of one regime, a new regime began with the election of John Maki.

I believe Pat McCarthy also resigned from his position as 2nd Lieutenant at about the same time. I think his job with the police department kept him busier than ever. For the first time in many years, we found ourselves promoting someone from within the ranks to occupy the two lieutenant's positions.

Randy Rogers was promoted to First Lieutenant, Terry Forsyth was promoted to Second Lieutenant, and Gary Crane was promoted to First Sergeant.

May 5-7, 1995 Pea Ridge, Arkansas

On property, literally a 'stones throw' north of the Pea Ridge National Battlefield Park, a maximum effort battle reenactment was planned, which would (hopefully) draw several thousand participants from the east of the Mississippi River.

Very rarely will you get any interest from eastern folks into coming all the way over into Missouri, Kansas, or Arkansas to do anything. *"The Civil War in the Trans-Mississippi was merely a sideshow as compared to the bloodbaths of Virginia,"* most eastern purists' claim. *"If I've got to cross over the Mighty Mississippi, you better make it worth my while."*

Only at the battle reenactment of Wilson's Creek (1991) and one or two Pilot Knob's, have we had more than token support from the east and the Western Brigade in particular. The maximum effort event planned at Pea Ridge was not completely supported by ALL members of the Western Brigade. Those who hailed from Ohio, Indiana or Kentucky claimed Pea Ridge was "was *too far away to drive to.*" Instead the event was being sanctioned by the North/South Alliance and sponsored by Video Post Productions of Kansas City. *This was the same outfit that filmed the 1991 Wilson's Creek reenactment.*

I'm not going to get into a whole lot of detail about the Pea Ridge event because with the exception of a couple of incidents, it was not that memorable.

Let me begin by saying Pea Ridge was planned as a three-day event, beginning on Friday. There was a registration fee of only five bucks, payable prior to April 5th. A person could wait until the day of the event and walk in off the street, but the price would jump to fifteen dollars.

I traveled to the event, which began early Friday morning, with Mike and Ralph Monaco and Jeff Perriman. Within a few hours, we were at the encampment.

The event was billed as a campaign style event, but there was a tent city and dozens of sutlers with their knickknacks. Like many of the curious, I think I browsed sutler row on the first day, but bought nothing other than Lucifer's, some stick candy, and some medicated crotch powder for a dollar. The powder was nothing more than a couple tablespoons of Gold Bond in a paper envelope with an old-fashioned label stuck on it. I was afraid I'd get chafed this weekend and had never tried Gold Bond before, so I dusted my gonads real good and basked in a wonderful coolness that nearly made me swoon.

I believe most of Holmes Brigade arrived with the plan to camp campaign style. One or more of the officers might have had an A tent and there might have been some dog tents set up. The majority of us flopped right down in an old field and opened up our haversacks and began sharing food with one another.

At some point we had to blow some cartridges in the first of three scenarios. A scaled down version of Elkhorn Tavern had been built on the event site. It looked no bigger than an old country out house. It reminded me of one of the plywood buildings that had been constructed for the 1987 reenactment of Lone Jack.

Later that afternoon word came that we would go a little hike. We would march about 3.5 miles south along the old Telegraph Road all the way into the National Park. Upon arrival, we would bed down for the night on hollowed ground where so much blood was spilled so long ago. This was nothing new for Holmes Brigade. We'd been coming here almost every year since 1987. Nevertheless, it was a neat idea to have nearly a thousand reenactors on National Park property.

I'm not sure if it was this event or if it happened during Red River, but during the march, Mark Strother and I decided we wanted to goof off. The battalion was taking a half-hour break so all the boys could catch their breaths'. At some point, Telegraph Road becomes Tobacco Road, with mailboxes, homes, and barns. Right next to where the army halted, there was a home (might have been a trailer on cinder blocks) with a trampoline in the front yard. I think the lady of the house was allowing us to use her garden hose so we could refill our canteens. Meanwhile, I approached and asked her if we could jump on the trampoline. She gave me an odd look, but said okay. Mark and I pealed off our traps and shoes and we bounced around for a good ten minutes. No one else was game. Afterwards I was giddy and out of breath and had a tough time resuming the march.

Approaching the National Battlefield Park from the north, Telegraph Road becomes a narrow passage with heavy timber on both sides. Footing also becomes an issue because the trail takes many turns over rocks, sinkholes, roots, patches of mud, and mountain streams. These streams are no more than an inch deep at best with the water as clear as glass, but algae covered rocks will turn your ankle out from under you if you ain't careful.

I think all the Confederate reenactors were planning on bedding down in the lawn surrounding Elkhorn Tavern. The rest of us marched almost a 'quarter-mile', turned into one of the fields and spread our blankets between two fence rows.

The Park Rangers were very particular and nervous about having us romp about on National Park property, but they allowed us to build a couple small fire pits right there. Each fire pit was only about a foot square and dug about a foot deep. The Rangers warned us to keep our fire contained to the assigned area. They didn't want to combat a runaway grass fire.

The men took turns edging up to the tiny fires to cook their rations. I think I had a skillet by this time, but not sure what I ate. More than likely my menu consisted of summer sausage, dead things from the sea, hardtack, and fried baloney.

At some point during the night, might have been after eating the health food, I felt the need to evacuate my colon. When doing a campaign event, you should always bring a change of socks, plenty of food and two or three handfuls of toilet paper from home. Nothing will upset a reenactor more than answering the call to nature and not having the necessary paperwork to complete the job. When confronted with this unpleasant situation, I've resorted to stuff like the paper the black powder cartridges are wrapped in and reproduction paper currency. I find that with age, my system does not always shut down and I am forced to make frequent trips to the sinks. A wise man will tell you that some lessons are learnt the hard way. If I attend a campaign event, I might leave the extra shirt at home, but I never do leave without an extra handful or two of 'squeezeably soft' Charmin.

It was very late that Friday night and the stars were out, but there was no moon, therefore it was blacker than the inside of a cow. However, I felt nature's call, so I rose to unsteady feet, found the park road, and walked like a blind man about a quarter-mile to where a row of five portable toilets sat. I think I met Randy Rogers coming from the opposite direction. I wanted to make sure I didn't use the toilet he'd used.

In hindsight, I suppose I could have leaned over the top rail of the fence, but the Park Rangers might have screamed bloody murder come morning had they seen human feces on a National Park.

Steve Hall told me that he and Maki arrived late and made the trip to the National Park after dark. Steve says Gary Crane was on horseback and led them through the forest, but it was a real challenge after dark. I imagine they stumbled around like blind men and banged their shins more than a time or two. Perhaps they were tempted to hold on to the tail of the horse so they wouldn't get lost.

Saturday morning there was some kind of ceremony, and then we took the road back to the event site. This meant we had to retrace our steps through the wooded trails and over streams the same route we had had come down on. Most of the trip this time was down hill, but the final one hundred yards into the event was up steep pavement.

In the afternoon it started to rain. It wasn't that bad at first. We sandwiched our muskets and traps under two gum blankets then we entered Terry Forsyth's A tent to eat peanuts. A few of the guys had ponchos and they were walking around with the rain dripping off their hat brims. Meanwhile, the rain was starting to fall much heavier.

I kept saying to no one in particular, that "surely they won't have a battle in this stuff!" The rain was coming down in sheets, when all of a sudden, Captain John Maki shouted for us to form up for the fight. We all were too stunned for words. We all looked like a bunch of wet dogs, but we formed a ragged battle line and fired our squirt guns for about ten minutes. I don't think there were more than a dozen guns that fired, out of three hundred in line. When some of these muskets fired, a black sludge bubbled out like a poorly inflated balloon.

Finally, and mercifully, play was halted. We sandwiched our wet muskets and traps back under the gum blankets and resumed our eating of peanuts inside Terry's A tent. The worst part of the ordeal was trying to find a dry peanut.

To say that we were all miserable would be an understatement. It was still raining like Noah's flood, so a consensus was taken on 'cuttin' stick.' Ralph, Mike, and Perriman were all for leaving, finding a motel, and eating hot chow. If I'd brought my own car or if I had my own tent to crawl under, I might have thought differently. Remembering Red

River I was reluctant to spend another miserable night in wet clothes, so I agreed with the majority.

The problem was that reenactor parking was at the bottom of a steep, slippery hill. With all my gear strapped on my back, I carefully navigated myself down the ridge. It was one hundred feet down this hell hill. Roots and tree limbs helped check my fall from certain injury or dismemberment. I believe we had plastic trash bags to put some of our stuff in and to sit upon as we drove away from the event.

About 20 miles or so from the event, the skies seemed to brighten a little bit. It was still raining, but not as heavy. We all debated about turning around and going back, but in the end, we all said "NAH!"

We found a motel where each of us had a hot shower, and then we changed into 20th century clothes, and found a restaurant (*that was serving cold beer*). Sunday morning found us back on the highway to Kansas City.

Between June and the end of October, Holmes Brigade attended some of the usual stuff including an event at Glasgow, Lone Jack, and Pilot Knob. I came to Lone Jack as a spectator, for some odd reason. I had something going on that weekend, but I did drive up either Saturday or Sunday afternoon to see the boys.

I don't remember a thing about the other two events. It was probably the same stuff as any other event, blow cartridges back and forth, but nothing stands out to warrant further discussion.

October 27-29, 1995, Spring Hill, TN

Event organizers must have learned their lesson from six years earlier. This event would no longer be held in early December. It's possible they didn't want people freezing or have another death on their hands (*as with the December 1989 event*), so the event was kicked back to the end of October while the weather was still reasonable.

I think I mentioned that the old 1989 reenactment site had been turned into a golf course. This year, the event would be held on property owned by the Saturn Automobile Company. In 1995, Saturn was still a new automobile. Most of us had never heard of Saturn, but they owned 1,500 acres near Spring Hill, Tennessee, that they would allow us to play on. I believe the property included land that was in the original 1864 fight. Registration was $6, payable before October 1ˢᵗ.

Steve Hall and I rode down in my Explorer and after a twelve-hour drive, pulled into registration to sign the usual waiver forms at the sign-in station.

I think there was a tobacco shop in a nearby strip mall, so I bought some smokes then we drove to Rippavilla.

Rippavilla was an old plantation house that had served as John Bell Hood's headquarters just before the Battle of Franklin. In was in this house that he'd had his famous 'shit-fit' with all his generals after he found out that the Union Army had escaped his grasp during the night of Nov. 29, 1864. The Saturn Automobile Company owned this house, plus all surrounding acreage.

Upon arrival, it was discovered that there had been some recent rains that had turned some of the roads pretty soupy. I think there was only one road leading into camps. People had to take turns going in and out of the muck, if memory serves me.

The parking was about 'a quarter-mile' from the camp. We unloaded all the junk, including A frame tents, and then I bravely took the vehicle up the road. I probably had the Explorer in 4-wheel drive getting around. The parking lot was on higher ground, so it wasn't too terrible.

Of course it was very late when we got into camp. The question is whether we arrived Thursday night or Friday night. It might have been Friday night, because just as we pulled into camp, some of the Union Army was marching out for the late afternoon skirmish. I distinctly recall someone asking if we were going to fall in, but we politely declined. We still had our civvies on and nothing set up yet.

Holmes Brigade had about thirty guys, but Captain John Maki couldn't make it. He was still employed at Mid-America Car (the railroad people). Trying to get a day off from that company, John once told me, was like pulling teeth from a chicken. Randy Rogers and Terry Forsyth ran the company.

We were on our own for rations, but I'm not sure what all was eaten. Did we eat together as a company or was it individual mess?

I was surprised to see Gregg Higginbotham at this event. He did not fall in with Holmes, but with another Federal unit who was doing campaign style camping, meaning no tents. It might have been a group organized by Cal Kinzer or the Mudsills. I believe he brought Greg Hildreth (*fellow from the previous Lexington reenactment*) and possibly Don Whitson or Dave Bennett.

The only thing I recall of the battle on Saturday and Sunday was we had to march a *helluva* long way to get there! It was two miles one way, at least!

We had to go through a green tree-lined park, and then once we came out on the opposite side, the battlefield looked like three football fields end to end.

I'm not sure who the Western Brigade commander was at this time. I think this was after the Shackleford era, but before the era of Chuck Warnick. The only battalion officer I recollect for sure, who was doing most of the shouting and running around, was a skinny critter named Chad Green.

I think Chad Green was a Colonel. He reminded me of a combination of Audie Murphy and Benny Hill, with a little Wild Bill Hickok thrown in. During the battle on Saturday, we were throwing volley after volley into a line of Confederates. Chad Green was darting back and forth like a wild hare, mostly with his hat in one hand and a saber in the other. His shoulder length brown hair danced in the air as he worked himself up into a fever pitch with loud shouts of defiance against the foe.

It's possible he was commander of our part of the Brigade, because he gave a shout at us to charge a Confederate field cannon, which sat one hundred yards at the bottom of a hill. Like Jack and Jill, we tumbled down the ravine and chased the fat Rebel gunners from their gun and we claimed the captured prize. Chad Green whooped and hollered and waved his Hardee hat in the air and shook his long flowing locks towards the admiring ladies behind the spectator tape.

This may have been the signal to conclude the play-acting because we found ourselves crawling back up hill to reform the Brigade in order to march off the field. It was while we were reforming our blue lines, I heard someone cry, "Bob Talbott!"

On the other side of the spectator tape, only about twenty yards from me, were three lovely ladies. Two of them were my cousins Patty and Clarinda Jo. The third was Patty's daughter, Erin. It had been almost six years since I'd last laid eyes on them, at the Franklin 1989 event. Erin had been about twelve, now she was almost eighteen. And what a looker! She was a raven-haired beauty if there ever was one.

Months earlier, I had called Cousin Patty and told her that I was coming to this Spring Hill event. She had just gotten divorced from her husband, Gary Fitzhugh, but still lived in the city of Franklin. Clarinda Jo was also divorced, had left Kansas City and had moved to Tennessee to be with her sister.

I had just barely begun a warm conversation with the girls, when behind me; I became aware of a stone silence. Spinning around, I realized that the four of us (*especially the girls*) had become the object of attention by the three hundred boys of the battalion. All the guys had laughter in their eyes and grins on their faces, while some started making innocent remarks. In essence, the guys were giving me grief over the attention I'd drawn by these three Tennessee beauties.

The colonel told me we had to march back to camp, but told me that the ladies were welcome to follow us. I felt a little red-faced as I rejoined the ranks; the guys were still poking good-natured elbows into my ribs for the female attention I received despite the fact I told them they were kin.

When a soldier is with the army, nothing warms his soul more, than being in the presence of the opposite sex. However not all emotions are carnal or vulgar. Most generally, the soldier is reminded of the loving mother, wife, or sister who is far away at home. Even the most bitter of men will feel his heart soften when he hears to soft voice of a gentlewoman directed at him.

The army marched all the way back to camp, at least two miles. I was awed by the fact that my cousins followed right behind us, like children following the Pied Piper. Once the ranks were dismissed, most of the guys assembled their cooking stuff and began planing their dinners. I had just pealed off my jacket and was standing there in my sweat soaked shirt, when the girls came into view.

When I called Patty months earlier, I'd suggested to them that they invite me to dinner. I suppose I was a little abrupt and was assuming they had nothing else to do that Saturday night. Clarinda Jo told me that there was some sort of "singles night" at the local church they'd been invited to, but since I was in town, they'd cater to my needs. To be honest, I felt like I was infringing on their personal time. Six years ago, I had been invited to eat dinner with Patty, her husband, and the two girls. This time, Patty and Clarinda were both recently divorced and probably had better things to do than baby-sit me. At the time, they couldn't think of any thing better than take me out, so off we went. I told Steve Hall and the entire Holmes Brigade guys not to wait up for me.

As we left camp, there was a guy in another company, who asked the girls the correct time. It just so happened he had his shirt off, which was merely an excuse to display a hairy chest. Of course the girls and I knew this guy was all about his personal vanity and his desire to display his physique. If the fellow had shown the girls his hairy ass, I suppose I would have been compelled to thrash him.

The girls took me to their car, which was parked about "a quarter-mile" away. I sat in the back and I think they had the windows rolled down, because I probably smelled like a hog. Young Erin sat in the back with me, but as far away as possible to avoid getting any of the funk oozing off me.

Despite the unpleasant vapors, we had a nice conversation. The girls drove me through parts of Nashville, past Dolly Parton's home, and a few other landmarks. We were on the road at least an hour until the car pulled up at a house and Erin got out. She was visiting a friend, possibly a boyfriend.

Further down the road we went until we pulled into a Franklin strip mall where we went into a Mexican restaurant and had Chimichangas and Margaritas on the rocks. I was feeling bold, that I ordered my Margarita in a half-gallon goblet. By the time I finished that pup, I had to be fork lifted back into the car.

About an hour later, I was driven back to the Rippavilla plantation. I don't remember the drive back; it's possible I was passed out. I said goodbye to both my cousins, gave each a sloppy kiss, and staggered back to camp. I got lost on the way and had to back track about a "quarter-mile" till I found Holmes Brigade.

Some of the boys were still up. It was around 10 PM when I staggered through the company street, making an ass of myself in the process. I was blasted.

I don't remember going to bed, but must have passed out after hitting the fart sack. The very next morning, I was feeling pretty low. I felt as if a hog had shit in my mouth and used my tongue for toilet paper. I don't think I had to puke, but I probably had to make a visit to the porta-johns to empty my screaming colon.

The Sunday afternoon battle was at the very same place where we'd had it on Saturday. That meant we had to march over the same ground we'd covered yesterday, just to reach the field for the opening kickoff.

In this exciting episode, we were compelled to advance across the same three hundred yards of open field and assault an earthen fortification held by 'Johnny Reb.' Act One began with a half-hour artillery duel followed by Act Two, a half-hour musket duel at long range. Each side had nearly a thousand men each. We fired as a Brigade, by battalion, by company, by sections, by rank, and fired at will. We must have blown one hundred rounds each.

Act Three of this drama opened with the gradual advance by the soldiers in blue, complete with flags snapping in the breeze and little boys going 'rat-a-tat-tat' on their drums. The Confederate vagabonds gave ground slowly with a few of their kind dropping to Mother Earth in that final embrace of death.

Carefully our lines stepped over the stilled bodies of both the blue and the gray. Medical stewards and assistants with buckets of cold water lingered to the rear to "attend to the wounded." Rags soaked with fake blood were secured to the heads and limbs of some of these wounded. Some men acted like they had been 'gut shot' and went through a whole Academy Award performance of writhing, groaning, screaming, and flopping around on the ground like fish out of water.

Meanwhile, I was in the rear rank of Holmes Brigade trying to keep my place in line. When in line of battle, on the advance, the order is to try to keep the line straight. In many cases, the officers will tell the men to 'dress to the center.' The Color Company, with the National and Regimental flags, is posted in the center of the regiment, so the idea is for the left and right companies to squeeze towards the center. When a thousand men squeeze, someone usually gets squeezed out. I soon found myself on the outside looking in, so I said to hell with it and remained to the rear with the file closers.

Finally, there came a command to advance at the double. *It's probable this command was given by Chad Green, who had his hat off and his hair flowing like Rapunzel.* To advance at the double means the men will break into a trot. There was about another one hundred yards to the earthen fortification. I was damned if I was going to run any more, so I stopped dead in my tracks. Perhaps the lingering effects of last nights half-gallon Margarita put jelly in my legs.

Under a cloud of rising dust, the gallant boys in blue stormed the earth works and engaged the defiant foe at close quarters. This meant some pushing and shoving was probably going on, as well as, harsh words said by both parties.

Rather than take part in the celebration of victory that followed, I made a complete about face and left the field. It was my intention to walk all the way back to camp, get the Explorer, and start breaking down the camp. To get to the parking lot would require me to walk the complete two miles all by myself. If anybody happened to ask me why I was leaving the field, I would tell them I was demoralized. Another phrase would be 'showing the white feather" or 'shell shock.' Nobody saw me leave and I didn't say goodbye. I just walked away.

It took me about a half-hour to get to the parking lot. I made frequent stops along the way, because my legs were feeling wobbly. Behind me I could still hear the sputtering of rifle fire from the boys still dueling it out on the battlefield.

A few reenactors had thought as I did and left the battlefield early. There were a few cars, pick-ups, and horse trailers moving around the camps. I parked the Explorer near our camp, packed a few things away, changed into my civvies, and catnapped until the army came marching home.

Following the event in Tennessee, Holmes Brigade next went to Prairie Grove, Arkansas. I've said much about this early December reenactment in Volume One of Chin Music. It is sufficient to say it is held as close to the original date as possible and on the same ground as the 1862 fight. I have nothing to say about the event held in late 1995; nothing out of the ordinary stands out other than the normal blowing off of black powder cartridges and sleeping on the cold, cold ground.

You've heard the expression, "Been there, done that." With that said, I must admit to you that 1996, with one exception, was nothing to speak of. We had a full slate of events on our calendar, from Fort Scott, Kansas, in early April, to Owensboro, Kentucky, in late October.

There was the Wilderness Campaign, held in Virginia during the weekend of May 17-19, but I didn't want to go all the way to Virginia. There was Fort Larned, Kansas, during Memorial Day weekend, but I wanted to stay at home during the holiday and get some work done around the house. There were also events in Nebraska and Oklahoma, but I wasn't in the mood for that either.

After Fort Scott, I attended the 'Bleeding Kansas' event in Lecompton, Kansas, the early war event at Cole Camp, Missouri, and I journeyed back to the northeast corner of Missouri at Athens. But with all these events, it was the same tune over and over, 'been there, done that.'

I realize I'm not giving 1996 its due. I'm sure a majority of the guys, in Holmes Brigade, would be able to paint a more exciting picture of this year. It's possible I've forgotten an incident relating to 1996, but as I attend the same stuff over and over again, nothing new stands out.

However, not all is lost. I would like to tell you of an event I attended in 1996 that DID have an impact on me, one that affected me physically and caused me to consider an amputation.

CHAPTER SEVENTEEN

The Wargasm of Ninety-Six

November 1-2, 1996, somewhere in Muhlenberg County, Kentucky

Just when I thought the reenactment season was over and I could look forward to a long winter's nap, what should come to my ears, but the cry of the war gods of Western Brigade chanting, "WARGAME! WARGAME! RAH RAH RAH!" The folks on the throne of power decreed that there should be at least one more tactical before the end of the decade. I think this tactical would be the last I would ever attend, plus it's one that has affected me the most, in a physical way, so it's important that I discuss it here.

By definition, the wargame or tactical is not meant to be seen by the public, but is solely for the amusement of the participant. Perhaps 'amusement' is too frivolous a term. There is nothing amusing about running about in unfriendly terrain, sleeping on the cold, hard ground, eating poorly cooked food, and firing blanks at an enemy. A tactical is a means to sharpen the 'on-the-field' skills of a soldier by placing him in a combat setting.

The difference between a tactical and regular battle reenactment is with a tactical, an impartial judge will determine whether goals are met, objectives are taken, and positions are held. During the course of the tactical, a number of points will be added or subtracted depending on how the unit performs. What will affect the performance of a unit in a tactical the most is when a judge begins deducting men from the ranks by declaring them 'casualties.'

The judges for this tactical will be Officer's of the U.S. Army Observer Controller Team based at Fort Knox, Kentucky. These judges have been briefed on the various weapons and tactics of the Civil War soldier. They will determine casualties, and critique our movements both on the march and in battle after the campaign for the day is over each day. Various judges will be assigned to EACH battalion of infantry, artillery and cavalry. Each of the 15 or so judges will be equipped with a hand-held radio so they could report the position of the troops assigned to them (from a bulletin published in October/November 1996 Holmes Brigade dispatch).

In the past I've attended a number of tactical's including those held during mainstream reenactments such as Prairie Grove, Arkansas, Brices Crossroads, and Champions Hill, Mississippi. Only at such places as Land between the Lakes and Red River have I experienced a total 'head to toe' military campaigner experience.

Based on a number of after action reports that I read, the Western Brigade seemed unhappy with the turn of events at Land between the Lakes tactical of 1991. Although most reenactors agreed that it was held on a great site with lots of good troops and good judges (although not nearly enough of them), once things got under way, no one had a clue what was going on. Just like in the real army!

Despite the negative feedback, we could have easily returned to LBL, but it's possible it was closed for the season, so a substitute site was chosen. We ended up going to the Wendell H. Ford Regional Training Center, training ground for the Western Kentucky National Guard.

"From its beginnings in 1969 as a 29 acre weekend training site, the Ford Training Center has been hailed as the premier mechanized infantry and armor maneuver training area east of the Mississippi River, providing effective and cost-efficient training facilities for National Guard, Reserve and active component units from every branch of service.

"Constructed on 8,500 acres of reclaimed strip-mine land, the Training Center has gently rolling hills and is relatively flat with open areas ideal for scenarios

demonstrating linear tactics. The site also feature live-fire ranges, hardened bivouac sites, a controlled humidity storage complex, complete maintenance facilities for military equipment, engagement skills training center, obstacle course and a 4,200 ft. grass runway" (from the same bulletin).

The National Guard would only let use about five square miles. We could not play with the tanks, the live-fire range, or the 4,200-ft. grass runway. Damn!

The Western Brigade had wanted to use 'Ford Field' in late October, but the 101st Airborne was having their own wargame exercise, so a second option for the reenactors was November 1st through 3rd.

Like I said, I was all set for a long winter's nap when this event was announced. I could have stayed home. After all, Higginbotham was not going nor was John Maki. Jon Isaacson was gone to Harper's Ferry; Ralph Monaco was running for State Rep, and his brother-in-law Mike Monaco worked as a sideline doctor for the Kansas City Chiefs football team. *Mike was one of several physicians who, on game day, fixed sprains, bumps, bruises, and other non-life threatening injuries as the football player came off the field.*

So here I was, undecided about going to Kentucky, when Mark Olson said he would like to go. As it turned out, there ended up being four of us who made the trip in my Explorer. There was Mark, Joe Hudgens (a kid just out of high school and on his way to study law just like Aaron Racine), Steve Hall (who had been elected to first sergeant at the spring muster at Ft. Scott), and myself.

There were general instructions, printed in the Holmes Brigade Dispatch, on how to get to the event, but I went ahead and printed out an 'idiot proof' map using my Rand McNally Road Atlas computer program. The Rand McNally computer program is just like having the big, floppy magazine version without the magazine. Today, most people would probably use Map Quest or some other internet service.

We probably left early Friday morning and arrived in Kentucky that evening. The sun was still shinning, even for the first of November, so it must have been around 5PM. We made good time.

An hour before reaching the event, I found a convenience store. It's possible we stopped because the guys wanted to look for some bacon, jerky, and 'Slim Jims.' If memory serves me, this store didn't have much of a variety of stuff. It was out in the middle of nowhere and was mostly a cold beer and fish bait store. I was looking for something to ease a headache I was developing, but the only thing the guy sold was GOODY'S HEADACHE POWDER. I believe the powders are nothing more than crushed aspirin pills packed in little wax paper envelopes and sold for about a buck. There were about ten wax paper envelopes per packet. I had never heard of headache powders, but they seemed to do the trick.

After a few more miles, we found ourselves within the 'Ford Field' complex. The area, I vaguely remember driving through, looked like a construction site in which a lot of earth movers had been at work ripping and tearing up the ground for no apparent reason. It was as if someone had taken a giant ice cream scoop to the whole area, then tossed the hunks of earth in haphazard directions. Stands of trees and wild brush grew on either side, plus a nasty road had been scratched out. This was no place for the timid, definitely Jeep country. I believe we drove past a whole bunch of mechanical vehicles, including half-tracks and tanks. It looked like a weird sort of military used car lot the way the armor was parked side by side.

The good news was that the Union camp was the first thing we bumped into. After a 'quarter-mile more,' we saw what looked like a refugee camp smack dab in the middle of several bomb craters. That's the only way I can describe the camp as I recall it. The whole area as far as I could see looked like the no man's land of World War One. I parked the Explorer about a hundred yards away, we changed into our duds, and then we manhandled our belongings over to the forbidden zone.

I was amazed at the sight of so many dog tents! *"Don't bring anything that you can't tote yourself,"* we were told yet here were the guys of Holmes Brigade with tents and extra blankets. I did not bring a dog tent, but unsure about the rest of the boys. This was supposed to be a tactical, one in which you carry everything on your back, including rations, weapon and at least 200 rounds per man. The organizers within the Western Brigade told us to, *"expect a good march and hard-core living/ campaigning throughout the weekend. This is a true hard-core experience, so make sure you are aware of the hardships involved, but it is the closest thing you will ever experience to the actual war."*

The organizers had good intentions when they wrote this event up, but when temperatures begin to fall, as they usually do in late October and early November, authenticity only goes so far. While our ancestors of 150 years earlier surely spent many nights on the cold hard ground, modern man will not always make that sacrifice and will scurry like a ground hog under the shelter of canvas.

Realizing that some people would bring Sibleys, walls and A frame tents, despite the attempt at a total campaign style tactical, event organizers decreed that these large tents would be located in a separate area known as the 'fixed camp.' These fixed camps would be located deep in the tactical area and would serve as supply depots. Ammunition and other supplies would be brought out to the Campaign Army via wagons from these camps. They would also, in a larger capacity, become an objective for opposing armies to capture or defend.

Who occupied these large tents? Well, some men brought their wives and/or sweethearts to the event. No matter <u>how</u> much you explain to people that this is to be a campaign style event, you'll always find at least a half dozen women who tag along just to be there. It's like they don't want to sit at home while the men are away at play (or so they assume). Even though my wife and daughter attended Civil War events with me in the past, they were mainstream events in which there were specific activities for the ladies and kids. At a tactical event, these gentle creatures had no purpose or role to play. However, that did not sway them from sitting in front of their tents for hours on end doing nothing, except knitting or hovering over a boiling pot.

Then there was the artillery camp. These boys with the red hat cords could not go anywhere with out rope beds, tent fly's, and mountain man chairs. Of course, one must realize that most artillerymen are overage and overweight. Certainly incapable of lying out on the cold, hard ground like their infantry counterparts.

Finally, we had sutler row. Actually, I only think there were three peddlers at this event. These vultures can smell a dollar bill a mile away. I'm pretty sure Fall Creek was one of the sutlers who were 'allowed' to attend. Of course, they had their circus tents set up with plenty of room inside for twenty or thirty boys to look over the merchandise that included ponchos and heavy wool blankets. Since this was early November, I'll wager that Fall Creek had plenty of both items and at an inflated price to tempt the hard-core lads who chose to sleep outdoors.

The Union Brigade-under temporary command of Chris Craft, our leader at First Manassas, Shiloh, and Gettysburg-was organized into three battalions, numbering about 150-175 men each. Holmes Brigade, about 25 of us, was assigned to Second Battalion, under the command of Chad Green, that flamboyant, swashbuckling madman of the previous Spring Hill event. The other units in 2nd Battalion included Logan's Brigade, the 47th, 48th, and 115th New York, the 21st Ohio, Willich's Brigade, and the 11th Kentucky. Sounds like a whole mouthful of boys, but the numbers suggest each unit had a strength of maybe twenty or less.

We also had an artillery battery (see early mention of red hat cord boys), the 6th Kentucky Cavalry (a dozen horses' asses), and the US Signal Corp. I think the latter group had fancy look-through telescopes and colored dishtowels that they waved to get someone's attention. Last but not least, we had the Brigade Quartermaster. He was in charge of supplies including straw, firewood, extra ammunition, the water ration, and anything else that wasn't nailed down.

As Mike Gosser remembers it: *"Before the event we paid a fee for firewood* (a registration fee of $6 per person covered such things as emergency medical coverage, porta-johns, radio communications, trash pick up, and firewood). *When we went for our firewood issue the Quartermaster was none other than Ol' Ed McDonald. As we stood in line he bellowed repeatedly "one stick per man per day". Ever since then we have referred to Ed affectionately as "Ol' One Stick".*

I don't know why they were so stingy with the firewood. There were miles of woods all around us. However, we weren't allowed to wander off and attack the forest of the National Guard Training Area. We could only use the firewood that was provided us. One stick per man per day didn't last too long.

You used up half that much just to cook. Let's say we used four sticks of wood to cook our breakfast, four to cook lunch, and four to cook supper. That's twelve. It got pretty damn cold at night (not nearly as at '89 Franklin). Those thirteen remaining sticks did little to take the chill off the bones of 25 guys huddled around its flames. I spent one night trying to thaw out frostbitten feet.

"Phil and Matt Curran and I hunkered in a dog tent for warmth with Phil in the middle and Matt and I on the outsides," recalls Mike Gosser. *"At least twice during the night Matt and I woke up to find Phil had rolled over and over in his sleep and was in a cocoon of all the blankets with Matt and me freezing."*

I already told you what a dummy I was for not thinking to bring a dog tent. I thought the rules were to bring only what one could carry on his back! Actually, a dog tent is nothing more than two shelter halves (measuring about 3 foot by 6 foot) buttoned together and tossed over makeshift poles. The shelter half is designed so each man can carry a piece. I could have made room in my knapsack for it, but I was still using my Mexican War hardback and it didn't have a whole lot of extra room.

Mark, Steve, and Joe might have had a dog tent or they might have shacked up with someone. I ended up sharing a dog tent with Jack Buschman, one of the 1st Colorado boys. I was mightily grateful for the lodging and he was happy for the extra body heat.

In trying to recall the events of the day at the 1996 tactical, it seems to me that it wasn't as exciting an event as LBL. We certainly didn't wander more than one mile from our lodging! Even when on the march or engaged in a skirmish activity we were always within rifle shot of our hovels. Unlike Red River where we marched so many miles then slept where we dropped, at the Kentucky tactical, we returned back in our little Hobbit burrow in no-man's land to spend the night.

Most of us, who spent that first night on the cold hard ground, spent it sleepless while praying for the sun to come up. With our teeth chattering and our limbs shaking from the bone-penetrating chill, we were very unhappy campers. Come first light on Saturday morning, we staggered like frozen zombies to form the Union Brigade. The members of each battalion appeared from different directions-over the lip of a trench, out of a crater hole, or from around a large boulder, to form one line on level ground.

I don't remember if Colonel Craft led the Brigade into drill. I seriously doubt it. This was supposed to be a tactical with the key to success being stealth and surprise. The last thing you want to do, to announce your presence to the enemy, is to have men marching around in circles with rat-a-tat drums. Even a man who is deaf, dumb, and blind would have been alerted.

We formed up on one of those man made roads that had been scratched out of the earth. This road curved around the biggest hill I ever saw in my life. The hill reminded me of Little Round Top and San Juan Hill all rolled into one. It was a grass covered hill and stood at least five hundred feet high. It was so big; I swear it looked as if it had a bit of snow on top. Much to my surprise and our discomfort, our first assignment was to march straight up that big hill.

The Brigade was spread out in one long line, about an 'eighth of a mile' in length. At a word from the Colonel, we advanced up the steep incline. Instead of rifles, we'd been better served if we'd had mountain-climbing equipment. The hill towered over us and into the clouds at an angle of 45 degrees or better. From the very first step, unit cohesion vanished. After a dozen steps, some of the 'big boned' fellows in the Brigade began to slow down. A dozen more steps and even the heartiest of lads were gasping for oxygen. A few of us were on hands and knees those last few yards, clutching handfuls of grass to pull ourselves forward.

It's a good thing the grass was dry otherwise they're might have been a whole lot of slipping and sliding. Could have meant broken bones for any man 'Jack' who tumbled down that hill. My own body was bent in half with my knee brushing against my chin as I made those final inches to the summit.

The very top of the hill was relatively flat for about fifty yards in one direction and thirty yards in another. What I thought was snow on top of the hill was in fact a large white hospital tent. How in the world did they get that big canvas tent, plus all that surgical equipment up that backbreaking hill? It must have been transported by burro or helicopter. The surgeon and his stewards looked too well fed to have manhandled the stuff themselves.

As we gasped and spewed out our early morning breakfasts, I think I spied our Signal Corp boys waving their colored dishtowels. Nearby was an artillery piece. I think it might have been only a mountain howitzer, but then again it could have been a full size Napoleon.

My memory is not clear on what happened next.

We did 'lolly-gag' up on that hill for some minutes while a judge explained about casualties. At different times, during the course of the tactical, a reenactor might feel a tap on his shoulder, turn around, and find himself in possession of a slip of paper, courtesy of one of the judges. On these slips of paper would be a brief statement declaring that 'the bearer of this note is dead' or 'the bearer of this note is wounded.' If you received a wound note, it would state the seriousness of the wound and how long you were expected to be 'out of action.'

The judge told us that someone who is 'wounded' would have to sit out the tactical for several minutes or several hours. Whether wounded or dead, the reenactor could not lay on the field. Instead he had to crawl back up the hill to the big hospital tent and park himself.

I was not a casualty myself, but I heard some stories from those that were, that once you got to the hospital tent, the surgeon put you on a detail of some sort. Maybe carrying firewood or pails of water up and down that damn hill! My guess would be that the surgeon would rather subject the poor soldier to some sadistic task than to have him lounging around getting a suntan.

After some time had past and we had farted around long enough, we received an order to go down the opposite side of the hill. Going down that big hill was almost as treacherous as climbing up it. At the bottom of the opposite side was the 'supply depot.' Here were the big Sibley tents, the ladies/civilian camp, Quartermaster stores, and sutler row.

No sooner had we formed up in the road at the bottom, than a wall of gray and butternut appeared from the woods fifty yards beyond the tents. Once they came out of the woods, their lines quickly came together and they poured a murderous volley upon us. There might have been a Rebel cannon barking at us, as well.

First and Third Battalions might have been instructed to reform on the other side of the tents. Meanwhile, Second Battalion was asked to form up at right angles until the whole Brigade looked like a lop-sided letter L. The enemy had retreated back into the forest by this time and our boys were about to give chase, when suddenly a judge stepped forward.

The judge said that the enemy had succeeded in inflicting some casualties in Second Battalion and he came to pull some guys out of the line. It just so happened that I was attending to a shoelace, so I escaped the lottery.

About six guys from Holmes Brigade, including Mike Gosser, found that they would have to take a 'time-out.' I was standing right next to Mike in line, but the judge missed me (he overlooked me as I was bent over tying my shoe). Mike got very upset and purple in the face about having to leave the field. He hadn't had a chance to get his musket dirty and now he would have to sit out the whole rest of the afternoon on top of hospital hill.

Once everything was all sorted out to everyone's satisfaction, Second Battalion was reformed and ordered to advance into the woods (we might have been sent in to draw out the enemy and force them to chase us into the waiting arms of First and Third Battalions).

Second Battalion was spread out in skirmish formation, with at least five paces between each man. The ground was densely wooded and broken up by tall brush. Instead of advancing cautiously, Chad Green had everybody at the double quick and just as he had done at the 1995 Spring Hill event, he was leading us into the jaws of death with a sword in one hand and the National Colors in the other hand.

What a sight he was! He was like a mad hare, running up and down the line, darting from brush to brush, shouting at the top of his lungs, and waving those colors like Audie Murphy in the movie RED BADGE OF COURAGE. Of course, he had lost his hat somewhere along the way. Every time he paused to shout another encouragement, he would thrust his chiseled chin upwards and give his flowing mane a teasing toss. It was as if he was posing for the cover of a romance novel.

This running about in the woods like a bull in a china closet had the desired effect of arousing the curiosity of the Confederates, who paused in their flight and gave us battle. Not sure of the order of events from here, but suffice it to say much powder was burned and at some point, Second Battalion was forced to give ground. We retreated, drawing the enemy after us like a moth to a flame, until the enemy fell into the waiting arms of First and Third Battalion.

An after action report was written some months later by Alan Rainey of the 3rd Kentucky and appeared in the Camp Chase Gazette. Although he was a member of First Battalion, Mr. Rainey has some interesting remarks about the skirmish. Since I did not keep a minute-by-minute diary of the event, I submit this spine tingling observation:

"The sound of skirmishing followed by the report of a field piece grabs everyone's attention. The crash of a volley nearby seems to indicate that the Second Battalion has engaged with someone. Realizing that subterfuge has been thwarted by the terrain, the Colonel opts for the expediency of a road and the column heads back to the track.

"The trees begin to thin and the ground on either side of the track begins to flatten out. Second Battalion is in line to our right and firing briskly into the woods at their front. We form a battle line on their left flank. We advance with the first company on the road, the rest of us strung out in a tangle of tall weeds, saplings and briars. The officers shout and holler for us to maintain our alignment, but the vegetation makes a mockery of our efforts. The men begin to drift towards the road and easier going. To the staff's dismay, the formation is now nothing more than a mass of blue moving forward.

"A general on horseback rides up. "Change front forward by the right of companies." We sense we are on the Rebel right flank and quickly form a battle line along the road. The boys move out, hot to engage. Someone spots a small field piece ahead and the line is halted and lies down.

"We crouch behind our works and watch as men from the Second Battalion begin to tumble back from the woods in our front. What's left of their battle line

assembles at the edge of the clearing that is our camp. As they loose a ragged volley, the shouts of "Cease Firing" are heard. The woods in front of the remnants of the Second Battalion are now alive with Confederates. They begin to cheer... evidently the judges have decided their charge has over run the Federal position. They have not yet noticed the men of the First Battalion lying behind the logs.

"As the boys of the Second Battalion work their way through our lines the Rebel commander appears, asking if his men can have a turn at the water in the rear of our camp. Much to his dismay, our commander shouts back that he may have as much water as he likes, as soon as he surrenders his command. The lads of the First Battalion roar their approval.

"With a shout, the Confederates start forward. Our cannon roars and the Battalion begins firing by rank "Rear rank... Fire!" "Front rank... Fire!" "Fire at will!" I roll on my back; pour the cartridge down the barrel, powder dropping in my eyes. Roll on my side, cap the nipple, and roll on my belly, aim, and fire. Repeat, repeat, repeat. After who knows how long, I am beginning to cramp. I stand up to relieve the aches and start to load again. I am tapped on the arm and a white ticket is handed to me. I glance down at it. I am killed."

Many times over the last two dozen years I've kicked myself for not keeping a detailed day-to-day diary of all the events I've attended. If I had, it's possible this volume of recollections would be even more exciting than it is. Thanks must go to Mr. Alan Rainey for fleshing out the story of the 1996 tactical with an old fashioned 'you-are-there' type of feeling. With his brief narrative, you can almost smell the gun smoke and the stink of his body sweat as he lies in wait for the enemy.

At just about sunset, all this 'tomfoolery' was halted. We were all just about played out, but we staggered back the 'quarter-mile' back to camp and collapsed like sacks of moldy potatoes in the dust. I seem to recall taking the time to boil water to clean out my musket. After running several small rags through the bore, I put everything away and prepared for supper.

I think Ed McDonald's wife was making a huge pot of chili and invited all the Holmes Brigade boys over to dine. By this time my dogs were barking and my legs felt stiff from all the running, walking, leaping, and squatting we'd been doing since sunup. Nevertheless, one never turns down free food so I hobbled 'another quarter-mile' to the civilian camp, with the rest of the boys, and ate my fill of hot chili.

After the chili dinner and back at our own camp, I pulled off my brogans and started massaging my toes in front of the crackling fire. My toes felt like popsicles so I wiggled and rubbed them only inches from the flames. I must have stubbed the big toe of my right foot because it was causing me some extra grief.

During the tactical, some of the guys had stepped in puddles of water. Hours later, their socks were still damp. Roger Forsyth (no relation to Terry) attempted to dry his socks by hanging them over the fire on a stick. He held the stick too close and managed to put a nice black burn mark on them.

Several of us sat around that fire for a spell and we wagged our tongues till sleep overcame us. I put on a pair of dry wool socks and soon found myself in the dog tent with Buschman for, what I hoped would be, an uninterrupted nap.

The bad thing about Jack Buschman's tent, which I neglected to mention before, was it seemed like it was set up on the tip of a hill. If I rolled to my left, I'd tumble down that hill. During the night, I awoke to see the roof of the tent only inches from my nose. I must have slid down during my restlessness. The only thing stopping me from tumbling out in space was the tent stakes on the side. I'd given up on resting comfortably, so I crawled out on my hands and knees over to the glowing fire pit in keep Joe Amos company.

Joe Amos was a member of the 'Gosser Gang', a motley collection of fellows from Kansas who'd joined about the early 1990's. When I originally met these men, it was probably at an early Ft. Scott event. We called them the 'Gosser Gang' because most of them were related to one another.

There was Mike Gosser and his brothers Tom and Ray. There was also Phil and Matt Curran (I think Phil was Mike's Uncle). Rounding out the crew was Joe Amos and Bryan Kent. Now I'm not sure about Bryan. He might have been a cousin of the Gosser's. Sometime in the middle part of the 1990's, Bryan suffered a back injury at a work site. As a result he did not stay in the hobby very long. I doubt he was at this event.

Anyway, it was too cold to sleep, so I crawled over to a weak and feeble fire to have a conversation with Joe Amos. Joe and I had something in common, in that both of us had attended the Tehran American School in Tehran, Iran.

It was at Ft. Scott 1992, the year I decided I was going to turn in my sergeant stripes for good that I jokingly stated that I wanted to by an officer. To back up that declaration, I told the fellows "I even brought my own sword." The sword I waved around was made of cheap hard plastic. It was about three feet long, came with its own scabbard, and had all sorts of Persian writing on it. It was a ceremonial sword that my Dad got as a gift while we were in Iran.

Later that day, Joe Amos asked me about that sword and Iran. I told him our family had lived in Tehran from 1966 to 1968. It was at this time that he told me of a similar stay during the early seventies.

My father was a member of the USAF and when he got his orders to ship out, he took us along. I was thirteen years old, Bill was eleven, and Mark was only four years old. At the time, our mother was pregnant with our sister, Carolyn.

I think Joe Amos' Dad was in the Army.

Back in the sixties and early seventies, there were all sorts of Americans living in Iran. Some were with the military, but most worked for the Oil Company. When they came to Iran, most brought their families with them.

I remember Iran as being dry, dirty, and looking like a desert. Only the wealthy lived in garden spots. This was the time of the Shah and his coronation on the peacock throne. Everyone loved the Shah, or so I thought.

While living in Iran, all the American kids, from K through 12, attended the Tehran American School or TAS for short.

That night, Joe Amos and I reminisced about the days in Tehran, attending TAS and our personal homes complete with swimming pool. Of course, being an American, you had to have a 'bodgee' in your house

The 'bodgee' or maid was a dirt-poor Iranian female who was hired to come into the home to cook and clean. The women who came to work for the Americans were pretty hard looking characters. Under all those black shawls, it was hard to tell how old they were. They could have been twenty or seventy. They all looked about the same. One step above the poor house. They were happy to get the work and the few dollars that came their way. The alternative would be to beg in the streets. I saw a lot of beggars. My brother Bill and I took a garden hose to one who came scratching at our back gate.

I don't know what time it was when I crawled out of Jack Buschman's dog tent, but guess around 3 AM. When Joe and I finished talking about the old times in Iran, it was just about daybreak. About that moment, Terry Forsyth crawled out of his dog tent and approached the fire to warm his toes.

"You bastards been talking about Iran all night," he complained.

It's obvious he didn't get much sleep. Was Terry's restlessness caused by our conversation about Iran or the extreme cold that turned him into a human ice cube? There aren't too many people who can claim they've lived in Iran. The odds are less if these two people suddenly find themselves, thirty years later, and sitting on opposite sides of a campfire in central Kentucky at a Civil War reenactment.

Most of us were already up, that early Sunday morning. We were just waiting on the sun to show up and thaw out our bones. We behaved like grumpy old bears that had been interrupted during the hibernation by a minor annoyance. There was a lot of mumbling and staggering about for the second morning in a row as the guys elbowed their way in front of the fire. One is reminded of a bunch of puppies that burrow together in a pile or ducklings that nestle under mom's wing. We were body heat vampires. We clung to each other like leaches on a corpse, regardless of individual body odor, in the hope that our limbs would unthaw.

Coffee was being boiled and a few skillets came out to cook breakfast. I fried up a piece of beef mixed with part of an onion and a green pepper and in a short time; all was right with the world. My big toe was still causing me some pain, but I thought it would be all right once we got back on the march.

Not long after breakfast, we were ordered back on the road. Not sure what happened during the morning, but we probably blew some more cartridges and wore out some shoe leather by chasing the enemy in and out of the wild woods.

Through a break in the trees, about a half-mile away, we could see a lone artillery piece inching its way up the side of a valley. Colonel Craft used his fancy 'look through glasses' and determined what he was looking at was a Reb gun and he wanted it fired at. It seemed our cannon was short handed, so a couple of volunteers, including Mike Gosser, ran over to assist in manhandling the gun and pointing it in the right direction. After a few minor adjustments with aiming, the artillery captain fired a 'blank' round.

As mentioned earlier, there were about 15 or so impartial judges. One was on top of this hill near the US artillery piece. Another judge was a half-mile away by the Reb gun. Right after the gun fired its round, these two judges began a dialogue via walkie-talkie. Based on all the information about range to target, type of ammunition supposedly used, the elevation, and other nuances related by the artillery captain, it was determined that the Reb gun had been disabled.

I think we were up on top of a high plateau when we paused for lunch. Among the items I'd crammed in my haversack, was a lemon. I'm sure I had some crackers, jerky, and some dried fruit, as well, but I distinctly remember sucking on a lemon. I had smoked several cigars over the course of the weekend and by the time I bit into that lemon, man, could I feel my taste buds shriek! My tongue and lips all tingled as I sucked on that bitter yellow fruit. That's the last thing I remember about eating Sunday lunch because the next second, we were called to action.

We must have thought we were on holiday without a care in the world. The air was clean with the scent of pine in the air. We assumed the Rebs were taking a siesta or perhaps enjoying a mint julep when suddenly word came that they were upon us. They must have slipped up the plateau by sliding unseen like snakes in the grass. I don't know how they got the drop on us, but word was breathlessly shouted for us to get into formation.

Our Brigade was scattered all over the field. The drummers sounded the long roll and we began running around in a panic, much like ants after its hill had been stepped on. Commander Craft did not have time to form the Brigade pretty, straight, or neat. As soon as ten men came together, an officer shouted for them to left wheel into line. Several hastily pieced together formations were thrown into the fray to slow down the Rebel swarm until the main force could be assembled.

Huge gaps appeared where our formation passed over mud holes and large puddles of water. Our blue lines could only manage a few feeble and uncoordinated musket volleys. Despite the frantic efforts of our gallant commander, the enemy succeeded in rolling us up like yesterday's newspaper. We fell back in defeat!

To no one's surprise, the judge declared that the Union Brigade had been routed and destroyed. We had had our fanny spanked good that day. I'm not sure of the overall score for the entire weekend, but with a few exceptions, I don't think the Union did well this tactical. I can only remember the few highlights I've mentioned and can't speak for those who might have a different slant of the event.

And so the curtain came down on the final act of the Grand Tactical. It was time to wrap things up and prepare the hard task of going home. In hindsight, I don't think this tactical was all that great as compared with the Red River adventure nor did it have the high drama as LBL, when thirst was our enemy. At this Kentucky tactical, we certainly didn't live off the land and do much hiking. It did get very cold at night-as cold as a landlord's heart. However, we had the luxury of retreating to tents and blankets in our own camp next to our own campfire each night. For a diversion, many browsed the wares of Fall Creek Sutlery, in most cases to acquire another blanket, and of course there was the chili. So, it wasn't much of a 'campaign' experience after all.

About a week or two after getting home, I noticed that my big toe continued to ache. I thought perhaps that I had bruised the bone in the toe as it began to swell and turn purple. I continued to get apprehensive about my condition because it became increasingly difficult to walk on it without wincing in pain.

It was then that I noticed that the toenail was growing oddly. No longer was it growing out as a normal nail would. Now it was growing thick. The nail was almost an eighth of an inch thick and causing me great pain near the first joint of my toe. At this point, I could barely put weight on it. The nail could not be trimmed, by conventional means, so it was then that I decided to see the foot doctor.

I told the doctor that I had probably jammed my toe on something while I was at the Kentucky tactical. He said the toenail was no longer growing as it should and would only cause me continued stress. He said the toenail would have to be removed.

Removing the nail off my big toe was like removing a wisdom tooth. A local anesthetic was injected into the toe and the nail was removed. Afterwards, a solution was rubbed into the wound so the nail would no longer come back. I had damaged something in my toe causing the nail to grow funky. Better not to have a nail at all than one that might cause me grief again.

I soaked my foot in Epsom salts for several weeks until the skin hardened up. A couple of years later, I suffered the same affliction with the toenail on the other foot and had the same procedure done.

My feet, particularly my toes, have lately been an unsightly mess. None of the nails look good (although not as horrible or painful as the big toenails had been). My little toes have developed a problem in that the bones have become crooked; the bones have bent inwards. There is a medical term for when the toes curl inwards, but I'm not that bright to recall it. Maybe my foot ailments are caused by all my years walking on a concrete floor at work or from the years walking around in brogans. I suspect the former. Oh well, the next best option would be to get my feet whacked off and get my legs fitted with rollers. Enough with my petty ailments, its time to conclude this book.

CONCLUSION

Yes, gentle reader, you have reached the end of this book.

In 1997, just as he had warned us, John Maki resigned as Captain. I just don't think he was that comfortable with this high position. He seemed more comfortable in just being one of the guys. A few years later, he would accept a position as company cook, with no rank.

Randy Rogers became the next Captain and held that post for two years.

By the strangest, and most controversial of circumstances, the 1999 elections were held at the Pea Ridge, Arkansas, living history event in early March. The membership at Pea Ridge decided that Terry Forsyth should be the new Captain. Since the millennium, we have had four Captains: Terry Forsyth, Mike Gosser, Tom Sprague, and Aaron Racine.

Ladies and gentlemen, I have not decided whether I will pursue a Volume Three. When I began writing Chin Music, Volumes One and Two, I began to feel a sadness. Perhaps nostalgic is more appropriate.

Noticing my melancholy as I began this memoir, my wife reminded me that, "you can't live in the past." To paraphrase Bruce Springsteen, after twenty-six years in the hobby, all I have to offer an indifferent audience is, "boring stories of Glory Days." Over the years, I've come to realize that there is more to this hobby than dressing up in a wool uniform and shooting a black powder rifle. I've met some great people and developed lasting friendships with many of them. I understand how lasting friendships can come about because of soldiering. I'm closer to my Civil War pards than I ever was to my blood relations. My kinfolk don't know my vices like my tent mate does.

Thank you for picking up this book and allowing me to share my own weird and astounding 'true' tales of Civil War Reenacting.

Printed in the United States
By Bookmasters